MW00640579

MOVEMENT TO THE HEREAFTER

BY MITCHELL KRAUTANT

For permission requests, write to the publisher, addressed "Attention:
Permissions Coordinator," at the address below.

Ingram Content Group
One Ingram Blvd.
La Vergne, TN 37086
www.ingramspark.com

Printed in the United States of America

First Printing, 2020

ISBN 978-1-952740-23-7 (Hardback)
ISBN 978-1-952740-22-0 (Paperback)
ISBN 978-1-952740-21-3 (EPUB)

mkrautant.com
mitchellkrautant@gmail.com

TABLE OF CONTENTS

INTRODUCTION	5
CHAPTER 1	7
CHAPTER 2	27
CHAPTER 3	35
CHAPTER 4	59
CHAPTER 5	81
CHAPTER 6	105
CHAPTER 7	137
CHAPTER 8	151
CHAPTER 9	199
CHAPTER 10	231
CHAPTER 11	247
CHAPTER 12	283
LAST CHAPTER	307
CHAPTER 13	349
Biography of Mitchell Krautant	361

INTRODUCTION

(These paragraphs in parenthesis at the beginning are in every book I am getting published. It plays a large part in the message I want to get across for every book.

First, let me explain a modification I have made in this book. I have removed all words of "evil" or "Devil" from it. I have asked Angels if those words are accurate. Their answer was that they are "arrogant" and "unlawful". I am a good person. And actual presences of those terms are going to be present big time in the final three phased missions I have been given by God to do.

So, I want you to realize that those terms are arrogant, unlawful, and using them will drive your mind to do negative, not-good things. So, I have changed those two terms to God's words of those events. "Evil" has been replaced, accurately, with "nothing". "Devil", has be replaced, accurately, with "arrogance of nothing". The reasons for those terms is explained, in detail, in the book *The Divinity of Angelhood 4: The Final Battle at the End of Time.*

The terms not-to-be used anymore were designed by Satan when he pushed Adam and Eve to eat of the Golden Apple. Those were Satan's terms, pushed by him to be spoken by humans to drive them to take actions to bring them closer to "nothing" ... which is what Satan is, at the core.

I encourage you to change your verbiage, as put forth. It plays a huge part in how you think, and how you will act now, in the future, in the past, and most of all, how you will be judged on Judgement Day, with a fate of either holiness or pain, forever. Pay attention. It matters more than anything else you can imagine.)

(Actually, it was too hard to do away with those negative terms as I wrote this document. They are a habit put forth into our human minds to say. Sorry! Please try to circumvent those terms... if you can... though. It is the just thing to do!

I guess that I am, at least, in part an unjust person. Read my stories within my many books.. and make your own decision about that criteria!)

CHAPTER 1

Introduction

This is a story about how I had been brought to the Hereafter and given direction of life by Angels of God. It is a full story. You will find, though, that the comparison between what had actually happened, and the mental proclivities of other Afterlife patients is different. Why?

Because I have virtually no memory of what had occurred.

This book is written with the names of the abusive parties changed, to avoid any lawsuit. The names used are: My ex-wife: ex-wife; ex-wife's husband: Brickface; girlfriend stripper: Grace; mother: Paris; sister: Downlow; woman involved with after Marines: Matrix;

veteran nurse of the Marines: Krishna; Krishna's brother: M; Krishna's other brother: A; son: J. The names of the lawless people within the Washington State justice system are actual, because they are on record, and frankly, they deserve prison time and suing. And I shall be giving this statement to the ACLU to try and convict them.

Here is what had occurred.

In November 2013, I was a victim off attempted vehicular homicide. And afterwards, my memory was erased from November 2013 to July 2014. When I awakened, I was inside of a space of the VA hospital in Loma Linda, within an area that was a psychological ward with two hallways separated from the rest of the hospital by two locking doors. I remember awakening and was walking down a hallway looking at a picture of the sign of Prisoners of War (POW's) within the wall surface. It was a picture of POW's in uniform moving in a POW camp with towers surrounding them with guns on them. I had immediately the sensation that I was in a POW camp myself, and that the section of the hospital that I was in was part of an incarceration camp.

The thought was extremely disrupting, and I felt like I had been captured in a way I did not understand. Now, such a level of thought was odd, because I had been out of the military at that time for a period of literally 14 years. So, my memory should have been different. The reason I was having those thoughts was likely because I had gone before the Hereafter and had been visited by Angels and equated it to my performance aboard the unit 1st Force Reconnaissance Company. That is a Special Operations Capable Unit of the Marines, at a very elite and high level of performance.

What is it that I wanted to do there? For one, I wanted to perform in ways unimaginable by the average person. I wanted to run faster, to do more exercise, and to exercise my will in levels far beyond what the average person was able to do. I wanted to shoot with precision and expertise, and to be able to perform anti-terror exercises with the whim of the fantastic. And I learned how to do that, too. Now, that concept was brought forwards by the fact that I thought I was in a POW camp; and my altercation of the substance of that thought was to revolt against the staff of the place. I did so by saying negative things to them.

For example, one day I was walking on the patio outside when a staff member, a psychologist, came out and began to ask me questions about what had physically happened to me. I told him the lie that I was seeing things that did not exist with my mind's eye, and that made me get the message to describe things per the concept of the idea that things operated on a Satanic religious basis and that all things were designed for destruction after we died of unnatural causes. The concept was extremely negative. Where did it come from?

Let me describe it this way ... In September, 2012, one year before my death in 2013, after I was released from an unjust prison sentence for a crime I did not commit, upon release I went before my roommate, Krishna, and asked the question of "what happened after I died in that hospital?" The fact was that up until then, I had not died in a hospital. But I asked the question. Why? Because the mind operates in a function of not only what has occurred, but also on what can occur, and isolate those concepts upon their own functions.

The answer was given to me on the computer I had, on a website. The reason I knew that information operated that way was because I had gotten, through religious presence, the concept that religious questions can be asked at random to random portions of writings, and the answer is put forth by God and His Angels in a way that answers the question. That works for known documents, but also unknown and new documents that have not been read yet. How so?

Because the spirits of the people who wrote the subjects are related to the written matter, in a way that allows them to move forwards with thoughts on a related person's inquiries.

The answer I got to the question was one that identified that I had been sent to God's Garden, within which I was approached by three Angels – two who were vociferous presentations of reality, and one who was the Angel of Death – the one who had drawn me to death within the Hereafter, and who afterwards brought me back to life.

Their communication to me was about what I was

to do after I died. I was to move forwards during life to knowledge about how the works of the Ark of the Covenant operated. Upon death, I was to be swept aboard with that knowledge, and upon the Ark I was to operate on a religious sense of knowledge about the facts of Heaven and Hell, and with that knowledge I was to isolate and judge people I encountered with the presence of their actions, their beliefs, their Angelic beliefs and the judgement of their Angels – the ones set on both of their shoulders, judging them through life – and with that information, judge them as a whole as being present for either getting sent to Heaven and a holy soul, or getting sent to Hell as a sinner.

Upon completion of that, I was also told the summary of how I was to do that. I was told that I was not at the surface a human. I was an Angel, who had been slain and transmitted to humankind upon the error, and thus began to live a life like other humans, when in fact I was an Angel. That was why I had an IQ of 142 points per the IQ test given to me by the psychologist of Force Reconnaissance when I had been accepted into the unit. That high intelligence allowed me to take on concepts that the average person would think was impossible. But I witnessed them and took them under stead of actuality per the concept of what was going on with the other party.

Now, keep in mind that I got that concept before I actually died in the coma in 2013. How is that? Because different elements of time have been found, scientifically, to operate differently than most people think. There is such a thing as time-travel, which includes the concept of the fact that a person can move through the concept of the future through to the past, and vice-versa. Thus, it is possible that a person can get the memory of things that have not happened yet! That is what happened to me: I got the message from the future that had not happened yet that I had been taken to God's Garden and met with Angels, who told me about my future after Death. A heavy and tall order, mind you. But the actual death occurred in November 2013 in a coma, after I had been the victim of attempted murder. They had damaged me severely, and I was found lying bloody in the road in front of the VA hospital. The photo of me that was in the newspaper was one that showed me laying in a hammock with serious blood all over my face and a bandage on my head with a neck brace on. The body of a man near death.

I was put in the hospital in a coma for two months. During that period, I died. I do not remember the death itself, but I remember the only memory I have of those six months. It is of getting sent to God's Garden, and there being addressed by three different Angels.

In November 2016, I began to get the concept of writing a book about the Hereafter. The memories of what had occurred to me were prevalent. One of the things I did was get a book titled: *Proof of Heaven: A Neurosurgeon's Journey into the Afterlife*. I asked the book at random, "why do I have no memory of the Hereafter?" The answer said, on page 86: "Om understands and sympathizes with our human situation more profoundly and personally than we can even imagine because Om knows what we have forgotten, and understands the terrible burden it is to live with amnesia of the Divine for even a moment."

That is what I was going through. I was getting the mental acquisitions of religion in a facet that would make one think that it was religious based, but I had no memory of it. And it hurt, because I would get some sort of idea about religion that I would know to be actual, but that did not come from a frame of mind that seemed like it knew those sorts of things. But it was present, and I knew those thoughts to be actual.

As a whole, I had amnesia of the event, and it was, indeed, a terrible burden. I was undertaken with the concept that I did not know enough about religion, so I spent a lot of time reading through random parts of the Bible and the Qur'an, the purpose for getting a solid proclivity of religion.

As part of it, I read over the part in the Bible about the Ark of the Covenant, inside of Exodus, and it became plain to me that I was to go aboard a part of the ship that was very pronounced in its construction and presence of souls aboard it.

In addition, when I was homeless in 2011 to 2012, I sustained the experience of being around Jesus Christ, who I found to be a soul that was capable of resuscitation repeatedly though time, thus becoming present in ways most people did not understand or accept throughout time. He led people on a very thoroughfare of reminiscence and that made them aware of the fact that he existed outside his time in their time and could lead them to success and enlightenment. I maneuvered along a level that I knew him, being him in a World War 2 concentration camp, and itemizing the guards as being evil. He escaped, with my help, and taught me about his mission there.

That was in part the religious ceremony that I partook in. There was more. But to itemize that, understand that I was tried and convicted of crimes I did not commit by evil forces within my presence.

Now, before those events of near death happened, there had been a history of negative things occurring. For example, I had been abused as a child severely. I had also been sexually abused as well. I know this because of my experience with my first solid girlfriend in Junior High School. Her name was Grace. When we began to date, I began to infiltrate her in ways that were extremely sexually negative, but I didn't know it at the time. For example, on one of the first nights I was with her, I took off her bra and sang to her a 9 Inch Nails song. I was rude and obtrusive with feeling her breasts. Now, what I did not know with that, as well as the fact that later, after I had been moved away unlawfully by my evil mother, that she had gotten married to a soldier. But she moved near my house, and I visited her, and she changed her mind and got involved with me. Then, one night, she was at our house, and I began to make out with her to the music of 9 Inch Nails, and she got very excited.

Later I joined the Marines, and she became a stripper. Think about that. I was involved with a stripper. That is evidence that I was sexually abused as a child. And evidence that I can have really bad judgement.

The episode of my military service lasted for nearly 11 years. And it was pronounced and remarkable. I started out in a Sniper platoon. Then I went over to join Force Reconnaissance, which is a Special Operations Capable unit of extremely high caliber. They are the highest trained Marines there are. And the training was difficult, strenuous, and high caliber.

But it was also near-lethal. In fact, it was lethal for some of the Marines. For example, there was a picture painted on the wall of the pool area, of a man in a parachute flying above the ground. What had happened was that he had failed to draw his parachute and had fallen thousands of feet into the ground and died. So, was that something us other freefall heroes had to face?

I know it is. Why? Because when I was in a freefall exercise, my parachute had failed to open properly and began to spin around errantly. Reacting to that, I cut it free and opened my spare parachute, which opened, and took me into the ground normally. Safely. But what could have happened was that my reserve could have failed the way the main did, and I could have died.

That wasn't all. During freefall school, at the beginning I was slated to attend a practice jumping in the Wind Tunnel. The Wind Tunnel was a length of passage surrounded by square cables around a floor fan that blew air around it. The air was designed to push up a person in front of it lying flat, in a way that was similar to what they thought they felt when jumping in the atmosphere. Now, as I was in there, jumping, two instructors flew above me, wrestling. One of them knocked the other one into me, knocking me out of balance. I began to fly upwards, strung out, and flew literally about 35 feet above the fan. Then my foot struck the squares on the cables and caused me to fall head-first. I hit the cushion on the side of the fan so hard head-first that my neck nearly broke and my helmet ruptured along my skull. I kicked myself in the back of the head so hard that I thought I broke my skull.

At the end, I went before the instructors and told them what had happened. The instructor asked me if I wanted to go to medical. I refused, stating that I was okay. I wasn't okay. My neck hurt badly, and it was nearly impossible to keep my head straight. And my legs felt very weak and disrupted from the errant flexing that had occurred in the knees and the waist.

But I was kept on jumping. "You're going to jump, Marine." The Instructor said: "and you will succeed at it, or you will come in and say you have an emergency!" He wanted me to land, regardless of what occurred. No failed parachute. Now, that was unrealistic, because if I had begun to fall errantly, I would have likely disrupted my parachute and caused it to malfunction. But his duties as an instructor was to make things as difficult, but realistic, for us as possible. So, he decided that I would jump.

And jump I did. And I kept everything cool the whole time, except landing, because the landing took a level of effort that involved placing the feet on the ground at a higher speed than usual, and because of my injury, that hurt badly! But I did it every time, and succeeded at it, in pain, and that made me a serious jumper with extraordinary skills.

There was also the time that I had almost drowned in the ocean. We had been on a mission to parachute into the water of the ocean, pulling our parachutes in a fashion that allowed us to steer clear of them in the water. Then we were supposed to flow in through the tidal waves onto the shore for the purpose of conducting a water survey of the beach. After we entered the water, we noticed that the tide was extremely high, with the waves at between 12 to 14 feet high, which was too much for us to be able to swim in. Thus, we released the cord, and began to swim in to the beach on our own.

Midway, in the waves, I began to become undertaken by the size of the waves, and they were pounding me down under the water without any air. And there was no way for me to get upright. I tried and tried, and no matter how much kicking I did, I kept on failing. Then, I sucked in water, and going black, nearly unconscious, I pulled my resuscitation valve and injected air into my vest. With air in it, it floated to the surface. And like that, I floated all the way to shore.

When I got there, my team leader came over to me, obtrusive, and said "you pulled the valve on your vest? Who the hell do you think you are? We are parachuting today! Get over it!" He was extremely rude. I brushed my hand off at him and ignored him.

That was how I concluded my exercises with Force Reconnaissance. My next command was the Mountain Warfare Training Center, as an instructor. The reason I went there was because I had the sensation after being on deployment with Force Recon and nearly getting sent to perform in Afghanistan that I wanted to prepare other Marines to get ready to go there. And I wanted them to send me there too, as an instructor, if possible.

Now, the average instructor of MWTC operated in training the Infantry. So, was that what they did with me? Hell no! They got from my command my fitness report that said that I had scored as a genius on my IQ test, so to expand on that, did they let me teach the infantry? No! They instead put me in charge of training the Infantry, of training Force Recon, or Special Forces, or Navy SEALs, of Air Force Pararescue, of helping to train the Mountain Snipers, and of developing a whole new class for Force Recon Marines! That is literally four times as much duty as the average instructor had! And did I receive credit for it? Hell no!

I eventually got out after that duty. The main reason

was because I had taken a serious injury from freefall school that was disrupting my climbing ability. My shoulder was so damaged that it needed surgery. I went and had it worked on. Afterwards it was so disabled that it didn't work properly. Thus, I decided that, for one, I was never going to be able to go back into Force Recon Company, so I was never going to stay in the Marines, due to the fact that the only place I could go was to Headquarters or the Infantry. And I wanted neither! I was a Special Operations Capable force operative, man! Not one of those lower-character haters!

Then, about 6 month later, I joined the job of Triple Canopy, which is a protection network for people of higher government that were working within the realm of warzones, like Afghanistan or Iraq. My job there was to provide security against people with firearms.

I got recommended by a peer leader to go to his occupation at a firing arms range within the city called Issaquah, right next to Seattle, Washington. I went there and went through a course that required us to shoot at targets shaped like people with firearms at their waists. The course was two days long. Upon completion, I called my very abusive ex-wife, to see my son, the 5-year old boy of mine. At first, I tried to get her to meet me at the police station, but she refused, telling me to go to his daycare.

When I went to his daycare, his teachers were viscous to me and told me things that were lies. They refused to give me any of my child's papers, which was against their own policy, except for one. And that one had the false statement that Brickface, who was my ex-wife's Fiancé, was listed as my son's Father. A complete lie! And one that those despicable daycare teachers were taking on their records!

I took my son for three days from there. During that time, he told me about how my ex-wife and Brickface had abused him steadily. Unknown to me, I felt the same diatribe as I had felt at the summary of the fact that my mother Paris had abused me steadily when I was a child. I felt there was nothing I could do. I realize now that those feelings were in error, but at the time there was nothing I could do. My ex-wife seemed unjustly overwhelming. I became suicidal, feeling as though there was nothing I could do for my son, who was abused as I had been when I was a child.

I went to my ex-wife's house that night to talk to her. At her arrival at the door, I had the mental intuition related to my job on the range, and I got the summary that she was drawing a weapon on me. So, I did exactly as I had trained to do in that situation, and I drew my weapon on her. About 5 seconds later, I realized that I was in error, so I unloaded my pistol and apologized, telling her that I was considering suicide for her abuse. Then I left.

I called the police officer at her house to turn myself in. His name was McNulty. I told him about how my ex-wife had lied about me to my command and committed perjury and financial discrepancies against me. He ignored me, and upon me finishing, he got with Detective Tawnia Pfaff, and the two of them wrote to the judge a full list of lies about what had happened. The things they accused me of doing are frankly impossible to do during a firefight, yet they were trying to engage perjury and malicious prosecution against me at my ex-wife's lying request.

As a result of McNulty and Pfaff's perjury and malicious prosecution, the prosecutor tried to use a phone message I had recorded about my ex-wife's lawless daycare behavior against me, and the Judge, Kessler, violated my 8th constitutional right against me and placed my bail too high for me to afford, let the prison unlawfully charge me money, and placed me under being tortured by the prison system. Violations and lies!

Then, when Victoria Smith, my attorney, brought me to attend a hearing about innocence. I told the judge that I wanted to plead innocent. He had Victoria Smith take me back to the cell, and she told me that she had been intimidated by the police and that I was forced to plead guilty. She told me that if I plead innocent – which I was – then the police would bring up additional charges against me and put me in prison for 15 years! So, against my will I plead guilty when I was innocent – when the charge was already too long in prison in the first place.

The prison system was atrocious. Those guards broke

the law against me in over 18 different ways. Finally, it created such a mental disability that I began to face severe PTSD. As a result, they transferred me to another psychologically disabled treatment center. On the way, I had to go to the bathroom, so the officers took me to a gas station and went into the bathroom with me. As I approached the toilet, the officer behind me began to threaten me with pushing me against the toilet, and I did exactly as I had been trained to do. I pushed him against the wall and went in to hit him. The other officer drew a weapon on me and threatened to shoot me. I went into the car and listened to those assholes shit-talk me to the local police, trying to get me re-arrested. They would have none of it, though, and told those officers to take me to the prison.

Those officers, the disgusting slobs that they are, told the staff at the prison the lie that I had "tried to escape" and to "put (me) in solitary confinement." So, the staff did that, errantly, in error.

Now, sometime after I was released, I read an online newspaper article titled *The Horrible Psychology of Solitary Confinement*. The article was clear in the fact that it determined it to be the equivalent of Torture. I can confess to that. I was there for a year and a half, lawlessly. The later chapters shall describe what exactly occurred there. The damage was serious, and permanent.

I faced prison unjustly from March 2005 to September 2009. From there I was released to my sister Downlow's house, with serious mental illness. And there, she forced me to face the abuse of her children, the steadfast abuse from her and Paris, the loss of my son, and the complete lack of justice I had to face. And not only that, but in solitary confinement, I had learned that God himself operates in that environment, drawing negatively charged people to either religion of justice. And it happened in ways that the average person would think is non-articulate. But it is a fact.

So, is that all that happened? Not quite.

After I was abused by Downlow and Paris, I finally had a revolt and got kicked out of Downlow's house. I was homeless for a day and found a remedy through the VA nurse I knew named Krishna. I asked her if I could live there, and she said "yes". So, I did.

The whole effect was troubling, because she had also been abused as an immigrant. She was also seriously Muslim, which made her remarkably religious. We got along with errors, true, but, overall, we did well. She took very good care of me.

And that happened from 2009 to 2011. Then the religious factor started to happen seriously.

What happened?

I was drawn severely to religion from the Solitary Confinement I had gone through. In college, I went through a process of getting deeper and deeper reminiscences on religious matter in-regards-to what we were being taught and what the students were thinking and doing. The full effect is described in a further chapter. But what I got was a serious effect of the message from God that I was to assist in his warfare against evil people within, you guessed it, the confines of the same place where my rights were at first conflicted ... the city of Seattle, Washington. There I experienced potential dangers to the environment that occurred on a religious level beyond understanding. Then I was sent to Los Angeles, the city of Angels, and there fought against evils in a manner possible and won. From there I went to San Diego, my military hometown, and there began to come into the influence of my real family ... religiously persecuted individuals with high power who had been separated from me at birth. And I also came to realize that the reason behind that was because I was actually an Angel before I was born as a human; one who had been submitted to the evils of the Devil when he began to sweep through the universe for the function of taking it over and making it slaves. Thus. God decided to create mankind and use them as a means to defeat the evils of the universe. A tall order, and that is what mankind has been facing ever since.

Upon completion, however, the evil forces influenced Paris, and she submitted me unlawfully to prison, trying to find me guilty of a 7-year sentence for crimes I did not commit. I wasn't released from the mental health sentencing prison until after 9 months had passed. And I was innocent! Ridiculous!

Now, going forwards, upon my leave in San Diego, I

came under the understanding that my real family wanted to be reunified with me. And the place they considered to do it was inside of Phoenix, Arizona. Phoenix, the name of the mythological bird that flew in the heavens on the old earth. There I was to find a way to unify us and get justice away from the evils. There, I found a way to the VA hospital, and was sent away without any support, totally against policy. And upon my departure, I was the victim of attempted vehicular homicide.

I have little memory of that event. In fact, it happened in November 2013, 14 months after I had the dream about it while surfing the message online about going to God's Garden. And I had no memory of anything regarding that until July 2014.

The introductory memory I have of it is that I was walking within the hallway of a sectioned off area of a hospital. In it at the end was a picture of a POW flag, with pictures of soldiers in uniform being held as prisoners of an enemy camp. And that is what I determined to be my fate at the time.

Now, the event of the attempted homicide and the memory loss is the "Amnesia" that was discussed in the *Heaven* book. The reason that happened to me, and the reason I have no memory of the Divinity that I was a frequency of, is because I have been selected to go to the Ark of the Covenant when I die, and to do God's work there after death, being made into an Angel again. That is an order much higher than any put forth in the Bible. It is because of my origins as an Angel. It is because I have been so subjected so far to evils of the world that it was arguably something that could have driven me insane if I wasn't an Angel. Literally. Think about it.

Solitary confinement is so wrong and illegal that it causes permanent neurological brain damage among average citizens. Then I faced fighting God's war against evils, with success. Then I faced another unlawful prison sentence conjured by Paris. Then I faced existence in the Hereafter after being a victim of attempted homicide. Plus, I was abused seriously as a child and teenager by Paris herself. And I finished the military being treated poorly by a command that tried to insult my intelligence. Any one of those six things, in and of themselves, is literally enough to drive a person mad. But I made it.

I am seriously religious now. I am a combination of Muslim, Christian, Hindu, Buddhist, and Jewish religions. I have found that each of them speaks a version of God's language.

This story is about how I faced those obstacles. It is about how, as a highly religious man, I have made it through the Hereafter and there got the message that I was to engage upon death upon the Ark of the Covenant and save humanity to Heaven as needed, to Hell where appropriate, and to Angelhood where necessary.

CHAPTER 2

GENERAL THEORY

This chapter shall describe the initial parts of what this book is about. It shall talk about the summary in rough elements, with the final chapter being followed near the end of the book. This is about a very rough idea of what happened in-regards-to the Hereafter and me, and it is based off of what intelligence I got on the subject from Krishna's very religious brother, M.

Let me start out with that conversation with M.

I approached him the day after Thanksgiving, while he was at Krishna's house, and said "I have a question for

A. The other day on the phone he said he would talk to me about the Hereafter, and I am wondering if he will do that now."

M said: "Let me answer that question. There are two duties among people who go to the Hereafter. One is that it is judged on their holy or unholy presence of doing things. The other is that if they do positive things for people, then that follows them into the Hereafter. You know that the Hereafter is what happens after one dies, right? I thought so! So, you now know that if a person does all sorts of holy things with his or her time and treats people right, then they will earn the presence of being sent to Heaven after they die and are in the Hereafter. And there is another aspect as well. What does it mean to go to Heaven? What is Heaven like? It is a presence of holiness that goes far and beyond what a person can sense or know about. It defies common sense. The emotions and the knowledges that come from there have a serious impact on the presence of people's minds! So when a person does things that are holy, they are swept to Heaven when they die and are put in a mythically proportioned aspect of well-being that allows them to see and hear and imagine things that are so far beyond the capability of the average person to imagine that it is phenomenal! Yet a person can also do negative things to others, too. Want to hear about that?"

"Sure. Thank you for what you've said so far," I said in response.

"When people do evil things to other people, that follows them through God's and his Angel's knowledge of that, and they use that data to put a person not in Heaven, no, instead the go to Hell! Hell man! That is the place where a person is tried and convicted of the crimes they have committed and face judgement forever! When I used to go to the prisons and talk about that to the prisoners, they would listen very solidly, because they understood what it was like to be judged!" He got ready to carry on. At that time I was thinking about how I had been unlawfully sent to prison, and the people there were definitely tried for not only their actions, but also what they had done inside the prison while being punished. Some of them were treated very unlawfully by the prison guards. I knew that for a fact, because I had endured over 18 different elements of lawbreaking by the prison guards during the time that I was inside. They even went so far as to violate my 8th constitutional amendment right on at least three different ways: overcharging my bail, fining me in excess by paying DOC what I had earned when they were, by law, supposed to be giving it to me; and by torturing me by unlawfully placing me in the mentally disabling and permanent year and a half effect of the what should be very unlawful solitary confinement. That made me severely mentally disabled after I was released for over four years later.

M continued. "So, people in prison understood that there was a place called the Hereafter, and that some of them would be going there. Now, to get there, a person has to either die or be on the verge of death. Have you experienced that?"

I came clean, getting a message from God in my forefront mind to be plain with M. "You may not know this, but in November 2013, I was the victim of attempted homicide. The driver of a vehicle hit me twice, trying to kill me, and left me severely damaged and near death. I had a broken skull, broken face, broken nose, broken back, breaks on both legs, broken knee, and nearly broken foot. I was bleeding all over the place, with severe bruises and contusions in my face and skull and neck. The picture of me is one of my head bleeding profusely with a bloody bandage over my head and a brace on my neck. The thing is, I have no memory of what happened, from November 2013 to July 2014. I was in the hospital for nearly a whole year. 11 months. I was in a coma for two of those months." God's Angels told me to continue, in detail. "When I was in the coma I died. That is the only memory I have. I was taken to God's Garden and approached by three Angels, and they told me about what I was to do after I died. I was to help God with Judgement Day, helping present people to either Heaven or Hell based on their holiness or sins. That is what I got from the Hereafter. Now, I have asked the *Heaven* book why it is that I do not know what actually happened to me in the Hereafter. I have found that God and his Angels will move my finger to the proper answer on random pages when I ask them a question, believe it or not, it happens, and the answer was this: (roughly) "on page 86, it said that a person who faces amnesia after being subjected to the Divinity of the Hereafter faces a certain mental disability that is severe and horrible." That is what it said. So, I wondered, why is it that such an amnesia happened? And the answer I came up with is the fact that the people who attempted to kill me, and the negative police who refused to view that evidence and get me justice, were all agents of Satan themselves."

"That is not the case with the police," said M. "They cannot go on public records unless they have an order from the judge. They should have gotten one, though. They were wrong. They should have brought you justice."

What I didn't want to tell him was that that was the interaction I had gotten used to from disgraceful police who do not do their jobs. For example, there was the felony perjury and malicious prosecution that the police who arrested me in 2005 committed against me. And the police refusing to get a judge's order in 2013 was another element of misconduct among the police. To exaggerate the problem, there had been news on CNN about a lot of Black citizens protesting or killing 5 Dallas police officers for killing unarmed black men unlawfully. And the fucking justice system was letting those officers get away with their misconduct, finding them innocent, even though they were proven to be guilty. The people were fed up with that and took up arms against the police for it. And that is what they deserved for killing innocent citizens and getting away with it.

"What you should realize is that you have arrived at

the Gate of the Hereafter. You have been brought back by God. Some people there who have done good things get sent to Heaven. Some get sent to Hell. Others are brought back to life, if they are seen as needing more time here on earth to do whatever they see as necessary. You are one of those. For some reason, God has determined that you need more time here, and he gave it to you! You have done things that are holy, I can tell."

"I treated people with respect," I said. "When I was a Marine, I treated my coworkers with respect. In High School, and even before, I treated the other students with respect, even when they threatened to fight me for not accepting their drugs. I treat Krishna with respect, too. She is a fantastic person!"

"That is right, that is right!"

The conversation continued, and he went far more in depth with what the perceptions of people in the Hereafter were.

Now, I do not know how he knew those details, but his descriptions of what was occurring was solid in my mind, and I asked the Bible and the Qur'an what his opinion was. The answer was: *Job 42, 23* "Its flesh is hard and firm, and cannot be penetrated. Its heart is hard as rock, hard as a millstone, ..." That was a solid presentation of how M had come across with his knowledge of the subject.

I also asked the Bible to tell me about how I had read over what M had said. It responded: *Ezekiel 47, 11* "So at the special feasts and sacred festivals, the grain offering will be a basket of choice flour with each young bull, another basket of flour with each ram, and as much flour as the prince chooses to give with each lamb ... the east gateway to the inner courtyard will be opened for him ...”

And finally, I asked the Bible to tell me about Krishna’s holy prestige, and what was going to become of her when her time was up. Because I had gotten word that I had been an Angel before I was made into a human, and because I was told my Angels that after I died I was to go onto the Ark of the Covenant to judge people on Judgement Day, I figured that it was possible that Krishna was also going to be made into an Angel herself. So, I asked the Bible, “Is Krishna going to be made into an Angel?” The answer was: *Mark 6, 6* “And he was amazed at their unbelief. Then Jesus went from village to village, teaching the people. And he called his 12 disciples together and began sending them out two by two, giving them authority to cast out evil spirits. He told them to take nothing for their journey except a walking stick – no food, no travelers bag, no money.”

Now, the details of what occurred after I was in the hospital is put forth in one of the final chapters. The full elements of the Hereafter, as I experienced it, and what it will mean to be a face on board the Ark of the Covenant is listed for your understanding here in this book. This is a very rough draft of what that chapter shall contain. It is led by the full diatribe of the evils that occurred before that death experience in the Hereafter. The reason is because I was formerly an Angel, and the evil forces have come to know that, and it was evils around me that tried to drag me down.

The events that happened to me are so severe that they would have made an average person severely mentally ill. And it did, to me, too. But I was able to supersede it with a serious religious perspective and my high intelligence. It was those things, and my duty to God and His Angels, that has allowed me to get past them so far. And God and His Angels are going to let me get equilibrium on the matter after I die ... even before. Why, you ask? How? Because God has made me, with my disabilities and near-death experience, He has made me an author, and this book, plus the other books I have written so far, called the *Cheetah on the Wing* series, are such that they cover all aspects, even to a religious foundation, of what has occurred to me.

This is the writing of an Angel. I want you to realize that, if you like it or not. And these things can happen to you, too.

CHAPTER 3

ABUSE GROWING UP

Now, one expects children to lead safe and protected lives, without errors or trials, within which their parents treat them with respect and dignity.

That was not what happened with me. I was severely abused. This chapter is that story.

To start out with, I was highly religious. I have a memory of going to a parade with actors from the church in it that were all dressed like they were wounded, and they were teaching first aid to the people that were attending.

"That wound needs a splinter, my friend! Get a

splinter from that kit and give it over!" To that he would get a first aid kit from his belt and inside, next to his bleeding ruse headwound, he would take out a splinter and put it on.

"That does the trick! Thanks, my friend. Ok, my head! My head hurts so bad! Ouch! Help me!" There was nothing to that for the man helping to do. So, frustrated, he would wave his hands and shake his head and mutter parables of healthcare that didn't apply.

I grew alarmed as I watched that. The so-called victim was a person saying things to itemize the mind of the caregiver in a way that was making him do things that were irregular and unnecessary. I didn't want to watch it. It was remarkable that the so-called victim had the mindset to become like a felon in their irregular presentation of what needed to happen.

So, I went up to the so-called victim and tried to call them out. And the man became abrasive and said a lot or rude things. "I am wrong? I am wrong? I am the patient, you oaf! Get that through your head! The patient can't be wrong! So, deal with it!" Rude and exasperating.

That ruined that, so I left, trying to put them behind me with the mental picture of being in the position of a helper of the wounded and being taken advantage of. That idea lasted a long time, too. I was in grade school, around the third grade, and the idea of plausible contracting between the caregiver and the wounded was such that it was being violated in mind. Rude, arrogant, and unnecessary.

So that was how that situation turned out. It was such that it had a serious impact on my mind. It was the first episode of that that I remember going through.

Right next to that time, Paris, my so-called mother, decided that there was a problem with my mindset. She thought I had mental problems. She decided to take me to a psychologist to get checked out.

The fact was that the only problem I had been having was with Paris's abuse. She would say negative, errant things to me that were totally in error, and I began to become aware of it and call her on her errors. She hated me for it and was so in depth with her false sensations that she wanted me to be silenced by whatever means she had available. So, she told the psychologist that I was saying a lot of things wrong, without telling him anything about what she had said, thus making him think that I was coming up with those things on my own.

In the *Proof of Heaven* book, I asked it in November 2016 to tell me about the abuse I sustained from Paris … what it was like. The answer was:

""What," I asked those who were assembled, "are you doing here?" To which Phyllis replied, "What are *you* doing here?""

What that means is that Paris would come in to my

room, for example, and say something negative to me, like "you think you're a villain hitting your sister (when I didn't). You will be punished for it!" or saying something sexually disconcerted, like "show me your privates, if you are a hero!" What did she mean by that? She said those things to manipulate or to harass me. What did I do? I immediately shifted to the chain of thought that she was saying something else, that meant something else, and I would say it. I was also in error, but it was for self-protection.

The real fact was that I was sexually abused, and because I saw a fictional power within Paris, I could think of no other way around it other than to change the event by mislabeling it. That changed the effects of it deep within my mind, in a way that allowed me to keep on going.

When I was young, it was very interesting to visit my father. When I was in the first grade, he recognized my intelligence and bought me a mathematics book at a level much higher than my classmates. I studied it hard, and he helped a lot. Because of that, I entered the highest mathematics classes in Junior High School and High School and ended up taking Calculus in my first year of college.

He liked to rent us movies, from time to time, and would explain them in detail. I do not remember the names of the movies we saw, but they were science fiction or medieval or a social rhetoric movie. Some were advanced. For example, at a very young age, he took me to see the horror movie Alien 1. It was so intense that it gave me nightmares, but I also got a present of an Alien action figure that I could play with. I also had figures from the Star Wars movie, that I really enjoyed.

He talked very little. The reason, I think, was because, for one, he was a genius that wasn't appreciated. Paris kept telling us that he had schizophrenia. I never once saw any signs of it, so I really think he didn't have it. Paris, when I went to High School, told all my teachers that I was mentally ill, a complete lie, and many of them believed her. That was why they were failing me. I'll get into that later.

My father treated me very excellently. The problems were with Paris. I will get into that next.

Now, my memory of the abuse is such that it is difficult to remember it. The reason is because I adapted to it by thinking something different when it was happening. Now, one of the things I do remember is that Paris kept trying to get me to study harder and harder in school. The reason was because she hated my intelligence and my ability to learn things. Upon graduation of grade school, however, I began to develop adaptation and evolution. I began to get different ideas about things, and I began to fight against her when she started to give me an opinionated answer about some form of abuse.

In addition, she was attempting to alter my mindset and insult my intelligence. She did so in a number of ways. For example, one day when I was 12, Downlow took one of my nun chucks and turned it against me, striking me as I ran away up a tree. She was yelling and screaming, and Paris came outside and cheered her on. Damn her! I eventually got down from the tree, and when I went inside Paris was telling me about how I should have let her strike me over and over again. I said nothing, even though I should have told her off. I went into my room and wept.

Paris wanted me to surrender to Downlow, to accept the punishment and to accept the pain. She wanted me to accept it! And there was no way that I would accept that. From that I could tell that Downlow was going to be a very abusive person in the future. And I was right.

My teachers in Junior High School started to become aware that I was a genius. They wanted me to face the probability of living a much higher lifestyle. They began to speak to Paris about it and based off of what my mathematics teacher and my world history teacher told me, Paris was trying to steer them away from it by telling them a lot of negative things about me, things that they knew were not true.

During my science class, for example, one day I wrote a report for class that was based off of DNA and gene theory. It was at a much more advanced level than what we had been taught. I got the material from a college book that I had gotten from the library. It was full of details and at a very high level of understanding.

I taught the subject in class with a picture carved out of a DNA molecule with the different four frequencies within it. It was an elegant picture, and I taught the subject to the highest level of my ability at the time. The class was genius. But the instructor did not like it. She thought I was lying, even though I wasn't, and wrote me up as having a score of a "D". A "D"! What the hell? I was deeply offended and complained to Paris about it that night. She decided that she wanted to take some form of action, in order to re-establish our trust, so she went before the instructor and argued, in difference to what she had said to the other instructors, she said that I had gotten an "A" and definitely not a "D" because, believe it or not, I was a Genius! Go figure, right?

Well, the instructor listened, and I got an "A". Afterwards, the other instructors started to give me limits to what I could present and gave me directions to do the assignments. They wanted me to exercise the genius skill and get a very high grade out of it.

That was how I had joined High School, in the 9th Grade. Now, at the time, I got involved with Grace, a girl who had a very bright skill level and who was very attractive. One figures that a teenager who is coming of age will have a mindset of seeking romance and equilibrium, but that is not what was happening with me. True, I was interested in the concept of romance, but my mindset, because of the sexual abuse I had sustained, was more related, in ways unknown, to the concept of sexual conduct. And the way I met Grace was unexpected and different than expected.

What I remember is that my friend S and I had learned about her location in a house on the street in Klamath Falls, Oregon. We went there one night with a car we had "borrowed" from his grandparents without their knowledge and threw rocks against her window to awaken her. She did, and coming downstairs was obtrusive and abrasive to us at first, then we realized that she was joking about the oddity of us throwing rocks at her window. She came with us to her friend's house. While we were there, I began to feel along her breasts, saying things about the mysteries of the band Nine Inch Nails, and prodding her at the same time. She was tight at first and it was unclear if she liked it. It was actually unusual for me to be doing that to her breasts, because nothing had led up to it. But she started to like it, so I kept on going, leading her into another room and making out with her there.

Then a soon day after, I got with her and she told me about how there were a lot of negative things happening to her. She told me about how her mother's boyfriend had killed a group of people and had been tried for murder. Then she discussed how her mother did abusive things to her, saying all sorts of things that were disruptive and not true. Then she discussed how her friend was trying to get romantically involved with her, but she couldn't do it because she was enraptured with me. Overall, the experiences were disturbing, and I wanted her to give me an answer to the subjects addressed ... a solution to the problems they created. She had none.

Later I found out that something negative happened to her, and she took a razor blade and cut through her arm in multiple locations, leaving scars and scabs of a tall order. I felt very sorry for her. What I didn't know at the time was that I related to her, because what she was doing was what a victim would do when being abused seriously, and I was that kind of victim ... I just didn't really know it yet.

Grace and I began to hang out in High School. She was in my trigonometry class, and there we discussed the theories and the mathematics behind it in steady earnest. She also would come out to my football practices and joke about the strategies we used moving through the field and striking the other players. She was very adept at it and joked about my uniform and how there were pads over my privates and how they couldn't be stricken by the other players ... right? "Man, you'd be all over the place if that happened!" she'd say: "gotta keep 'em separate!" A real joker!

I enjoyed out time together, and she seemed like a much higher standard of woman than one would expect.

But then I got moved away, unlawfully, and everything changed.

Upon the end of the 1st semester of 9th grade, there was a serious error that changed my life forever.

Paris had been driving her car downtown to do things at the stores there. One day she came back to the house with a sense of urgency.

"I want you and Downlow to get your things and get in the car. We are leaving." She was obstructive and rude and immediate with her request.

"What for?" I asked.

"JUST DO IT!" She yelled!

We did, getting luggage with clothes and property in them, and put them in the car. Then we began to be driven far, far away. "Where are we going?" I asked Paris, when we began to cross the border into California.

"Your father almost killed me. I was parked in the city downtown, and going into the County building, and he came at me at the car and tried to beat the window open. So I put it in drive and drove him down! Can you believe that? He was trying to kill me!"

I did not believe her. The statement she said about what he had said to her was a lie. And the concept of my father wanting to talk to her about raising us was one that would not lead him to damage her. She was lying and I knew it.

"You ran him over? That is attempted murder, Paris! A crime!" I said angrily.

"You have no idea what you are saying! I did no

such thing!" At that it was clear that she was taking us elsewhere to escape justice. She belonged in prison. "I am taking you to your uncle Bundle's house in Concord, California. There you will go to school and I will be fixing this problem."

She was totally wrong. I had no desire to go to Concord. Lose my friends? Lose school? Lose my place of life? Having to live under the rules of a different person? Face the fact that I was no longer going to be near my father? What the hell?

When we arrived at uncle Bundle's house, he seemed like he didn't want us there. He could identify that there had been a problem, and that Paris needed help with it. But realize that she had attempted murder? I don't think so. Paris likely learned from our conversation that if she talked about the details of what happened, then she would be accused, and she didn't want that. So, she kept the conversation away from what happened, saying that instead of coming to her car, he attacked her in the building. And she removed the part where she tried to run him over.

Bundle put forth a set of rules for the house. He had three kids. One was in Junior High School, one in 9th grade in High School, and one a High School Graduate. That left me in the middle. His older daughter took me to the side and offered to give me impetus on how the school worked. Then she offered me drugs. Marijuana. I took none of it, but wanted to be her friend, so I told her I would take her up on the offer later, even though I had no idea to.

Regarding drugs, up until then, I had done none of them. I had been offered Marijuana and Heroin in Junior High School, but I turned it down every time, and the people offering them got feisty and threatened to kick my ass. I stood up to them, telling them that I would flat-out destroy them if they even tried, and they listened, aggressive but faulty. The experience was highly negative ... and left me wondering if drugs mattered.

Then I was forced to, after leaving the Klamath Falls High School, I was forced to attend a Concord High School there. It was fabricated and faulty, with the classes underneath knowledge and know-how. For example, I was put into an art class. In it the instructor told us that we would not be paining pictures like a regular art class. Instead we were going to have to fabricate a design on a piece of cardboard that we cut into the shape of a house. We had plain glue, and a set of rough paints to paint it with, and that was it.

I didn't want to get in depth with it ... right ... so I went and instead of putting normal fabrics on mine, I created a rough and haunted atmosphere with sideways and slanted boards, rough and broken windows, alien creatures within the windows and the doorways (which were open and slanted), and ghosts climbing over the roof. The picture was remarkably horrible! But I made it solid and plain, like a device from a novel by HR Geiger! Rowdy and ready for a spell of serious haunting!

The instructor liked it. At the same time, there was a woman in the class that began to associate with me. She told me that she had in the past been overweight and showed me pictures of her fatness. Now she was remarkably skinny. I realized that there was a name for that disease, where a woman gets too fat and can't control it, so begins to starve herself to do away with the weight, at the expense of her health. I can't remember what it is called. Online it says it could be "diabetes or hyperthyroidism". That alarms me, because I have been diagnosed as having diabetes, as shall be put forwards in one of the last chapters.

I went through the Concord High School like that for two semesters of 9th grade. During the time, I began to do artwork during my time off from school in my room. The artwork was very different from that that I had made before. Before, my artwork was solid, spacious and presentable, with a solid themes and format on them. Afterwards, inside Concord, with the trouble of Paris on the horizon, I began to make artwork that was similar to what was done by Iron Maiden. Strict lines of fraudulent facial features and errant body positions and room materials formed in the presence of altered space.

The picture I painted was wholesale in its pictorial sideways presentation. I wrote it as an example of what was happening to me. The errors of the picture were presentations of the errors I had gotten from Paris's speech, from Downlow's false justifications of her behaviors, of Bundle's list of rules and erroneous speeches to me about school and life and cleaning, about his older daughter offering me drugs on a regular basis, you name it. The errors were such that I saw them as altering the presentation and behavior of characters in a picture on a tall order; making them fraudulent and false and in terrible presentation for no good, for an evil, reason.

Evil. That is what I deduced Paris to be, as well as Downlow and the characters they came into contact with.

Upon completion of the second semester, Paris came back after a months-long break to Concord. There she told us that she was "successful in being transferred to Washington State and we were going to be going to school there." She had gotten her job at Weyerhaeuser transferred over to Puyallup, Washington State, and wanted us to go to school there.

So, we transferred up there. Me, grouchy and seeing things horribly, with the mindset of things going to get a lot worse for me. And they did.

For starters, I was put into a middle school that covered three different grades instead of two, like Klamath Falls and Concord had done. They had the 9th grade in that middle school ... the Junior High. And the grading system was different from where I had been before. The classes for mathematics was totally different than what I had done in other states, and the other classes were so fraudulent that it was almost impossible for me, a genius, to go anywhere in them because of their stupidity. For example, one of the classes they forced me to take was a Home Economics class, in which we were supposed to learn about how to use frying pans and pots to cook in. Horrible and stupid! Anyone taking that class would know to put soup in a pot! Yet those fools worked on trying to cause us to have a greater degree of probability for success by telling us so many fictional details that it made learning it nearly impossible ... because of its stupidity!

When I was there, sitting one day between class in the hallway, away from people, I was met by a girl named Kara. Kara liked me a lot.

"What are you doing out here in the hallway? You should be learning in class, man! What is your name?"

I was very alert to her, because since I had from moving a fall-through with Grace, and I had been involved with no other women (besides the one I made out with in Concord), I was interested in if she liked me. She then said she did, complimenting me on my clothes and my physical fitness. We began to date, with my subtle thoughts on the sexual misconduct I had been subjected to by Paris.

We started to date, and I would go to her house. One day, we were sitting in the back yard in a kid's pool, and while there she started to feel me up. We went into a side room, and there began to have sex, for me for the first time. It was very rapid, and strenuous, and I came inside of her by accident. She took a towel and began to wipe herself off, saying all sorts of sexual things to me about how good I was and how she wanted to do it more.

That continued for a spell, and Paris became aware of it, I think, by reading my body language. I ignored her on the concept, and told her good things about Kara, which she didn't like. Upon completion, that December, on Christmas, I went to Kara's house, and there learned that she had sex with another man.

"We're in a romantic relationship, one you have no duty in trying!" She was extremely obtrusive and rude, and wanted me to forgive her and have sex with her too. I refused, telling her that I wanted nothing to do with her.

And if you think about that erroneous relationship, and the one I had with Grace, the soon-to-be stripper, then it becomes apparent that I was seeing the similarities to the sexual misconduct I had to life to per the errant behavior of Paris.

I had serious behavior problems. I got transferred to Roger's High School for the 10th grade. There I made friends with some punk rockers and joined their band. There I ran into additional problems, with Paris taking away all my property and leaving me with a room with nothing by an art-desk and nothing else in it other than a blanket on the floor. She was totally in error financially. She worked at Weyerhaeuser, and should have been paid a decent amount, but she got an apartment she couldn't afford, making it so that we were unable to have any significant furniture or cooking materials. I have no idea what she was spending her money on. Some sort of sin, I am sure, and one that paid nothing significant back.

She moved us away from that Roger's High School in 11th grade. I got totally fed up. The new school I was sent to was horrible, and I am convinced that Paris had gone there and said a lot of negative lies about me to them.

One day, my friend from Klamath Falls came up there to Puyallup for a visit. We went to a restaurant down the street, and there watched the TV. I saw on it a news channel that was talking about how American soldiers had invaded Iraq for the purpose of stopping global warfare. The program was about how the Marine Corps and the Army Rangers were moving through the country, taking it over with arms fire and tanks. I was alarmed and amazed and drew from the program the conclusion that there was a higher power that would bring forth justice to those who violated the laws and rules of the universe. It was clear to me that my presence in the Marines would be one that would force Paris to act responsibly with me. They would give her that message or make her pay the price for her errors. I really liked that idea.

"I'm joining the Marines, man. Screw school. I am going to go fight wars. That is what I do best at." I told S that I thought he should join too.

"I'm joining the Army, you fool!" He responded.

"You've got to be kidding me. The Marines is the most elite unit there is. Why join someone else?" I said.

"Because watch the TV, you fool, and you will see that the Army is much better!"

The argument carried on. I told S that I was going to the recruiter's officer tomorrow. And that is what I did.

The drill instructor was vapid in is responses. He asked me how I was doing in school.

"I'm dropping out," I said.

"No you're not. You're going to school at the school of my choice. No one enters the Marines as a drop-out. Take my words, and you will graduate!" He grinned and gave me the fly-card for Gates Secondary School. Gates was the equivalent of High School ... but done on a special level. When I went there, the instructor told me that I was not required to do homework like a regular school. Instead, I was to do the handouts of a packet that had questions on it, and after I did those at home or on the computer for a month's worth of time, then I would be required to take it to the school and turn it in. I looked at the pamphlet, and it was very simple mathematics math without anything even remotely close to those questions asked in my Trigonometry class.

Now, you may be wondering what else I did with my time. I was living inside of a house in Federal Way, a town north of Puyallup and next to Seattle. I lived there with S and F. F was a fat slob who was probably abused by his biker father, who drank a lot of alcohol and smoked a lot of cigarettes. While there, I spent my days learning the Gates classes, or working at the Construction Supply Company I was at.

Also, during that time, I found out that Grace had gotten married to a man there in Washington. I went to see her, and we immediately had parables, and got a relationship going again. Horrible now that I think about it. She should have stayed with him. Instead she started to come to see me. At the time, she had a young daughter. She didn't like the fact that I was joining the Marines, and wanted to go to school, even though she had bad memories of it. So did I, so I could relate to her. I had almost dropped out of High School because of the abuse I had sustained. It was a miracle that I was able to continue at Gates Secondary School.

To train for the Marines, I began to run to work. It was three miles downhill there. I ran the whole way day in and day out. Then when I was off, I had to run up the hill to the car, another three miles. That was six miles total per day. The exercise was going to pay itself off in ways indescribable. I shall cover that in the next chapter.

At the same time, S was having gambling parties in the apartment. I was involved and kept the people from fighting. At night, I began to have sex with Grace. Unknown to her was the fact that I had been sexually abused by Paris. I didn't tell her. I didn't think it mattered at the time, but it did matter a lot. It strenuously affected how I perceived Grace, and how she perceived me. How that was will become evident later.

My job at the Construction Supply Company was to cut and bend rebar for construction crews to use for making concrete sidewalks and housing bands. I worked outside, next to the parking lot, on a cutting machine that carved the rebar into shreds of planks. Another employee, Tim, came outside one day and told me to take my Marine Corps hat off because it was no place for veterans.

"I was in the Marine Corps myself, so I would know. You are going to fail their tests. They give you such strenuous tests that there is no way to complete them. They are physical! And if you think you can shoot, well guess again! You can't shoot good enough to be an expert! You're a novice rebar cutter! What makes you think you can shoot a rifle?" He was obtrusive and rude as Hell. I got fed up with him immediately, and took a roll of rebar off of the holder and started to put it roughly into the cart for it ... and it bounced off, went over the fence, and collided with the hood of his truck.

"What the hell do you think you are doing?" He asked me abruptly.

"It was an accident man. And you can go to Hell yourself, you prick. I will do far better than you ever hoped to do in the Marines!" I was angry with him for his faulty diatribe.

He got irate and complaining went inside to get me fired. It didn't work. The boss liked me.

I finished working that day and ran up to the car, knowing that, for a fact, I would do much better than he had ever done in the Marines.

And I was right.

First, I graduated from Gates, about half a year earlier than I would have gotten in a regular High School. The teacher was fantastic to me and invited me to give them a speech at the end. I did, and it was elegant. I got good grades, too. Odd, considering that the classes there were made for abuse victims to handle, and were much, much easier than those of the regular High Schools. And I had been getting bad grades in the regular High School, anyways. The reason was because I had been abused so badly for so long, but I didn't know that at the time. And because Paris had said a lot of negative things to my teachers, they had treated me like I was someone who didn't belong in class. Those idiots took her side, at my expense.

I finally got sent to Boot Camp on Camp Pendleton, California, next to San Diego. And I went free of Paris's errors.

I shall be brief about what Boot Camp was like. It was a life-changer. The exercises and the drill and the evolutions and the teamwork was so literate that we found ourselves doing what we were instructed to do literally all day long, with no breaks at all, from rising up straight through to going to sleep, every day for three whole months.

There is a website on the Marine Corps Bootcamp that discusses what all occurs during that 12-week period. If you want knowledge of it, go there. I shall avoid writing the details here. But here is a general description of what occurred.

First, we had to go through classes on what Boot Camp was all about. At the same time, they processed us with physical fitness and health tests, and gave us some classes on things like gear and uniform and equipment. Then we started the actual training. It involved running, physical fitness, cardiovascular exercises, a variety of made-up exercises within our board room, boxing, pugil sticks, martial arts, rappelling, the obstacle courses, the rifle range, and others. Overall, the training was excitable, fun, ardent, detailed, and full of verve. We had to do things nonstop from the time we woke up to the time we went to sleep. Nonstop! And we had no breaks whatsoever, either. Imagine going through that every day! And that is what we did, every single day of boot camp, with no breaks and no hesitation whatsoever.

Now, consider the problems I had before then with Paris, and the abuses I had sustained along with the episodes of getting nearly dropped from school just month before. Yet, I did well. So well that I got a perfect 300 points on the Physical Fitness Test at the end (the PFT) which involved pull ups (I got over 20), abdominal crunches (I got over 100), and a 3 mile run (that I did in under 18 minutes). I also had shot a perfect score on the range, as the only recruit to do so over a very large period of time. The recruiters, upon completion of the course, told me that I had done a fantastic job, and that I would very likely be recommended for extra duty as an elite job having soldier.

And think, that is how I did after having been abused so badly that I started to get bad grades in High School and was near getting dropped out! That performance is proof that if Paris tries to sue me for writing this, then she will fail, because the fact is that she DID abuse me and literally force me to 5 different high schools in a three year period. And I was a genius. That is proof that she was abusive so badly, and my performance in the Marines was so prevalent that it showed the effects of that abuse, and the effects of my genius in a positive military environment put on by the Marines!

I graduated with Paris present. She said a bunch of negative things about my command and drill instructors, about the troops, and about our movements. I got fed up and complained to one of the Drill Instructors about her, and he told her facts with the verge of getting her to stop. Then I went to a Hotel room with Grace, and there she told me that she was leaving home to go become a stripper. A striptease dancer!

Go figure that the girl I was dating would do such a thing. It was due to my mindset after having been sexually abused by Paris for years, and I didn't know it. But it was what drove me to a severely abused woman who eventually took on dancing naked for men for money as a job role. That was because she and Paris thought the same way ... I just didn't know it yet!

I left Grace that night, and our relationship was over.

The actions of Grace and Paris were so negative that they made it clear that being around them was extremely negative, and I wanted no part of it. And my success in the Marines was so prevalent that it became obvious that it was definitely a solid job designed to give the highest profiles of care and competition to its recruits - and that was what I wanted to do.

So, I began my Marine Corps career. And I excelled in ways that a person would not think was possible. And at the same time, I faced threats to my life that almost killed me. Yet I continued. That is part of the argument about the Hereafter that this book is about.

CHAPTER 4

MARINE CORPS

Now let me describe what an elegant career my time in the Marines was like.

At my first unit, I was told out of Boot Camp that I was going to be sent to the elite unit Sniper platoon within 2nd Battalion 5th Marines. There I was immediately sent to Scout Swimmer's course, then upon completion with no rest, I was sent to Sniper School.

You may not know this - I didn't when I was sent there - but Snipers are some of the most elite soldiers in the Marines. They have a skill with shooting that is elegant, and they are able to shoot at targets far, far distances away. The range at Sniper School had us shoot at 1000 meters away, and that was not even the maximum range!

The course was solid and elegant in its presentation. We were made to do sniper related tasks or do studies of it daily, from sun up to sun down, and the only breaks we got were at the range, in between firing. The physical fitness also was elegant in its steadfastness and presentation. We ran, did cardiovascular activities, or physical exercises like moving sandbags through the class daily. At the end, we were made to stay up literally for five days straight without sleep, while exercising, moving, doing classes, doing patrols, and doing drills. It was very rough! Can you imagine not sleeping for five days? It is almost impossible to imagine!

I graduated with honors. Not only that, but I had gotten a perfect score on the range, shooting so high that it went beyond what even the instructor's thought was possible. I got a reward for it, and a big fat 50 Caliber Hogs tooth. A Hogs tooth is a bullet with its casing shaved off, that is placed on a band for a necklace or bodily wearing brace. They are fantastic looking, and think about it ... what is the reaction of a person who witnesses someone wearing a Hogs tooth? They think they are assassins, that is what they think, and they are right! Snipers are some of the best assassins inside the military!

Upon completion, I went through the training very readily. I went on two different deployments to the West, near Japan, on board Okinawa. The training was resolute and solid. And so was the exercise. The problem was that after my third year in, I began to get injured every year.

The first event occurred while I was on a patrol for the Sniper platoon. I fell down a tall cliff above a creek bed, about 30 feet, and crashed down in the bed, nearly fracturing my legs, neck, and back. I had to crawl up the hill to the front with my pack behind me about 2,000 meters to get out. It was rough, and my neck hurt badly, but I did it, getting to the Humvee at the top of the hill on the road up there for extract.

Then, I was supposed to be on light duty for three months. Instead I started to do cardiovascular exercises, in preparation for the Force Reconnaissance Indoctrination that I was going to attend that January.

I recovered faster than anyone expected. Then I went to take the Force Reconnaissance Indoctrination. And I did remarkably well at it. Now is that story.

Now let me tell you about Force Reconnaissance.

They are an elite Special Operations Capable unit that has some of the highest presences of any unit in the American military. They are as adept, and some Marines argue even more adapt, than Army Special Forces, or Navy SEALS. They have an extremely high profile with elegant training that goes on literally every single day they work. And they work a lot more than the average Marine does. And Marines work more than people within other units. That says a lot about their performance.

The Force Recon Indoctrination was an acceptance episode that each Marine was to go through to prove that they had the endurance and capabilities to go through the training. I had already been to Ranger school, so I had an idea of where they put forth the duties that they did.

Now, the Indoctrination was composed of a solid series of exercises that started at 6:00 AM and went until 4:00 PM that night. That is a long time for exercise! Most people couldn't do it all. I shall not tell you here exactly what those exercises were. Just know the details of a few of them.

For example, there was a run for about 10 miles in the end of it. To start the run, I had to have a backpack on. The strap around my shoulders broke, and the pack collapsed as everyone else were able to keep on running. I immediate decided to fix it and fixed it with a lever from cord within my pack that I had. Then I put it back on and 5 minutes later began to run behind everyone else.

I caught up with almost everyone running. At the end, I saw I was behind another man who ran before me to the Humvee. I thought he had beaten me. I found out at the end from an instructor that he didn't beat me, in fact. He came in first because I was five minutes behind from the pack malfunction, but the instructor took the time off my time, so I actually beat him. I had come in first place.

In fact, I came in first place on the entire event. I was the only one who completed every single obstacle on the course correctly, who beat everyone on the run, and who competed every single other exercise. For that I was given first place, and the command of the place, who gave me a final verbal test, were extremely grateful and appreciative for my skills and abilities.

The next day I was approached by a Force Recon psychologist, who gave me an IQ test. Out of 100 questions possible, I got 98 of them right. She said that I was a genius, who had a higher intelligence quotient than virtually everyone in the company.

Extreme! Now, that proves that I should not have been on the verge of being kicked out of High School! I had come in first place in the competition for an elite Special Forces unit that did things that most High School students have no idea of how to do or perform! And I was a genius! *A Genius!*

You may not know this at this time, but as you read this you will get the idea of how many different ways I was tried and punished for crime I didn't do. I came near death on multiple occasions. The things I faced would have driven an average person mad. But I am not an average person. I got through it all on the level of genius! That is what got me through it all!

Now let me tell you about how there were even more injuries, and risks of death involved in that job. Now what one would expect, I figure, but it happened, and they actually could have been much worse, as I shall put here in the next section.

In Force Recon, I almost died on more than one occasion. I shall describe them here.

Those near-death experiences were the opening of my mindset for adaptation to such proclivities. It was the opener to my adaptation to the welfare that I began to experience regarding the near-death experiences, with followed me throughout life on a level far beyond what the average person would think was even possible. The summary of me being punished unlawfully by many people was not just the effects of negative people, no, they were agents of Satan himself, seeking to turn them against me with sinful actions that denied common sense and justice.

As you will see in the part about my actions during the warfare of God against evils, the demons and evil Satanic souls of the fallen had become aware of the fact that I used to be an Angel, and was going to be placed by God against them on Judgement Day. That is true, and what they sought to do was to kill me away from life so I could not move forwards in that direction. But I shall.

I have plans. I am engaged in a multi-million-dollar lawsuit against the VA of Phoenix, Arizona, for putting me in the fire of that Satanic villain who tried to kill me. When I win, which I shall, I think, I will be using portions of that money for trips to Israel, for the purpose of finding and learning about the actual Ark of the Covenant. It may be there, and if it is, perhaps I can get an agent to let me go near it and learn what I can about it.

I shall tell him about my fortune, and explain to him this book so he can get the understanding that I have learned from God and his Angels how to fight against evil forces, and have done it in the past, and will continue to do it full-scale in the future!

Now let me tell you about how I nearly died in the Marines.

First, there was the time that I almost fell and broke my neck inside of the Sniper platoon.

Then, in Force Reconnaissance, we did a special swim in the ocean along the tidewaters of the waves on the beach. We got there by parachutes, jumping into the water. I did that successfully, then we were to swim along the waters of the tide in holding the safety band for a water-depth meter. When we arrived at that tidewater, it was so thick, nearly 14 feet tall per wave, that it became obvious that we were not going to be able to do the drill. So, we all began to swim into the shore. On the way, I got swept under the waves over and over and over again, with no time to breath underneath each time, and I was beginning to drown. Now, to prevent drowning, we had safety valves on each safety vest we each wore - and depressing the safety valve would put air into the vest and make it float. I was beginning to drown and put my hand on the valve. And then I began to black out.

I woke up with my vest inflated upon the top of the waves. So, I survived, but barely. After we got ashore, my team leader came over to me and criticized me for using the safety valve. Then he told me to get ready to jump via parachute in the fields of the camp. I refused, I had had enough energy wasted, and was certain that I would be unable to jump properly. Besides, I had almost died. He didn't care. But we didn't jump. The platoon sergeant got my story and listened.

Then I went for a parachute jump in a field on base, and the parachute malfunctioned. It and my reserve both opened, and the main was crooked in such a manner that it was floating below me. The risk was that if both parachutes started to go towards the ground, then they would cause me to collide with the ground at too high a speed to survive. So, I finally was able to eject the main, and the reserve gave me good flight.

What could have easily happened was that when I tried to eject the main, it could have steered into the reserve, or caused it to steer incorrectly, and the loss of both canopies would have caused me to lose my life. There was a high probability of that occurring, too. It didn't, because I was lucky.

Then, during freefall school, we were to start out by learning how to fly inside of a wind tunnel inside of a building. The wind tunnel consisted of a circular group of fibers of parachute cable in a circle along the edge of the wind tunnel. The wind tunnel was made of a wind-blown fan in the floor, blowing upwards, surrounded by a mat of bracing fiber that one could fall on.

When I was in the wind tunnel, in flying position

floating flat, two instructors flew above me and began to wrestle. One of them lost body position and fell into me, forcing me to lose bodily position and start to float upwards. About 35 feet up, my foot hit the circular fibers and got stuck, pushing me head down. I then fell 35 feet head first into the mats, hitting so hard that I felt like I had broken my neck and had kicked myself so hard in the back of my helmet that it ruptured into pieces.

I was so hurt from that that I could have died. Instead, the instructor wanted me to go to medical, and I turned him down, instead requesting, in a Force Recon survival mindset, that I continue to jump. So, he let me while I was injured. It was so hard to keep my body posture because it hurt every time, but I was able to do everything correctly ... with difficulty, true, but correctly. Notti left the class injured.

Then, with the freefall injuries, I went to Mountain Leader's Course in the mountains. There the injury was so bad that I fell and could have almost died falling.

Then I went, about 6 months later, to be a Mountain Warfare Training Center (MWTC) Instructor. While there my shoulder was so injured that eventually I couldn't climb the cliffs with it, and thus no longer was able to teach the students, so the Gunner Sergeant of the Company told me to go get surgery on it. So I did. And the surgery was so horrible that it did not allow me to continue because of its continued injury to my shoulder.

That was the final element, in part, of why I got out

of the Marine Corps then. The synopsis of the surgery was that I was never going to be in shape to rejoin Force Reconnaissance again, so there was no reason to stay in. I was a genius, and there was nothing other than Headquarters that I could work that wouldn't give me the same anti-terrorist training that I had learned to do inside the Force Recon Company.

The other reason is because, before I got out, I had gotten back in touch with Grace, and had gotten her pregnant with twins. And she had become a subject of Paris's abuse and turned me away from them. That is a story coming up.

First, let me tell you about what was going through my mind with each injury and near-death experience.

Each experience, when I became injured, was such that it made my mind rush forwards to the concepts of doing things or moving my body in a rapid sense of time to do something different that would give me stability, or leave me uninjured. That is what allowed me to rapidly move my legs and arms in such a manner, for example, during the fall on the cliff or in the wind tunnel that allowed me to take the bodily position that allowed me to strike the ground in a way that allowed me to do so without breaking my neck. And both times I came close to breaking my neck, too, and would have if my bodily position had been any different.

Then, after the injury, my mind always went to the

same place; a management of what it was that I had previously planned on doing but could not now because of the injury, placed next to what was happening. And what was happening was that I was having to move on the injury and take it into account regarding what I was going to say and do for medical treatment to the authorities that I was working for. Upon the conclusion of that, it was such that I would find some sort of medical care, which was something initially far from my mind, or I would move and exercise in a way that allowed me to continue to recover while assisting my physical fitness. Now, people often did not agree with me exercising while injured, and the fact was that I shouldn't have been able to. But my mental state was so pronounced and accurate that it allowed me to do that. I shall explain how.

The mental concept of operating while injured is one that defies common sense. The normal person sees the injured area as being one that has movement on its own that must move less in order to heal. They see it as being unable to move in the way it normally does because the injury would become worse as it is flexed and moved around. But me, to me that was not the case. I was still able to move my injured legs in cardiovascular exercises even though the joints hurt from the injury, but the concept of moving pain away from affected areas was such that I was able to flex, under pain but control, even though I was injured. That was why I was able to do cardiovascular exercises injured in preparation for the Force Reconnaissance Indoctrination, and even on the verge of being injured, I had performed so much and so well that during the Indoctrination I was the only one to pass each and every single event during a full 10 hour long exercise episode.

So that is how I got past the injuries I sustained. And also, one of the things was to want to avoid further training because of seen disability present. For example, after I nearly drowned in the ocean, we were supposed to go on a parachute jump right afterwards. I didn't even think about it while or after I had nearly drowned, but when my Team Leader came up and mentioned it, I was taken aback and told him that there was no way I was going to jump. Jumping and nearly drowning were so prevalently different in exercise that one made it nearly impossible to do the other in a near time span. So ... I refused.

That answers that concept.

Before I tell you about the twins, let me tell you about the unnecessary and unauthorized duties they gave to me as an instructor there at MWTC.

I went to the Mountain Warfare Training Center as an instructor for training soldiers to go fight in Afghanistan. Based on my last Force Reconnaissance deployment, we had been taken under the auspices of the command to participate in the new wars in Afghanistan and Iraq. But we did not go ashore, and I felt very irate because of that. I believed in those anti-terror exercises a lot, because I had worked on anti-terror operations seriously within my platoon. We did fire-fire fights against aggressor actors that were so profound and solid that they went beyond what, we were told, even the FBI does for their SWAT members. We were at the most elite method of combat within the US military. Now, Navy SEALs and Army Special Forces may disagree with that, but we, as Force Recon Marines, had trained with both of them, and saw ourselves as being more profound and concise than they were.

When I arrived at MWTCC, the Gunnery Sergeant of the command told me that he wanted me to do more than the average instructor there did. Why? "Because you're Special Forces, Marine, so we expect you to be capable of a lot more than usual!" He then put me in charge of not only doing what the average Marine there did, which was teach the infantry or the corpsmen tricks about climbing, but he also put me in charge of training Force Reconnaissance, Special Forces, Navy Seals, Air Force Para-Rescue. He also told me that in addition to that, I was to assist another Marine instructor, who was a Sniper, to train Marines in his Mountain Sniper Course. And that is not all. He also wanted me to start to prepare the computer software for the Force Reconnaissance Mountain Leader's course, which at that time did not exist. A tall order! Any one of those programs were organized and slated to take up all of an instructor's time!

To make it plain, the average instructor worked literally four days out of the week on their package, with the other three days off. I, on the other hand, was made to work literally 23 days straight, to only two days off, during which the arrogant command was trying to make me go to my room and clean it for their inspection on my days off. I refused and told them to eat it! The Staff Sergeant of Unit Operations was the one to do the inspection, and he got feisty when I refused him. I went before him ready for confrontation, and told him in plain terms that I was working far more than any of his other Marines were, and if he had a problem with that, then I was going to get him fired. He saw me as absolute and stopped harassing me. Instead I caught him trying later to say a bunch of negative things about me to the other instructors, and I let them know that he was lying.

At the same time as the instruction went on, I was having the episode of shoulder injury coming forth, from the injury that I had gotten almost a year earlier in Freefall School. One day I was supposed to engage in a competition against another Marine of the Force Recon platoon training there, where we were to climb up a rope with protection faster than the other. About halfway up, I was beating him, and suddenly my shoulder started to ache so badly that it became rapidly impossible for me to move it upwards. I slid to the ground, with my shoulder up in my sleeve, and called the Captain over.

I told him about what was going on. He said, "you've done good, man, but you are too injured to keep on going. You need to go to medical."

I went to the Gunnery Sergeant of the MWTC

command and told him about what happened. He arranged for me to get surgery on it.

So, I did. The damage from the surgery was so pronounced that the doctor said that I was never going to recover enough to rejoin Force Reconnaissance ever again. And it turns out that he was right.

Behind the physical injuries I had sustained, the fact that I was never going to be able go to back to Force Reconnaissance, the errors of training me too much that they put me under, and, not yet mentioned, but the even more severe abuse I sustained from Paris, my divorce errors and abuse from my ex-wife, and the abuse I faced from Grace, any one of those things would have been too much for an average person to be able to handle with dexterity and lawfulness, but I did. And I was punished lawlessly for it by the so-called authority figures of the State of Washington. Those portions are to follow next, in the rest of this chapter, and the next chapter.

Now I shall tell you about how I erroneously married my ex-wife, and how she abused me lawlessly, Then I got divorced from her for it, and got in a repeated romance with Grace. And I got her pregnant with twins. And at Paris's request she separated me from them. Flat out evil.

You will see here that Paris, my ex-wife, and Grace are all agents of Satan himself.

Now, let me back up to the portion where I married my ex-wife. That occurred right after I had joined Force Reconnaissance Company, back in 1998.

I wish I had seen the errors in it from the beginning. I got involved with her in part because I missed Grace (the stripper) at the time, and had just been accepted to Force Reconnaissance Company, which was far more pronounced in effort and leadership than what I had experienced in High School. Think about it ... in High School I faced the erroneous judgements of the teachers who had been told a lot of negative things about me by Paris ... which were lies ... then four years later I joined Force Reconnaissance Company and there was seen as a Genius! Go figure, right? So, I wanted to celebrate, and at a college party near San Diego, I encountered my ex-wife, and there she hit on me and I very stupidly went for it.

My ex-wife is arrogant, faulty, aggressive, and has no concept of what right and wrong really are. I got her pregnant with my son, which she had while I was on my first Force Recon Deployment, and my first contact with him was kind and fabulous on my part, and aggressive and trying to steer me away from him on her part.

Over the following years, she did the following abusive acts: (I have a limited memory of the things she did, specifically, because remembering the details put my mind in the frame of creating counter-arguments, and when I did, Paris or Downlow would take her side counter to common sense and in error against me. That is because they are abusive and Satanic people, and they seek altercations against the Good.) My ex-wife: tried to kill me on the road running with little J, tried to force me to pay for child support early, accused me of saying negative things about her abuse to her roommates, accused me of cheating on her (when I hadn't), accused me of seeking death through training, accused me of child abuse when I hadn't even spanked my child but once within his first five years of life, she tried to force me to pay her more money than what she was entitled to, she even complained to my command trying to force them to make me pay her more money than she was entitled to, and she contacted my command trying to get them to kick me out based on a false claim of an assault against her that never happened. That was a felony account, on her part. The fact is that I had never gotten kicked out of any unit in the Marines, ever.

Eventually, at that last count, I got fed up with her and got divorced. She tried to force the Department of Child Support and the MWTC Command to force me to give her more money. They didn't, not until I was in prison later (as put in the next chapter) and did it illegally. And even then, she was trying to force me to give her more money than she was entitled to.

If I remember right, we were married in 1998. We got divorced in 2002, when I was sent to be an instructor at MWTC. Then, in late 2002, I got involved, by accident, with Grace again. Now here is that story.

For starters, in late 2002 I got an email from some unknown author of a boat in the water that was full of rifle cases. I was certain from getting it that it had come from Grace at an address that was ineligible. It did not have my name on it or anything to identify me. But it was the sailed convolution of a vehicle that was outside of the realm of reality. And that was where I felt I was, with the faulty premises of evil people trying to do negative things to me, while at the same time I was pervading it with Special Operations Capable operations that were full of success and promises.

Then, I don't remember how, but I got an email from Grace. She wanted me to come and see her. So, I was at MWTC, as an instructor, and took some time off of work to go see her in Oregon, in a small town I shall not name here.

When I arrived, I was in a costume of spiderman. It was a full-bodied rendition of suit, with the red and blue threaded spiderweb looking design on the front, and a picture of a spider in the middle. The reason I wore it was because I wanted to appeal to the fabricated nature of Grace in the realm of the imaginary, which I was used to getting from her in our speeches about things. What I didn't realize, was the fact that many of those things we talked about were negative things. Things like the fact that her mother's boyfriend had murdered some people, or that she had gotten separated from a military service minded man, or that she married his friend to get away from that, or that she had decided to become a stripper, when that was in fact her manner of saying how she had been influenced by the abuse of my mother against me.

We interacted well. She said a lot of odd things to me, trying to draw my attention. Then she forgave me for whatever she said I did to make her become a stripper. I accepted the apology, when I should have held it against her, and we ended up having sex upon her bed.

And I got her pregnant with twins.

That was what occurred after my ex-wife and I had been divorced because of her abuse, and she had held my positive parenting against me for no good reason. It occurred while I was facing injuries, surgery, and inoperability within the command of MWTC. It occurred during a time that I was facing the errors of Paris's abuse. Yet I got Grace pregnant.

That was God's way of testing me. I don't know how, yet. But somehow, I am succeeding. I have looked at a random page in the Bible asking what is going to become of me after I die. And it said that I was going to be made into God's Son, the way it was done for Jesus Christ, and I was to be a King over mankind after that. Heavy. I don't know how that is supposed to happen. I told Krishna, and she said, with great awareness, that God is going to give me ideas on how to make it happen when the time arrives, because He always helps me out that way. And she is right. She has a knowledge of the subject that only a person with the heavy compliance of religion can have.

I called my ex-wife and got her to let me see little J

there at Grace's house. She refused to drive halfway to see me, forcing me to drive an extra 4 hours away to get him. In addition to that, she kept on saying negative things to me, trying to get more money and saying, inappropriately, that I was "abusive to J."

At the same time, Grace was interfering with my parenthood. For example, one day little J was out in the play pool in the yard, and he was so excited that he didn't want to come inside for chow. I told him to get out of there and come in. He pitched a fit and began to cry for no other reason than that he was upset that he couldn't stay in the pool. So, I sat him down and began to, using my military mindset, say kind things to him to unify his mind with the concept of eating a good meal instead of staying in the pool. It worked. Grace didn't like it .... though and had a lot of negative things to say about it at the table.

The reason she did that was because she was so used to being around her abusive mother that she had gotten that method of prescription away from her, and it was remarkably negative.

Paris came up to Grace's house right before she gave birth. She told me that it was to help her. But when I arrived, Grace told me that Paris had done so many negative things that she couldn't even begin to number them. One of the things she pointed out was that Paris had taken her own kitchen table there and replaced Grace's table with it. "That was in error," Grace said.

Then I went into another room with Grace, and she started to say all sorts of negative things about our relationship that were not true. She said she hated me for getting her pregnant. And as she talked, she kept on mumbling and saying things in total profound error. I came to realize that she was so irate because she was getting ready to have the children. She was having seizures and going through the effects of giving birth.

We took her to the hospital. When she was in the surgery bed, she pushed out the girl, then immediately refused to push forwards on the boy. She was trying to kill him.

The doctor talked to her commands to deliver the boy, and she finally listened to him. He had to resuscitate the boy and bring him back to life.

Afterwards, I sat with her as the adoptive parents came forwards and accepted the births of the twins as their own.

A few months later, I was at my command at MWTC in California, and I got a message in the mail from Grace. It was a disc of rough songs on it and a letter that said that she wanted me to take no part in the children's lives at all. It was a hateful and evil letter, and I am certain that it was a result of the interference of Paris, who probably told her to take no further part in me.

Her actions are the actions of an abusive mother, who seeks to abuse the father of her children. Who seeks to separate an honorable man from his children for no reason other than to listen to his severely abusive mother?

I have, since the incidents that follow, in November, 2016, send a message via email, from Downlow's account, to the adoptive children's new father that I wanted to be kept in touch with the twins, and that I had been abused by Pars, so to pay no attention to her. I received no response. Probably because he chooses to listen to the negative lies of Grace and Paris and Downlow. In error, and something I do not deserve at all.

That concludes this part.

Now, think about it. Those behaviors are enough to drive a sane person mad. And I soon found myself unlawfully sent to prison as-a-result of those lies. Following is the story of the complete lawlessness of the Washington State justice system. (It is erroneous to call it that. It is a System of Fancy and Fraud. That is what it is!)

CHAPTER 5

ILLEGAL ACTS OF THE JUSTICE SYSTEM
FROM 2005 TO 2009

After I got out of the Marine Corps, honorably, I went and joined a protection agency called Triple Canopy. I went through their firearms training, with the impact of learning how to protect government officials from terrorists or warmongers within countries that we were at war with. We were to be prepared to go to a Taliban occupied country, like Afghanistan, or to a terrorist or warmonger occupied country, like Iraq. I trained very well there and was one of the best shooters they had.

The training ended in December 2004. Then I was put on hold from being deployed for them for the reason of there being an airwing problem in Afghanistan that prevented them from sending new troops there. So, I went and accepted a job interview inside of Issaquah, Washington, which was next to my ex-wife's town of Seattle. It was two days of small arms fire in a police station at a range there.

The targets on that range all looked like they had the body posture of a terrorist drawing a firearm from his or her belt. Pay attention to that, because it applies in ways you will not believe at first, but it is true. They looked exactly like the targets that we had learned to fight against inside of Force Reconnaissance. I shall explain how it applies later.

Then, upon completion of training, I went and called my ex-wife and asked her to meet me at the police station near her house to exchange my son. She refused and told me to go pick him up at his daycare, Small Faces. So, I did.

When I arrived the teacher there refused to give me a copy of my kid's daycare records. Then I told her that their policy online made it clear that both parents were to have access to all the student's documents. So, what did they do? They limited it to giving me a document about my son's grade level. What they had forgotten, or didn't notice, was that the document told me that my ex-wife's boyfriend was listed as my son's father. I had no idea, because they had refused to tell me! The fact of the matter was that it was arguably illegal for them to have done that in the first place!

I called my ex-wife and complained about him being listed as my son's father, and demanded that she give me access to my son's records in the daycare, since it was obvious that she had told them to "keep it secret," against their own policy. And those idiots were doing it!

Pay attention to that, because later a prosecutor refused to acknowledge that I was complaining about my ex-wife violating the law against me, which she was, and that idiot chose instead to use it against me!

I took the little one out of there for three days. During that time, he made it clear by talking to me that my ex-wife and her boyfriend had abused him over-and-over again, refusing to let him watch television after school was over and forcing him to study over and over again after hours.

I got suicidal at that, because the error of the staff of the daycare and the fact that they were taking my ex-wife's abusive side was extremely obtrusive. The fact that they were abusing my son swept in my face because I had gone through life abused, and my ex-wife's continued abuse was too much for me to handle. At the same time, there was the mental effects of what had happened with Grace taking the twins away from me at Paris's request. And upon all that, I was still facing the inequities of what I had to face with the accidents and injuries and near-fatal renditions and unjust tasking within the Marines. I felt like dying. I felt like I was going to die. So, I wanted to get it over with.

It was March 17, 2005.

I went to my ex-wife's house that night and knocked on the door. She opened it up and I told her I wanted to go talk to her about parenting at the local coffee shop. She refused and told me that I was abusive to my son. At the same time, she put her hand on her hip, and when she did that, she looked exactly like the terrorist targets I had just shot at only three days before, and for months in stringent duties inside of the anti-terror unit of Force Reconnaissance.

So, I did exactly what I was expected to do, thinking she was drawing a weapon on me, and I drew my weapon on her, prepared to shoot if necessary.

Now, pay strict attention to what I am about to tell you. In Force Reconnaissance Company, we did anti-terror drills that literally lasted for about 6 months straight through. We shot literally for 12 hours per day for weeks in a month at a time, against targets that were within 25 meters away and that were holding a firearm in front, or on their belt, ready to shoot at us. We engaged in counter-terror operations against actors of the Marines who were acting like aggressors within buildings, who would present and fire a weapon at us within 5 seconds of us entering a room to clear it. 5 seconds. Let me make this clear to you ... that is not enough time to think about what you are doing, that is not enough time to move, that is not enough time to dodge bullets, that is not enough time to do anything at all other than draw your weapon on the target and be prepared to shoot if they are armed. That is all the time you have! And one of the things you definitely do not *ever* do is take one hand off your firearm so you can push or prod the enemy into the door or wall or floor, or pull their hair, or do anything whatsoever, because frankly put, taking one's hand off the firearm leaves you presenting it with only one hand, which makes it virtually impossible to be able to take aim and shoot at someone getting ready to shoot at you. And you would miss if you tried. So, we never, ever took our hand off the pistol or rifle. We always kept it on. Always! And to be frank, doing anti-terror exercises against actors literally for almost every week within a 6-month period with that keep-all posture being the hallmark of your activities is a sure way to make sure it happens, every time!

The reason I am telling you that now is because the police who got involved lied to the judge about what happened. It is a sign of their complete ignorance. What they did was a felony against me. Pay attention and I will make it clear here what they did. The reason is because I am going to be submitting this portion of this book to the ACLU, for-the-purpose of suing those fucking officers, and sending their asses to prison for at least as-long-as they sent me there with their lies, when I was innocent.

So after I spent 15 seconds clearing the room that my ex-wife and her boyfriend were in, telling her boyfriend to get on the floor instead of hitting me, which he was trying to get ready to do, and he did get on the floor, I realized that they were not drawing a weapon on me after all, so I unloaded the pistol, apologized for the error, told my ex-wife that I was going to commit suicide because of her abuse, and I left.

I began to drive to Weyerhaeuser, which was Paris's old place of work when we lived there. I wanted her to accept responsibility for the suicide, because it was equally her fault that I was doing it.

On the way, I called my ex-wife, and a police officer answered the phone. His name is listed here in actuality, because that is what is on the court documents regarding the so-called "crime" they accused me unlawfully of. His name is McNulty.

I told McNulty about what had actually happened, telling him the truth. I told him the truth about how my ex-wife had violated the law against me. I told him about how my ex-wife had tried to, unsuccessfully, get me kicked out of Force Recon with her lies about me assaulting her. Then I told him about how her boyfriend had illegally listed himself as my son's father on his daycare record. McNulty ignored me, so I hung up, telling him I was going to commit suicide.

Then I got to Weyerhaeuser and tried to shoot myself in the chest. The trigger pulled, but the gun did not go off. The round did not fire. So, I tried it again, and again, it did not go off.

So, I went and called the police asking for the direction to their office so could turn myself in. The officer instead told me to go to a gas station near the officer compound and turn myself in there. I did, and then about 12 officers showed up in their cars and held me at gunpoint, threatening to kill me. Go figure! They did the same thing to me that they were arresting me for in the first place, and they threatened to kill me when I was trying to turn myself in! What the hell did that officer that I talked to say to them?

I bailed out for a lot of money ... everything I had ... $150,000.

Within a week I got an order at my house in Nevada to return to court. I hired an attorney to see me there. Here name was Victoria Smith. That is her actual name, it is on the court documents if you choose to take them from the files on record.

At the hearing, the judge had my attorney go into his room, while having me sit in the other room outside of being able to hear what he was talking about. I was there with a local bail bondsman. The hearing was held without me present, and my attorney then came down and told me that they were refusing my bail and re-arresting me and taking me to jail. The bail bondsman had never seen anything like that before, and said it was in error. I believe him, because Constitutionally, I should have been present at that hearing. And I later found out from Victoria why that was.

For one, the judge violated my 8th Constitutional Amendment right on three different counts. First, at the prosecutor's request, he raised my bail from $150,000 that I had paid to $500,000, which was impossible for me to afford. The 8th Amendment states, "the United State Constitution prohibits the federal government from imposing excessive bail…" Putting the bail so high that it was impossible for me to afford it was making it excessive.

The other ways judge Kessler (his actual name) violated my 8th Amendment right is to put me on a charge of a nearly 5-year prison sentence, during which the prison staff violated their own policy by giving all my money to either DCS or DSHS … when their own police stated that I was to receive at a minimum 10 percent of it. The 8th Constitutional Amendment goes on to state "… excessive fines …", which is what that was. And then the prison went on further to put me unlawfully in solitary confinement, which should be seen as the torture that it is, when the 8th Constitutional Amendment states "… cruel and unusual punishment." That is what torture is, you fucking prison administering idiots! And the same goes to you, Judge Kessler, who put it in writing that I was to undergo that!

Let me go even farther with what else occurred during that hearing. The prosecutor also wrote down the following. Let me remind you that it was actually proof of me complaining about my ex-wife very unlawfully putting her boyfriend listed as my son's father at his daycare. Yet, the prosecutor used it against me instead of using the law on my side, as he should have! Here is what it said:

"The voice mail message left by the defendant on

February 18, 2005, regarding some documents he was attempting to obtain concludes, "I've asked nicely. I made it a point to ask nicely, over a good period of time. Earlier in 2004, earlier in 2004, what happened (her name), what happened? I was asking nice. But what did you do? You blew me off. You balked. You told me I didn't need to have that information. So fuck you. Now, I am going to continue to bother your ass until you provide me with it because, guess what, that's the only way you provide it. Think about it."

The fact is that the things I was wanting was records regarding my son's education, and she was refusing to give me any of them. She was refusing to tell me what grade school she was trying to put him in. And she was telling the staff of Small Faces to avoid giving me any of my son's documents, even though their own policy said I was entitled to them, and that despicable prosecutor, Norm Maleng and Scott A. Marlow, WSBA #25987, refused to use that statement to bring me justice against my ex-wife's lawbreaking against me and instead used it to violate my 8th Constitutional Amendment right!

The prosecutors went even further with their lies. They tried to say it "is unclear where the defendant obtained the handgun ... and presumably would not have been able to bring it with him on the plane." A flat out lie! I checked the pistol on the plane on baggage when I got on! Everyone has that right! Those fucking prosecutors were trying to create out of mid-air another reason to convict me of a crime I didn't commit!

Those prick prosecutors and Judge Kessler each deserve to be sent to prison to force them to pay the price for their violations of my Constitutional Right.

It gets even worse than that. Let me describe what lies Officer McNulty and Detective Pfaff conducted against me, with their letter of felony lies, felony perjury and felony malicious prosecution they conducted against me.

Pfaff wrote a *Certification for Determination of Probable Cause* against me to Judge Kessler. In it she wrote the lie: "(My ex-wife's name) was shoved to the floor." The fact was that if I had done that, I would have taken my hand off the pistol against what I had learned through strenuous anti-terror exercises in Force Recon. She also wrote the lie: "Mitchell took a few fast steps towards (my ex-wife's name), grabbed her by the hair and slammed her against the French Doors." Again, that did not happen. A person has only 5 seconds to respond to the concept of someone drawing a weapon on them. There is no time to take a few fast steps anywhere, and again, we were trained to never, ever take a hand off the weapon and grab someone by the hair. That is totally in error.

The fact that those officers would make such novice, stupid mistakes with their taking on of what actually occurred is proof of their total ignorance and incapability to fight a firefight with anyone. They did the same stupid mistakes as done by cops talked about on CNN in 2016, who were from police behaving like those of Cleveland, Chicago, Baton Rouge, Ferguson, who killed innocent, unarmed black men by gunshot. And they were found innocent in the courtrooms even when proven guilty. That is the same sort of stupid error that those despicable officers, McNulty and Pfaff, did, by lying and maliciously prosecuting me to the judge.

It is even worse than that. They also said on that document the lie that "He was ultimately forced out of his Marine unit because of a "High Profile Assault" against (name of my ex-wife)." That was a complete lie, and I shall explain why in the next chapter. But know this, those despicable officers were telling that lie even though I had told McNulty the truth about it, that I had never gotten kicked out of any unit, and that fucker chose to lie about it to Pfaff! And she chose to lie about it to the Judge! And that despicable ass listened to her and the lying prosecutor and violated my Constitutional 8th Amendment right over and over and over again! What the fuck?

Let me make this clear to you. My military records are proof that I did not do those things said by McNulty and Pfaff. The problem was that I didn't have access to them because I was in jail, and then in prison, so I wasn't able to see their truths until afterwards, during the time when I was so mentally discombobulated that I was unable to write down those truths. Until now, some 11 years later. That was distinctly due to the mental illness I got from solitary confinement, which is arguably, within the website newspaper article called *The Horrible Psychology of Solitary Confinement*, which said that it was torture, and caused permanent damage to the minds of those who have to do it. Now I shall tell you about what my military records say about me being innocent.

First, my DD Form 214 states that I was sent to the following schools as well: Amphibious Reconnaissance 1998, SOTG Qualified Urban Sniper 1998, Sergeants 2000, Summer Mountain Leader's Course 2000, Special Forces Military Freefall 2000, SOTG Close Quarters Battle 2001, Instructor Training Course 2002. I was married to my ex-wife from 1998 to 2002 when I was in Force Recon company, so if I had assaulted her and was kicked out of that unit, as McNulty and Pfaff lied about, then do you think I would have continued to go to Force Recon specific schools, as I did, during that time? That is not all. There are more records.

Second, I earned *Certificate of Good Conduct* medals during that time. My second award was for the period 30 November 1996 to 29 November 1999. My third award was for 29 November 1999 to 28 November 2002. Do you really think they would have given me Good Conduct medals if I had gotten kicked out of a Special Forces unit for a High-Profile Assault against anyone? Hell no they wouldn't have! Pfaff and McNulty were lying!

And then there is the proof that they lied about my conduct inside the house, taking a hand off the weapon and assaulting my ex-wife ... again, flat out lies! If I had performed that way at all when I was doing counter-terror operations in Force Reconnaissance Company, then I would have been kicked out of the anti-terror operation itself. That never happened. Instead, I received a very high-quality assessment from the commander of the unit on my last Fitness Report. His name was Colonel Gunther. The reviewing officer was Colonel Smith. He wrote: "Continued outstanding performance by an exceptional Marine – ideal Force Recon Marine – smart, tough, and aggressive. His consistently superb performance over the demanding MEU(SOC) deployment had been critical to achieving mission success. His leadership and ability to conduct the entire range of sophisticated reconnaissance missions demanded by this type of assignment marks him as a genuinely exceptional Marine. My strongest recommendation for promotion and assignment to instructor duty."

Now, do you think I would have gotten that recommendation from the commanding colonel as my last fitness report from that command if I had gotten kicked out of that unit for any reason whatsoever? I don't think so! McNulty and Pfaff had lied, severely, committing felony perjury and malicious prosecution against me! They deserve to be sent to prison for at least the same amount of time that they sent me to prison, when I was innocent, and they are not!

To make matters worse, they were sending me to prison in Washington State, when I was a resident of a different state – Nevada. For that reason, I should not have gone to court or state prison there. I should have been sent to federal places. If I had been sent to federal places, then the police would not have been able to intimidate my attorney into making plead "guilty" when I was innocent.

I am going to be sending this to the FBI as a complaint against those officer's felony misconduct against me. I know the Washington State justice system is full of fraud. We'll see if the FBI is, too. They probably aren't.

We'll see.

To make matters worse, my attorney came by the jail and took me to a hearing in front of another judge, where I was to plead either innocent or guilty. I told them that I wanted to plead innocent, which I was, and Victoria Smith took me immediately out of there and back into the holding cell, where she told me that, for one, the police had intimidated her so there was no way for her to protect me, because there would be consequences. Plus, she said that, based on the paperwork (with the lies that I have mentioned, that I hadn't seen yet, but that had been delivered to her ... which is another error on her part) she had no ability to defend me. A lie! I had severe PTSD at the time, and had been abused so severely, as explained here so far, that I felt suicidal. And I had attempted suicide on March 17, just a few months earlier anyways. Did the court pay attention to that? Hell no they didn't! So, when I went back downstairs, Victoria told them that I was pleading guilty. When I was innocent!

So, I was convicted as guilty. I am taking this before the ACLU about the injustices done in that regards. I am giving them a copy of this document, so they can have it to use to plead me as innocent and correct my record.

And I want Victoria Smith to be fired from the BAR for what she did. Oh, wait … in 2012 she *was fired* from the BAR, for failure to represent her clients. She did the similar thing to them that she did to me. The fact is that she should have been fired back in 2005. I am going to tell the ACLU that, because her clients after the fact should have-the-ability to petition for retrieval for her mis-performances.

That is a description of the severe lawlessness of the Washington State police, their prosecutors, and their judges. It gets worse. They violated the law against me in over 9 different ways. The staff of the prisons, however, what did they do? They violated the law against me in over 18 different ways in 5 years! This next part is about that atrocious behavior.

Keep in mind that they were doing this all to a suicidal abused honorably discharged Marine who had risked his life to defend them from terrorists for nearly 11 years. And they chose to find me guilty, by lies, of crimes that I was innocent of. They convicted me of assault and burglary, both of which I did not do; both of which were based on the lies told by McNulty and Pfaff! What the fuck is wrong with those people, man? They deserve punishment for what they did!

I am slated to be on God's crew of justice-finders when I die. My duty has been told to me that on Judgement Day I am going to be slated to determine which people, those that are alive and dead, have done things holy to get sent to Heaven, or evil to get sent to Hell. And I shall tell you this, each-and-every one of those responsible for convicting me when I was innocent, they are going TO HELL, FOREVER! That is what they have earned, that is exactly what they deserve!

Now, the errors of the prisons. But first, the other police misconduct that they were trying to conceal that occurred on the same night, March 17, 2005.

Go to the AR15.com website and read the article titled *Kerlikowske in the news again*. It reads: "A Seattle police officer who said she accidentally fired her gun on Capitol Hill during an off-duty confrontation with a panhandler has received a reduced penalty, even though the panhandler told investigators the officer twice yelled, "I'm going to kill you." The officer was Penelope Fulmer, a 35-year-old officer, lied to other officers about what had happened. It continues with ""The department's captain of internal affairs, Neil Low, doubted Fulmer's account after reviewing the case. "The preponderance of evidence tends to support that she shot at him and did not have an accidental discharge," Low wrote in an Oct. 25 memo. "Fulmer not only cannot explain how such an accidental discharge would have taken place, in theory," Low wrote. "She accepts no responsibility for her actions."" And, also "Police Chief Gil Kerlikowske agreed with the officer, Penelope Fulmer, that her discharge of her personal handgun during the March 17 incident was accidental. He had originally planned to suspend Fulmer for 30 days without pay but reduced that to 15 days after meeting withher." Kerlikowske, already under scrutiny for reversing disciplinary recommendations, rejected the conclusion of a top commander in internal affairs, who believed that Fulmer deliberately fired her gun."

That whole episode is atrocious. Penelope Fulmer was guilty of attempted murder. And the police chief let her go with only a 15-day suspension? Yet my case, where I only did what I did because I felt like I was being threatened with a firearm, and I fired no shot and apologized, yet those police officers protected their despicable officers who committed felony perjury and malicious prosecution against me? While they were protecting an attempted murderer?

That is proof that the cops of Seattle are of the same low standard as those officers of Dallas, Cleveland, Chicago, Baton Rouge, Ferguson, who killed innocent black men by gunshot. They are guilty of protecting the attempted murderer Penelope Fulmer while committing felonies against me, an honorably discharged Marine who was innocent.

Fuck the Seattle police. Hell is what they have earned. Hell is what they deserve.

Now let me tell you about the wasted lives of the prison guards who broke the law against me.

Here is a summary of the 18 different ways the prison guards violated the law against me. Put these items together over the course of 5 years, with the last year and a half being mind-frazzling solitary confinement, *and you will see torture.*

The prison guards:

1. Destroyed or stole my legal papers repeatedly,

2. Found me guilty of infractions that their staff created for the purpose of unlawfully punishing innocent men, and I complained about it to the runner of the prison, who showed up as I was about to be transferred to Clallam Bay, and she said nothing to me: she very likely lied to the officers while she was ignoring me and sentencing me for an infraction I didn't do. That is one incident of multiple happenings,

3. Threatened me,

4. Tried to force me – a Genius with an IQ of 142 questions right – into going to GED class, when I have a High School diploma, then refusing to allow me to do college work,

5. Forcing me into classes that were obstructive of me moving forwards with my education,

6. Took my property with legal papers, art materials for my son, letter writing ability; they took it away from me and never gave it back ... which is illegal; and I had no funds and no way to replace any of those products for literally two and a half years. I was unable to even

get a snack. That had not happened to any other inmate, and the inmates who saw it happening said "those officers have given you a "Death Sentence"". The people who did it were either DCS or DSHS at my abusive ex-wife's request.

7. I complained to the Authorities of Property about the loss of my property, and those vindictive fools tried to lie to me and tell me that no such property existed,

8. With no college books in my possession and no money after the stealing of my property, I began to get books from the library. Then one day the staff put me into solitary confinement based on what members of the gangs were doing (a flat out lie), and while I was there, the officers went into my cell and took all of my library books. They did not give the library books back, no matter how much I complained. Then I went to the library and tried to check out a book, and they didn't give me a book ... they gave me a bill, that said I owed them $1140.00 for one of the books that, like the other books, wasn't returned. What does that prove? It proves that the staff were working together to steal library books and force funds from me that they were not entitled to. The bill was illegal, and they deserve to get sentenced for what they did ... stealing my library books, taking away my ability to read and go to college, and falsely billing me for their thievery.

9. I was called a "Terrorist" by a McNeil Island Captain, in response to my complaint about the staff

doing illegal things, when the fact is that I am an honorably discharged hero who trained against terrorists at a level far above those disgusting pigs. It happened after the manager that I had sent the complaint to had come down to my cell and ignored me, for the purpose of lying to the officers and telling them the lie that I wouldn't talk to her. The Captain of McNeil was probably the one who called Clallam Bay and told them to treat me like a terrorist. Then he drew me to his office and called me a terrorist himself! So, what did they do at Clallam Bay? Laughing at me, they placed me into a cell with an inmate who had put a Qur'an on my desk and told me that if I read or moved it, he would assault me. I went and spoke to the manager of the unit I was in, and that prick got hostile and tried to start a fight between me and his officer. They moved me to a cell directly on the same side of the counsellor's office, which made it so that when she made me go to court inside her office, the inmates saw me at her desk during the trial. They thought I was ratting them out and threatened to beat me. That whole episode was done by a lot of evil officers who were trying to force me to be beaten when I didn't deserve it ... all in order to prevent me from explaining to the upper staff the lawbreaking they were doing. Every one of those pricks deserves to be sent to prison for what they did!

10. I was forced into a staff member's office to attend a hearing against my ex that was open by a window to the living area of the inmates - and the inmates who witnessed it thought I was ratting them out and threatened me ...

both things that the disgusting staff member should have known,

11. I was told over the phone that my father Don had committed suicide, and the prison staff tried to talk me into fighting them by saying it was something I deserved,

12. About a month later was sent to another prison, where they put me into solitary confinement for nearly a year and a half; what the press has said about solitary confinement is that it causes mental injury within the inmate forced into that sentence, a permanent one,

13. There Paris tried to talk me into attempting suicide, because that is likely what she had done to David,

14. One day a group of officers hit me with tear gas, then, walking me over to the medical unit, one of them gave directions to the other to push me into the floor: so he did and hit my head on the concrete so badly that it caused my head to bleed: the doctors tried to give me an X-Ray and the staff that did that tried to talk me into moving my head so that the X-Ray wouldn't work,

15. The psychologists and staff members of that prison wrote false reports about me, saying unlawfully that I had said things like "assaulting officers" when I said no such thing,

16. I was spoken to poorly by the psychologists, who gave me no assistance with finding a better avenue with thought. I had serious PTSD, and those despicable officers refused to help me cure at all. That is what they do to inmates within solitary confinement: they provoke

and beat them, deny them their property, let them move elsewhere for only one hour out of the 23 hours forced to stay in the cell, they make fun of the inmates who speak out erroneous speech all day long, 24 hours per day, all day long, in such a prominence that it obstructs other inmate's ability to think or feel positive or think of something positive to say. Solitary confinement is such a horrible avenue of torture that the despicable guards who make it happen deserve to be placed inside cells like those forever, and never allowed to leave!

17. On my day of release, they directed me to speak to a psychologist who tried in depth to talk me into stating the desire to assault a member of the grocery store who was threatening me; they were trying to invent a reason to keep me in prison past my release date, and I am sure that it was in retaliation for me calling for them to be held accountable for me complaining about them breaking the law, when the fact was that they were guilty and deserving punishment!

18. The day after release, I was sent to the VA hospital in San Diego for the purpose of having surgery on my stomach after the deep and long hunger-strike I had been on in prison. It nearly killed me, and I was put into the VA hospital for about a month to recover from it. I was also severely mentally ill from the unlawful solitary confinement they had me on.

That concludes the 18 different ways the prison staff broke the law against me. The treatment was unjust, and torture, and those who did it deserve to be found guilty of their lawbreaking and put inside of prison as inmates themselves. And they deserve to be sued, for a lot.

I am submitting this to the ACLU for the purpose of putting forth a lawsuit for justice in this area.

Think about this as the way the damn prisons operate before you commit anyone to them for any reason. There is a reason why criminals, or people who are innocent who are treated as criminals, take up arms against the prison guards and police. This is why. They deserve it. Those assholes tortured me when I was innocent. I put my life on the line to protect them in the Marines. I deserve justice, and they deserve to pay the price for what they did to me.

They almost killed me. Think about that for a moment.

CHAPTER 6

ABUSE UPON RELEASE

First, let me tell you about the generalities of solitary confinement, so you can understand why it drives people crazy. An inmate is put into a cell in solitary confinement for literally 23 out of 24 hours per day. The only free hour they get is usually in exercise room that has nothing in it whatsoever besides a basketball and a net. They spend time in their cells by themselves, away from everyone. Counsellors come by the window in the door sometimes, talking about the sentence. They are forced to listen to the other inmates in cells around them talk, or yell, about things regarding their crimes, police illegal actions, the illegal actions of the justice system around them, of being abused and treated poorly, and above all, reoccurring reminiscences of the crimes they had been found guilty of.

To listen to such diatribe, literally for 23 out of 24 hours per day, every single day without break for a whole year and a half is enough to drive a person mentally ill. And the inmates going through it were, many of them, mentally ill from being in solitary confinement for so long.

I sought as many ways as I could to relieve myself of that. One of the things I started to do was read the Bible and the Qur'an over and over again, trying to ignore what was being said. And there were errant speeches going on that had the context of serious bodily injuries in them, talking about it in such a way as to make a person think about how to do many radical and crazy things with their bodies. And because there was no time for rational thought, those speech episodes became prominent.

Now, I had been sent there because I had been showing signs of severe PTSD, and I was supposed to be getting fixed. Did they do anything to fix me? No, they didn't! To make matters worse, when I spoke to a psychiatrist about what was happening to me, and telling him the truth about it, that despicable fucker told me that I was lying! What the hell? And to make matters worse, I am certain that they took part in lying on the records about me being an "escape candidate" and "extremely destructive". Complete lies! And they got away with it!

It got even worse, considering the fact that my father

had killed himself while I was in, and Paris came by later for a visit and tried to talk me into committing suicide. And I did. I tried to hang myself on two different occasions after that. She deserves to be tried and convicted of that.

The newspaper article online, titled *The Horrible Psychology of Solitary Confinement* had written in it the following:

> *"In the largest prison protest in California's history, nearly 30,000 inmates have gone on hunger strike. Their main grievance: the state's use of solitary confinement, in which prisoners are held for years or decades with almost no social contact and the barest of sensory stimuli.*
>
> *The human brain is ill-adapted to such conditions, and activists and some psychologists equate it to* **torture***. Solitary confinement isn't merely uncomfortable, they say, but such an anathema to human needs that* **it often drives prisoners mad***.*
>
> *In isolation, people become anxious and angry, prone to hallucinations and wild mood swings, and unable to control their impulses. The problems are even worse in people predisposed to mental illness and can wreak long-lasting changes in prisoner's minds.*
>
> *"What we've found is that a series of symptoms occur almost universally. They are so common that it's something of a syndrome," said psychiatrist Terry Kupers of the Wright Institute, a prominent critic of solitary confinement. "I'm afraid* **we're talking about permanent damage***."*

So that is a summary of what occurred inside of solitary confinement. Now, one of the surviving characteristics of that was that I got extremely religious. People may not realize this, but God and his Angels work big time within the concepts of solitary confinement; either to save and preserve a falsely accused person of being swept under the auspices of injustice, or to condemn and punish a sinner who knew they were sinning and did it anyways, committing the crime they were being punished for. The presentation of thought within that environment, while having to listen to others talk inanities, was such that it, plus reading the religious books, was such that it put a person's mind in the realm of religion (if they were clean and holy-finding).

As a result, I got a very serious religious mindset. I became a combination of Christian, Jewish, Muslim, and I was already Hindu and Buddhist from my time in the military in Japan. Of note, I met a man named Lee inside of the VA hospital in November 2016, when we were there to pick up medicine for the diabetes. And he told me that my last name of Krautant is Jewish. Imagine! So I looked online, and sure enough, the name Krautant is listed as Jewish there. Amazing! That is supposed to be the forefront religion of all religions! Now, the fact is that God has seen a lot of different ways to bring faith around, which is why each religion is different in some ways from the next, but that is designed to accept the differences in raisings and cultures of humankind.

Keep those religious materials in mind as you read this book. It came into huge presence after I was released, for years. Let me begin describing it here, upon the conversation about what it was like to be released from an unjust prison sentence after being subjected to mentally disabling conditions and highly religious conceptualization.

The very first thing that happened upon my release was my movement through the airport with Paris present. She had arrived to pick me up from the guard car that had driven me there, with the guards placing me under an electric restrictor around my ankle in the car. Upon arrival they removed it and wanted a female police officer to guide me through the airport. I refused. I started to go with Paris to the airplane.

On the way I stopped at a book store in the airport. In it I looked hard at the books, getting from them messages via their writing about the religious ramifications of people around the area. It was clear to me, from the book, that there were forces of evils around the area, and they were seeking out a way to destroy the people there.

Then we went and sat at a coffee shop. The airport began to vibrate, like during an earthquake, and Paris looked around like there was something going wrong. I then saw a man walking, who was stating the parables of a story about people travelling to a new place. I could tell immediately that it was the Archangel Michael. He was bringing about a form of disaster that we could not see, that was not solid or plainly evident to us.

I didn't find out until later that there is a way for Angels to bring about disasters to places on the earth, with the intent of killing numerous people, but that can, in a parallel universe dimension, seem like it is not happening in the same place to a different set of people. That is how Angels bring forth justice in a world that flies in multiple dimensions, that people are just starting to understand, but that exist for everyone.

Then, on board the airplane, I saw on the television a message from President Obama. And from it I gathered the concept that I, too, was being sought after to become like the president, in charge of the nation. The concept was plain and clear to me.

Now, if you think about it, it seems like I should not have been getting those concepts. But the fact of the matter was that the solitary confinement episode had been highly religious, and from it I learned about how to pervade the concepts of multiple dimensions at the same time, mentally. That is a tall order of concepts, but that is what I was doing! I shall describe that far more in detail as this chapter progresses.

I was taken to Downlow's house in San Diego. She introduced me to her two children, a boy of about 4 years old and a girl of about 5. They put me into a side space of a room there to sleep. They also gave me a couple sets of clothes, some cleaning gear, and some tooth brushes.

It was extremely difficult for me to function. It was radically different from the cell I had in solitary confinement.

Then the next day I was taken to the VA hospital, and things went seriously wrong, but also right in a way.

I was taken to the Veteran's Affairs hospital (VA) in San Diego for the purpose of getting me articles of treatment for some of the problems I had in the military.

What I didn't know at the time was that I was near death from the hunger strike that I had been on in the prison.

While we sat there in the waiting area, me and Paris and Downlow's two kids, we were there for almost 8 hours. I was having mental projections of a religious format. I was reading rapidly through a book and getting ideas about unseen world security problems from the fiction that I had. I got the idea that the kids had a mental prescription of what needed to happen on a religious basis, that they knew how people would uphold the 10 Commandments or conduct themselves in sin. Now, they were too young to know about the details, but they had the ideas of it set in. Then I saw on TV and the pictures on the wall the message that the people running the hospital were doing experiments on the patients there.

So, I began to move rapidly through the hospital. I went into a room on the third floor and broke in there a picture of some bad hospital employees and took a business card that had their information on it. Then I went downstairs.

I took Paris and the kids outside, telling them we had to leave immediately. The girl said some negative things about her brother, and I could tell, from Paris's directions to her the previous night, that she was being conditioned to be abusive to her brother. So, I pushed her down.

Then I ran across the parking lot. I was later arrested by a VA guard and taken back to the hospital.

I was engulfed with illusions of a woman being held

captive within another country. Then I was diagnosed as being near starvation and sent to the surgery ward. There they did surgery on my stomach, if I remember right, from the hunger strike that I had been on in prison.

I was submitted to the locked down psychology ward of the hospital for nearly two months. During that time the doctors did a lot of headlong evaluations of me, and I showed them that I was seeing things on a scientific level far beyond what the average person would see in things. I was seeing and hearing sounds and colors of things that the average person did not notice. It was highly religious based. Unless a person is religious, then they would think it was in error. It was not. It was the product of the religious factors of the solitary confinement in action.

When I was there, I met a very kind and pleasant nurse called Krishna. She took me to the back and gave me a snack, while listening to me tell her about the mental ramifications I was having. She listened and gave me the head's up on some ways I could study the dictionary for new words or the book of indexes on global proclivities in-regards-to what people on earth were saying or doing in their countries. What she didn't realize was that I was reading solidly into what was written. And I have an IQ of a genius, which made it so that I was able to draw conclusions about what was written that the average person would not understand or agree with, but that was in actuality what it meant on a global, large world faceted basis, as seen by a person who, by religious finding, was able to transmit their thoughts globally to other countries and get the ideas of other people in other countries. Countries on the other side of the world.

That worked out nice. Krishna was a veteran of the USMC, just as I was, and had a deep appreciation for the facts behind what I had been through. She understood. And she said she wanted to visit me after I was released from the VA hospital. I accepted.

Then I departed after about 2 months. And the abuse and religious affects got even worse.

The first thing I did when I got back to Downlow's house was to start to write about the negative elements of the prison sentence that I had to sustain. It was long, detailed, and full of rife and rowdy remarks. It was plain and clear ... those officers had violated the law so badly that it became apparent that they were mentally disabled and seriously in error.

To make matters worse, I had access to my military records for the first time within the last 5 years, and on them was plain evidence, as put forth here, that the police had lied and committed perjury and malicious prosecution when they arrested me. Overall, it became plain to me that the police, the prosecutors, and the Judge Kessler all violated the law against me to satisfy my ex-wife's lies.

But I had the permanent mental disability from being tortured in solitary confinement, and PTSD so severe that it prevented me from writing anything else about it. Not literally for 11 years, all the way until 2015.

Then, recovering from a death-dealing case of brain hemorrhaging due to attempted vehicular homicide I survived, in 2013, I wrote the full story, seeking assistance from the ACLU. This is one of those stories.

I began to read a Bible that I found there. Within it I very experimentally asked it a question about what my place was in religion. I opened it to a portion that was talking about a character named Mitchell... my name! Then I asked it to tell me about the Angels that I was involved in, and the back random page read an article about the Archangel Gabriel. That made it clear that I was being seen from time to time by an Angel of the Lord, and it was the proclivities of the Angel that helped me get through prison with a religious finding.

Reading that, I remembered the girl I had been in contact with in Junior High School, named Gabrielle. I didn't know until then that she was an Angel. I asked the Qur'an in 2016 if Gabrielle was an Angel. And it was clear that she was. Amazing.

And to think that God's Angels had contact with me the whole time. Their purpose is put forth at the end of this book.

I learned that Paris was teaching the children to be abusive. How?

During the daytime, in the morning, Paris would be

teaching the kids how to write letters on the board in the front room. She would say all sorts of negative things to the boy, while being friendly to the girl.

"Keep it, keep it, damn you, keep it clear! You don't know what you're doing, you horrible boy!"

He would respond in frustration and angst. "I do know, ma'am, I do know! I'll try harder!"

"You'll try nothing you terrible boy. Write those letters down now ... and do it right for once!"

The little girl put forth her version. "How is that miss Paris?" She would say it with a smile.

"That is great honey. That is great! Tell your brother how to do it, if he would even try."

He responded: "I am trying, ma'am, I am trying!" He was clearly frustrated, and he deserved to be. She was speaking to him horribly.

I said nothing. I listened. I was so used to her abuse that it became plain to me that there was nothing I could say to stop her. And at the same time, I was thinking about how she had told me in prison that Don had committed suicide, just one week after I asked her to give me his phone number so I could call him. It became clear to me that she likely called him and told him a reason to kill himself. I was certain that he had killed himself because he couldn't handle the idea of me being in prison. And then a month later she came for a visit to the prison and tried to talk me into committing suicide. And it nearly worked. I tried to hang myself twice after that. As a matter of fact, at the end of my sentence, I had created a noose the last day and woke up with the intention of hanging myself. The guards came in early and took the noose away, and they let me go.

It became plain to me, as I thought about that, that Paris was an evil creature, and it was her intention to cause those children to become so abusive to each other that they would be unable to go through life without handicaps.

Now let me tell you about the severely religious handiwork I conducted that was life changing. It happened on Halloween, 2009.

On Halloween, 2009, I was invited to go with Downlow and my younger sister to the parade grounds of San Diego for a concert. Paris put forth for me to wear an outfit that made me look like a seer or an avatar of the ancient Greek times. I didn't want to wear an outfit, but I decided that I didn't want to piss her off.

We went there and as we walked around, I kept getting solid religious concepts about the people there. Were they priests who did holy things for others? Some of them talked and acted like sinners, looking hardcore at people of the opposite sex around them and saying errant things like saying bad things about people's thoughts or actions and how they should be "judged". They were acting like viscous, terrible-minded prosecutors with criminal mindsets.

I noticed on the ground were flyers being walked on that were pictures of elements of Tarot cards and it became plain to me, as I used my religious, genius mind to read them in detail with the convolutions and speeches of people around me, that they were a guidon for people to move through space and time to something more pronounced in their existence.

Downlow and my sister left me there alone, not wanting to be around me. They said they were going to the Greek restaurant and bar down the street. So, seeing the carnival of music taking on the costumes of naked ladies, I went there to meet them. They were not there.

Inside, I was approached by a man who liked my costume and said I must me a very intelligent man. At the same time, I was looking as seeing portions of the bar that were indications of the idea that I had gotten from the Tarot cards. They were pieces of silver from people's wallets that had fallen on the floor, and it became plain to me that someone seeing the positive aspects of the place would be able to use their mindset to make their fortunes come to life.

So, I left and got in the Jeep that Krishna had let me have. I went driving, and wound up, using my mental force power of directions and direction to a higher purpose, I found myself driven to a graveyard. And it was the place that I was thinking of, on a very religious basis, even though I had never been there before and before then didn't even know it existed.

I got out of the Jeep there and began to lay, at night, on the ground near a picked out grave. I had recognized the name on it as a Biblical name, Joseph. There I began to think about what it was like to die and go somewhere else, and from those thoughts I got the ideas that came to fruition later, later, in 2013, when I died as the victim of attempted vehicular homicide.

In the meantime, I had a lot of other thoughts about the graveyard. Pictures of motions through the gravestones and of spirits walking along the grave lines and saying things regarding history and the future. I was in depth there with the concepts of souls of the dead having a presence among the living. Why was that?

Morning came, and then the answer started to come to fruition as I walked along the graves, looking to see how many names I recognized from some mysterious aspect of memory. And as I looked, past hundreds of grave names, it suddenly dawned on me, from the level of names that I knew about, that the graveyard I was at contained the souls of many of the people that I knew from a previous life of religious finding.

As the morning progressed, I came to the gravesite of a group of military veterans holding a ceremony for a dead Marine. I knelt and paid special attention. Then I saw on the ground a coin upright, and it became plain to me that it had been sent there by the dead as a token of their appreciation for my efforts there. It was a sign of holiness. As I picked it up, a man came over to me and said "He was a special soldier. Do you think you know him? Probably not, but you seem like a good soldier yourself. Do yourself a favor and keep up the good work!"

A solid rendition of respect! I thanked him and wished him the best in life. He thanked me, and we went on our way.

That was my first illustration of how the dead play a large part in our lives, how there is life after death, and how they have a penance of delivery after the end of times. That effect became plain to me after I was the victim of attempted murder, as shall be put into the last few chapters of this book.

Now I shall tell you about how I used knowledge I had gained from there to try, unsuccessfully, to tell religious stories to my younger sister.

What had happened was that during the daytime I had walked over to the San Diego library. There I was driven to find books of a religious nature. By what seemed like sheer accident, but on a level that was the religious findings of God and his Angels driving me to success, I came across a Jewish version of the Torah.

The Torah, also at the time called the Tanach, or the Hebrew Bible, had in it a story about a man who went in a parallel dimension, or something like that, and found elements of Biblical leadership there in the source of Angels. It was also about how he had gone to the

Hereafter and had found reminiscences of himself in a near-death afterlife experience.

I wanted to tell my teenage sister about that, for the purpose of making her aware of the fact, which she was denying, that there was such a thing as positive religion, and that the God therein was looking out for her. She had a lot of complaints about Paris and her unruly methods of performance, her negative speeches, and her ways of holding things against me. My sister told me that Paris had tried to use my prison record against me, and although I had explained to her that I was unjustly convicted, Paris denied it, saying that I deserved it for "holding my ex-wife at gunpoint." She refused to acknowledge the fact that I had done it appropriately, thinking that she was drawing a weapon on me. Yet Paris said I deserved that very lawless sentence. She probably also thought that I deserved to have been abused by herself as I had been.

I called my young sister to the side downtown and began to tell her the story. She did not understand what it was about. She even refused to acknowledge the fact that I told her that it had come from the Torah, as given to me by God himself. She chose ignorance and acted angry and hostile at me for even bringing it up and trying to put it forth to her. That was just her having hateful remarks about the religious semblances I was telling her vice understanding and accepting the glory of God.

That was the error of my family as a whole. And a big part of the reason was because those women were all trying to itemize themselves according to the wherewithal of negativity put forth by Paris herself. And they used it against me, counter to my contradictions of it.

They are just as evil as Paris is.

At the time, I had a book about Quantum Theory and Stars in the Sky. It was a scientific book that talked about how it was that the elements of space travel are symbiotic with magnificent force and the ability to maneuver in ways that the human mind can barely comprehend. After the negative impact that my young sister had on me with ignoring the religious aspects of the talk I tried to have with her, I went to a bar near the house, drank wine coolers and read the book I had.

The concepts of the story were so in depth and broadly related to my higher intelligence that I began to see how certain elements, like the descriptions of the light coming out of stars in the universe, were such that the light resembled in my mind the same lights that were reflected on the alcohol bottles on the bar. They resembled the synaptic firings of light from the wall of a black hole, which I saw reflected the portrayal of shape and color along the borderline of a sketched graphic along the bar's surface. The transportation of a ship through the atmosphere diagonally, then sideways through the space and time of the solar system, then down into the gravity well of a different planet was deeply reflected in the achieving, placement, movement, then table setting of each and every drink made by the bartenders.

The full impact of the concept of space and time became so pronounced that it became evident that such principles applied also to people travelling through different dimensions, travelling through space in altered locations. It reflected what they did when they died, their souls when they left the bodies, and were moving either upwards to Heaven, or downwards to Hell.

To that the concepts of what I had learned with the religious aspects of the graveyard became apparent. The movements of the souls of the dead were making sense to me then, in how they got the ideas, through the patterns and rules of hyperspace, for example, to itemize the functions of their senses in ways that made them realistic after they had no more human body and were moving my soul alone in the Hereafter.

And that is what this book is about. It is about the summaries of what I attained in knowledge of a religious nature regarding the rules of the universe and how it affects the Hereafter. The reason I had so much knowledge on the subject is three-fold. For one, I acquired that knowledge when I myself almost died multiple times. Another, I got that knowledge from my global experience, being my knowledge and intelligence, steered towards the sciences of space travel, the afterlife, and religion. And finally, it was granted to me by God and his Angels themselves, by itemizing my thoughts in ways that made it plain what the related thoughts meant, based off of science, experience, telling by greater souls or other souls, and such.

What was the summary of this new knowledge going to be? Was I to become a priest? A Rabi? Was I going to go through the Hereafter to another dimension, like to Heaven? Or was I going to use it to fight a War against evils for God?

It was all of those, but I didn't know it yet. Read on, and you will see descriptions of all of those.

I went to the movie theatre and saw a Star Trek movie. I noticed that the USS Enterprise has the number NCC-1701 on it. The number 1, Biblically, represents the number of an individual. 7 is the number of Angels. Zero is the number of mysteries. And the final one is what happens when they are all three, the 1, 7, and 0, are all contained within one body. That of a super-Angel. That of a super-hero. And that is what the crew of the USS Enterprise is. They are heroes. And some are arguably Angels.

I was sent back to the VA hospital after that by Downlow, for no other reason than to get my medicine updated. She didn't like the religious visions I had been having. What she didn't know is that I was getting messages from God about the idea that there was a potential apocalypse approaching. I heard inside, as we drove by, the sound of trumpets barely playing on the realm of the Mormon Church nearby there. That was an indicator of the signal put on by God's Angels that the Apocalypse was coming.

There inside of the psychological ward of the hospital, I ran into Krishna again. I thanked her for buying me a computer, which I had used to type my messages about the prison on, and for the Jeep, which I had been using to drive to places like her house to visit and to the graveyard for religious purposes, and I thanked her for the treats and food that she had so kindly bought for me during my visits with her during breakfast.

The staff were trying to do kind things to me. I noticed that they were giving me special plate meals during chowtime upon a specially designed and special looking box that was different than those of other patients. They were giving me special meals. I think it was because they remembered that I had almost died a few months prior to that from the hunger strike that I had been on.

One day Paris came by for a visit, and started to say a bunch of negative things to me, trying to say I was "inappropriate" for bringing up religious issues with my young sister, and saying a lot of negative things about me having been in prison. She thought I was going to do something violent against Downlow, for no reason, when I hadn't even thought in that manner!

I got fed up with her lies and started to yell at her. She got irate and went before the doctor in charge and complained to him, telling him a bunch of lies, that he later told me she said. I told him to ignore her from there on out. She was no longer invited to attend for any reason whatsoever.

The staff kept on trying to get me to take different medications. And they kept on asking me questions about things like movies, and speech, and why I heard and saw letters to the sound of their voices. What they refused to understand was that there is a higher plane of existence, in which certain rules of the universe move along in ways people don't yet understand. If you doubt me, read over any book about Quantum Theory or Superstring Theory, and you will see that the rules of that verified science are such that they at times fly in the face of common sense. There is such a thing as time travel, for example. And one of the solid theories of it is that a person can move not only forwards in time, but also to the past, on different levels depending on how they go about it. It is real, and it flies in the face of what people in general have come to believe from their experiences and mentalities here on earth. I tried to explain that to them, but they refused to listen. "You're a genius, right? Then you should know that is not true," they said. They were wrong. It is true.

After a replication of errant thinking there, I was released. And the religious format of the presence of things became extremely plain in how it was also migrating through other religious folks. Here is how.

God speaks to me in rudimentary knowledge and puts forth facts. In November 2016 I was thinking about writing this part of this book and on the radio came on the Squirrel Nut Zippers song "Hell". It went:

"In the Afterlife

You'll be heading to some serious strife,

First you make the scene all day,

But tomorrow there'll be Hell to pay!"

That is definitely a song about what it is that I am writing about. So ... it goes. Keep that in mind as you read the next part of this chapter. The next two parts talk about the religious ramifications that I had in-regards-to how different people were acting religious in special and unanticipated ways. There were a lot. I shall only describe a few of them here. Know this, though. The religious format that I was finding was so present and so thorough that it defied common sense.

One day I went to the mall, getting the mental images of the fact that it was occupied by exceptionally religious people. To move my mind in the presence of it, and them, I began to think about what sorts of things a person would buy there inside of Macys. I had images of style and certain aspect of shirts, like their color being in a uniform pattern of vibrant purpose, for the purpose of enlightening the mind of the viewing party along the line of what was written on their hat or jacket. The illustration of mental thoroughfare was such that it became apparent that a person would get different ideas about what was written when they read in in articulation with their reading of the colors of the design on the shirts. They equaled the total meaning of the subject, which was one that could have been talked about by the wearer in a way that changed the perceptions of the listener in ways that amounted to understanding of the strange but uniform methods of the topics discussed.

Here is an example of that ability to transfer writing to design. Say one had a hat that read "Marines: First In, Last Out." As they read it, they may come under the influence of a yellow shirt with the fronted shapes and colors of a rhythm of other colors within their own shapes along the front. They could be shaped like bruised circles, pieces of green triangles with layers on them, or blue spots that are small but readily available. The summary of the design may amount to the listener hearing the speaker talk about how there are a lot of different shapes of bacteria that can be found in the ocean, and at the beginning of time, there was probably a time-travelling branch of Marines, scientific Marines, who went and channeled energy away from the negative forces of Creation, thus making it so that they would not change the structure and ability to procreate among the new humankind.

And that could have begun at the beginning of time, thus the saying "First In." And on top of that they may have stayed through the whole evolution, going all the way to Judgement Day, thus making themselves the "Last Out." The United States Marines, being present for the positive preservation of the universe from the beginning of time to the end of the story. Highly religious. And that was what I was looking for there at Macy's in the mall.

I saw in a mirror on the floor a reflection of specifically appropriate clothing within. That was proof that the staff there was trying to make it so that the buying customers would have a prefix of what was good and necessary in the mirror, thus being able to turn around and buy the item.

But the mirror went farther than that. They were a reflection of the shape of the face and illustration of the features of the face, the expressions, and made it clear through the spacing of the other items in the mirror, features of suits or ties or shirts or whatever that were wanting to be bought but also played a large role in the presentation of the person wearing them, they played a large part in a person being able to itemize their description to one that described the function of what they were trying to accomplish. The reflection in the mirror was good for some people, read as bad for others, and left one thinking whether their affects with doing certain things that were either appropriate or inappropriate was necessary, and justifiable. Accurate!

I was able to tell those things about how the place was operating through my magnificent mental effects of knowledge on a religious basis. A large part of my ability to do so was due to the solid readings of the Bible and the

Qur'an that I had done inside of the prison element of solitary confinement.

What happened after I left the mall? The person I came across was highly religious and presented me with knowledge about the subjects that one would think the person would not have access to. But he did. And he left a deep impression.

I encountered him on the street that Downlow lived on, between the bus station tracks (or the train tracks, I don't remember which), which was under a cable for power that had a box from the bus or train attached to it, migrating power and electricity along it to the vehicle.

Here is what he said:

"You just went to the Mall having no idea why you were there, huh? I am a partaker of the hospital here in San Diego. You would not believe the ways those doctors are! For example, I went in there earlier this week, with an error in my brain. I was feeling pain there, see? But what did the doctors do? They gave me medicine for a heart-attack! One has nothing to do with the other, but they said it treated the same thing. So, guess what ... I went into my house and got my gun and was going to take it there when my girlfriend called and said that I couldn't drive the car I was driving. Why not? Because I would get in a wreck! Now, she wasn't really talking about the car, was she? She was talking about the gun! So, I didn't take it to the hospital. Now, on the way there was an electric storm. And electric storm! And as the trees and branches and clouds moved through it, it struck!" And as he said that final part, suddenly, a bolt of electricity rolled over the top of the bus moving down the road next to us on the tracks. It shocked the whole atmosphere, putting out light and noise! Where did it come from?

It came from that man talking about light and noise from electricity. He had transported it there through a religious function of his speech and sound! Amazing! That was the first time I had ever seen something so convincing in the realm of mental power that was unspoken and seemed impossible ... but it happened!

After that, he said I should get a car and start driving. I realized that he was talking about the vision I had of the Apocalypse coming as I was being driven to the VA hospital by Downlow. He was itemizing it in a function that I should be paying attention to that.

I walked over to the house of Downlow, went inside, and read over a book about tantric episodes. And I got the thought and impression that I was going to be met by a superior being soon. And guess what. That is exactly what happened.

Now I shall tell you about the first time I met the resurrection of Jesus, here, in the year 2009, over 2000 years after his life inside of Israel.

The first person I met there in San Diego was a car parking salesman who was a bum who was homeless. He was working at a place right across the street from Downlow's house. I ran into him while walking downtown one night.

He immediately asked me a question about what my reaction would be to someone talking about Jesus. I didn't know. They he joked about it and said that, because Jesus is a holy creature that is arguably on the same level as God, that the people wouldn't know about what he was actually doing.

Then we went walking around downtown, and he told me a lot of different factors that one could say were religious.

We went before a nightclub there, and in front of the place we were approached by a man who asked us if we wanted to pick a random card from a deck of cards he had. So, I did, and he asked me what it was. I told him it was an Ace of spades, and sure enough, he pulled up an Ace of clubs as the next card up. He was doing magic! Kay didn't really like that concept, so he told me that there were tons of ways to get people to do things, regular things, and magic was not one of them.

We departed that night. Later, I went in my room and looked at a different card that I had. It had numbers on it that equaled what I had drawn as numbers of travel inside the prison element, in the Bible. I was drawn outside, and as I walked down the street, I came across a man with a book in his hand that called me over.

"I'm a homeless freak, man. Nevermind. I have been getting these cards down in Mexico, and I think they are about space travel! Keep that in mind when I tell you this next part. You are being sought to travel in space, man. That is your purpose! The priests and prophets of God have all been up there. Now, keep that in mind, and you will find yourself there. That is all!" And at that he left very quickly.

I immediately got in mind the vision of the clouds and sky above me opening up, putting forth the rays of stars in them, and drifting upwards through the atmosphere. It was a very realistic vision, and I felt like I was being drawn by Angels upwards to Heaven, through space to a new realm. Then I suddenly got in mind that what was happening was very wrong, and I immediately drifted down.

The reason, I was sure of, was because there was an evil spirit nearby that had knowledge of what was occurring with my travels. I went with that in mind trying to find them to the other side of the building, and as I did I saw a rough looking man walking on the other side, and got it in mind that: be careful! That is Satan himself!

I went over to his presence, and pretending to draw a pistol from my belt, pointed it at him and called out the sound of shots being fired. The man flinched and began to run away. It had worked. I knew that my memory of doing it in the Marines made it so that when I pretended in this dimension, it made the actual even happen in a parallel dimension. And from that I had defeated Satan!

I went then down the street to Ralph's grocery store.

Outside there was a man standing, a bum with stringent hair and nice pants on. He said to me: "Keep trucking along like you are, and you'll find your way to China, or somewhere you want to go!"

"Are you homeless? Want some help? Let me buy you some groceries." I wanted to help him. I liked the guy. I could tell that somehow - I knew him - but I couldn't tell where.

"No thanks. Save your money. There are realms of existence that you may not know about yet. But you will. You will! Now, I have seen you walking around with a fellow soldier. Do you like him? Different people here have different ideas about things. Some are accurate. Some are not. I know you went in to save some souls in that bar down the street, didn't you?" I had, a few days before. "You did a good job. Keep up the good work, and you will be rewarded!"

And at that I wondered for a moment why he was talking to me like that, and then the sense of who it was became plain to me mentally. It was Jesus Christ! Holy shit, man, can you believe it? I asked myself that, and sure enough, I did believe it!

I didn't find out until three years later that Jesus had been resurrected in the Bible after he was unjustly killed, and then it ends. But did he maintain that ability? He did! The fact was that Jesus resurrected over and over again, living the life of eternity that we, as average humans, do not understand. But it was true!

And it wasn't until later that I came to understand that there are such people who are immortal here on earth, that we do not know about. But that is a different story.

So, I met Jesus in San Diego. And he told me that I was going to be rewarded for saving souls. That plays a large part into my future. One I have read about in the Bible. I shall explain what it said at the end of this book. Read on, and you will understand!

The channel of things that happened right after that are alarming but were actually in line with what was seen by God himself as being appropriate for me. Here is what happened.

Back in Downlow's house, one day she was at work and I was sleeping on the couch in the front room. I began to have a dream about the felons of the prison assaulting me, hitting me hard in the head and face and saying all sorts of negative things. Then I woke up, and Downlow's cat was clawing me in the face. I didn't know what I was doing, because I was still having the dream about being beaten, so I threw the cat on instinct.

I threw it so hard that I broke its neck. I felt very bad about that. I also got the vision that I should handle it religiously. So, I opened the Bible to a random page, and say in it a portion about animal sacrifices, or lambs. I was certain that it was directing me on what to do about the cat. To make it a sacrifice and please God. So,

I took it into the bathroom and skinned it, preparing it to be cooked.

I went over to the stove and put the dead cat in there. Then I was cleaning a part of the stove, and Downlow came home. Alarmed, she refused to talk to me and took me to a hotel, gave me enough money for one night, and told me that she was kicking me out of her house.

I was homeless for the first time.

Frustrated, because I was truly sorry for what I had done to the cat but dissolved over what the reason was for her to kick me out of the house, homeless, with no money. That was cruel and unnecessary.

I got on the phone and called Krishna. I told her what had happened. She listened to me and realized that I had good cause to be angry about getting kicked out. She invited me to go stay with her at her new house in Temecula. Temecula is a small city to the north of San Diego by about an hour. I thanked her and appreciated the kindness. What I didn't realize was how kind Krishna actually is. She is fantastic, and I shall put forth the methods of how in the next chapter.

Read on! The next chapter is a positive one!

CHAPTER 7

THE HEROISM OF KRISHNA

Krishna lived in Temecula, California, but also had a cabin near Green Valley Lake. We went up there right after she had invited me over to stay with her.

While I was there, I started trying to talk to her about the religious format of knowledge I had gotten, and how unjust the prison system in Washington State was. I said something about the abuse I had sustained, and to that she said that if I really wanted to, instead of arguing over things I could just hit her. Now, she was joking, but I didn't know that at the time. So, I left, and began to walk down the hill a very long ways to a place at the bottom of the mountain where Paris was coming to pick me up.

Krishna and I got past it. I began to live with her full time.

During that time, I began to go to college, at Mesa Community College, down in San Diego. I got really good grades there. I also began to have severely religious visions during school. I shall write more about that at the end of this chapter.

Let me describe what Krishna was like, though. When I was going to college, when I came home, she would talk to me solidly about what I had learned. She was very excited about my French class, and wanted me to talk to her in French, even though she couldn't speak it herself. She also listened to me when I came home and took breaks during the commercials of the *Morgan Freeman: Through the Wormhole* show and wanted to talk to her about the science that I saw on there. It talked about all sorts of things, like Superstring Theory, which I am very interested in. She gave me a heap of compliments. And not only that, but she also paid close attention to my health.

Krishna is a nurse with the VA hospital in San Diego, and she does a fantastic job at it. She became aware of the fact that I was abused as a child and teenager, and it was so pronounced that, as you shall see in future chapters of this book, she too was abused by Paris and Downlow. They shouldn't have, because Krishna did not only help me to live fruitfully, she was pleasant and very religious and didn't take crap from anyone.

First, let me tell you about what she did to help

around the house. For one, she did not make me pay rent or pay for the house. I was able to live there for free. In addition, she also helped me to eat out a lot. Now, the only income I had was a very scarce Social Security paycheck and a very tiny paycheck for a minor disability that I got from the Marine Corps. Now, realistically, I should have gotten a much higher amount, because it had given me severe PTSD, but they wouldn't pay me that. I was also injured so much in Freefall school that I had to go have surgery on my shoulder that I still haven't all the way recovered from. That is another disability check they should be paying me. But they aren't.

To help me out financially, though, not only did I not have to pay for rent, but I also didn't have to pay for groceries, or for eating out much, and that helped me out a lot. I was able to eat meals at the restaurants! And that definitely helped me out a lot.

It helped me out even more when I got the diabetes, because it allowed me to eat tasty sugar-free foods required by the diabetic patient.

In addition to those positive things, Krishna also was highly religious, and gave me religious parables of a Muslim demeanor in-regards-to education, health, and care.

Krishna went even farther than that! She did things that no average person would even think of doing for anyone. I shall explain in the next-to-last chapter about how she took extremely good care of me for the diabetes episode, which almost killed me. I shall also explain in the near-death chapter how she arrived when I was in a coma and attempted to take care of me after I was extremely sick from the attempted murder attempt that I survived. Add to that how she was my nurse in the VA hospital when I almost died there from the hunger strike in prison that I had been on. That is three different episodes of near-death experiences that I had that she helped me to survive. And during one of them, I actually did die.

During the near-death experience as a victim of attempted vehicular murder, I was in the hospital for 11 months. 11 months! That is a full 10 months longer than the neuroscientist who wrote the book *Proof of Heaven: A Neurosurgeon's Journey into the Afterlife*. He was in the hospital for only 7 days in a coma. I was in a coma for nearly two months! And I had nearly died about 6 different ways during 6 different times! That is the most in-depth description of the Hereafter that I know of! He said his was medically significant and thorough … what about mine?

Afterwards, she still listened to the fact that I am highly religious. I am not religious like the average person is, though. I have found that God, or Allah, or Jehovah, or Yehova, whichever name you want to use, they are all the same being who explains the religious aspects to different people in different ways that they could understand. Since my release from prison, I have studied the Bible, the Qur'an, and the Torah in such a way that it became evident to me that they were *all right*.

Thus, I am a combination of Christian, Muslim, Hindu, Buddhist and Jewish.

To expand on her support, after I survived the attempted murder attempt, I could not walk right. I needed a cane, a walker, and a scooter to be ambulated. Krishna got me and paid for each and every one of those. The scooter cost literally about a $1000 sum. She spent $1000.00 on me! And it was to take care of my health. I shall describe how they work in the later chapter.

Now, it is the year 2016 as I am writing this. Donald Trump has been elected president of the USA. That asshole has tried to say a bunch of negative, evil things about the Muslims in this country. What that idiot needs to understand is that, for one, I am a Hero of the United States Marine Corps, Special Operations Capable and Anti-terror unit Force Reconnaissance Company, and I am a very close friend of another Marine Corps veteran and VA nurse, Krishna, who is Muslim. If he really thinks that a Special Operations Capable operative of the Marines would get involved with a terrorist, then what the Hell is he thinking? Trump is an errant fool, a partaker of evils, who wants all sorts of negative things done against good people he doesn't understand. Why? Because that fuck is evil!

It is worse than that. Krishna is worried that Trump is going to rule that she is not a citizen of the USA, or commit her to a concentration camp, because of his unnecessary and unlawful hatred against Muslims. And to think, he is turning against two USMC veterans of honorable quality, for no good reason. What were those idiots thinking who voted for him? It is a sign that the USA is facing a degree of corruptness that is so far beyond what is acceptable that the people are going to find us in a war that we will certainly lose. Against China. Or Russia. Or Korea. Or someone who hates the presence of that idiot those idiots put into office. And Trump would go to war unlawfully, too. He would, thinking he would get away with it.

That is a summary of how Krishna treated me. A tall order, I think, that she has elegantly upheld in a much better fashion than most people would.

Now let me tell you about the religious effects I had at college, and the big portion of decision making it had on me.

College was remarkable. I began by going to an advanced mathematics class, in preparation for calculus. That was because when I was in high school, I had done a lot of advanced mathematics classes, all the way to preliminary calculus. So, I felt it was appropriate, and so did the teachers there.

I also took a French class, a chemistry class, and a physics class. The reason I took those science classes was because I had in the Marines books about Superstring Theory and was very much in depth with the scientific aspects of the rules of the universe and planet and how they functioned.

The chemistry class and the physics classes were solid and well taught. The teachers knew a lot about the subjects and were very much in detail with what they were about. I got A's in both classes. In-regards-to the French class, there was a girl in the class named Jessica who talked to me a lot, in French mostly.

Now, from the in-depth presentations of the subject matter, I got from the instructors many different views of what was actually occurring. In the French class, I got the episode of thinking that there was a distinct line of thought that allowed a person in one culture to think and speak in the language of another. It got me to thinking about how the Greeks and Romans and Israelis all had different languages, but there were altercations and warfare between them. The foreign language concept was one that had the religious basis as well. How?

Because Heaven, and parts of the earth, are supposed to be occupied by Angels. If Angels are connotations of a different species or different form of life, which they are, then their ability to speak and understand words would be much different than ours. Their ability to speak the language used by God was one that the humans hadn't taken on yet - or would never be able to take on until they get to Heaven. So, what did that mean in relation to the class of French I was taking?

I thought it meant that the teacher of the French class

had a much higher aspect of knowledge on the subject of foreign speech than the average citizen did. And why? Because she must have been in the higher realm of speech than we as students were! She may have been in touch with God herself!

So, I studied. I studied hard. The mathematics class, too, was one that put the pre-calculus concepts on a religious basis. It is in ways I cannot describe here. In order to do it, one must understand what was going on inside of the religion, while also seeing the actual formulas put forth in the books, to include the actual structure done.

In between classes, I would go out to the field next to the classes, and lay next to a tree, looking at the walkway and limbs of the tree on the other side, and think about what was taught. Due to my element of being around the religious elements of Christianity and Islam in the prisons, I spent my time there thinking about how the functions of the birds and squirrels in the trees had something to do with the creatures put her on earth by God himself. Or his Angels. Either way, they had a lot of messages to give me about religion, how they perceived the environment and how they saw to move through it. Also, there was the thought of how they interacted to the speeches about the classes or hobbies or sports talked about by students or teachers. What would a squirrel do if they heard a coach talking about football? Would they change the way they looked for nuts or fruit? Would they change the way they moved?

I thought so. And the messages I was getting from the religious aspects of my thoughts told me that I was accurate.

One night, I went down to San Diego in the Jeep, and went to Denny's. There I was reading one of my science books, drinking coffee, and listening to other clients talking. The thought that came forwards as I read was about a tree called the Devil that had a certain aspect of poisoning the squirrels and ants that came up to it. The method put forth showed that the scientist that wrote it had a solid impact on what the plants and animals were doing, with a firm understanding of how they articulated themselves through nature. It was similar to what my perceptions of the animals on the campus were doing and thinking.

As I read it, the people next to me began to say something that I do not remember, but it was a discrete knowledge of what I had been studying in the physics class. I got up, alarmed, and left after paying.

I walked down the street to a building there in the night that had a fence around it with a stone tablet sign separate and in front of the fence. Next to it were tall flowers. So, I went behind the sign and sat down behind the flowers, and there I began to read over my Bible. It had portions in it that I knew would be talking about the mental images I was getting on the campus.

The part I randomly turned to be the part about the kingdom of David. And there I saw and got word of a lot of what had been happening to me. The theories and rights of the college were becoming plain. Let me describe what I had seen there to explain some of it.

In my chemistry class, then later the calculus class, the instructors brought up the idea that there was a very rough time finding a place to park in the parking lot at the college. And each time they did, there were a group of students who complained that they didn't find any place to park. That was not what had happened, I thought, because I had not only found a place to park every day, but I had also seen places for other people to park as well. So why the separate diatribe of what was occurring?

It was because there were multiple dimensions in that school. One that was apparent to each student, and one that was apparent to other students. The concept of multiple dimensions is a new on that is scientific in the realm put forth by Stephen Hawking in the book *The Grand Design*, or so I think. I haven't read it yet, but I remember seeing something about that on its cover. That shifting of dimensions, that there are multiple universes parallel to this one that have different rules of science in each and every single one of them, plays into the concept that the educators of the college were aware of both of those universe parabolas - the one with parking in it and one without parking in it – and were speaking in those terms to the students. Why?

The conclusion I drew was that they were doing that because, due to their actions and speeches, certain students were facing getting ejected from school to a different time. Those were the students who said they had no parking. The other students were accepted at that college because there was room for them to park.

There were other elements that occurred there, that brought the religious affects full on steam. It began to invade my mind in such a way that it was becoming extremely difficult to concentrate on the classes. Why?

Because I was being drawn by God Himself to move to a different community for the purpose of fighting one of his wars against the forces of evil. And I was to do so as a newly found priest. Where was I supposed to go?

I was supposed to go to the same place that caused me severe injustice. And the place that began that was Seattle, Washington.

So, I got in the Jeep and left to go there. I did not tell Krishna where I was going. I didn't want her to know what I was doing. She would worry.

Now let me tell you about what the trip was like to get there.

Now, the full story of what occurred during that war for God is contained in the *Cheetah on the Wing* series books numbers 3 and 4. If you want details of that, feel free to read those books. Here is a much briefer, one-chapter long version of what had occurred as a presentation of the basics of it.

But going up there, I took a side road along the mountains to I5. On the way I saw a sign that said something about Satan being present to lead people along a paddling ceremony. It was a full-on evil rendition of what it wanted people to do to be swept up in that mix.

I kept on driving. The next place I wound up was on I5 next to the city of Yreka. In the Bible, there was a portion about the sexual infidelities of a woman, and I could tell that it was about Paris. Then, I got a call from her.

She wanted me to drive over there to Yreka, where she was living. I refused, telling her that I was doing something else.

Then, as I drove, I started to get seizures, from my head all the way to my feet. The hands got extremely sensitive, as though there were burning fibers of gun shell casings inside of them. Above my head I saw a glimmering light in a circle, like a halo, is what it looked like. And then I thought aloud that I wanted God to save me from crashing, because I could not steer. And then I saw it.

It was a car next to me, passing me, with the license plate (one number) GOD (three numbers). It was a vehicle of God himself, and the Jeep was steering itself around the turn.

When the car vanished, I came back to normal again, with my hands shaking.

I drove to a grocery store in the next town. There I got to thinking about my episode with God himself. It was plain to me that I had been granted salvation for my distinct religious efforts I had put forth.

Not only that, but God had also put in my mind that he was making me into a priest.

The next day I arrived in Medford, Oregon. There the warfare for God began. It was an introduction to it. I shall explain the brief elements of Medford, Seattle, and Los Angeles in the next chapter. After that I was sent to prison, again, for a crime I didn't commit. If you have any doubts as to whether the evil forces we fought against have the preface to do such things to people, this will answer your question.

CHAPTER 8

WARFARE FOR GOD AGAINST EVILS 1

The religious elements of Medford, Oregon. The first place I went to was a hotel that had a room with two pictures in it. I got the sense that I was to choose between the two pictures and do what the picture said. One picture was of a cowboy near a horse. The other was of a group of fighters in a pistol fight.

The next day I drove down the street to the VA. When I sought treatment there, the woman inside the place seemed like she was possessed by a demon. She did nothing to help me, and even said that I was going to have to stay there. I left with no medication.

Then I went to Safeway to get some money. The

woman at the cash register ignored me, telling me that I had to have them call her. I went outside and called them, and they refused to talk to her, saying a lot of lies about getting the money. So, I went inside and argued with her. Eventually, she gave me the money.

Then I went to a casino that was near Safeway. Inside, I came under the presence that the gambling machines were operating on a level that made them capable of reading the mental powers of the players. To test it, I thought and read of things that I wanted the players to think while I was looking at the screens of the machines. They listened, unknowingly, and started to hit the buttons. It was in order, and they started to win, all at once.

I went up to the counter, and the woman working there was named Jessica. Now, pay attention to that name, because it became evident to me, on religious terms, that we were related. It did not occur to me there, at that time, though. It occurred later, inside of Seattle.

I went outside and there was a man who was having problems with the machines inside. I let him know that we had found a way to beat them. He appreciated it. I thought he may have been a portion of Jesus, and that is what my senses told me he was. He liked my solution to the problem, and said he was going to his house to figure it out.

From there I walked over to the college, and there met a girl named Marian. She talked to me about very religious aspects of the school, in a way that I had not seen before. I appreciated it.

I had no place to stay, and no money to afford a hotel. So, as I walked next to the river, I saw a bridge and walked under it. Underneath was a line of blankets to sleep on and a case for clothes. I opened the case and found in there a note with the name of Christa on it. Christa. That was the same name as Christ. And it made me wonder, based on the information and previously meeting his reincarnation, and having had met a version of him at the casino, I wondered if it was possible for Jesus to resurrect as a woman. Was it possible?

I got from her very religious answers that the answer was "yes", it was possible! And that makes sense, considering that males and females are virtually built the same, with only minor changes in structure. Ones that may likely be able to be changed during the very religious process of resurrection and reincarnation.

The place I got those answers from her were at the coffee shop right next to the bridge with her stuff.

After my very positive interaction with Christa, it became plain to me that we were going to be able to work together.

("When I die and you lay me to rest, I'm going to go to the place that's the best. Never been a sinner, never sinned, I've got a friend named Jesus!" That is the lyrics to the song that is on the radio right now as I am writing this part about Christa being the resurrection of Jesus Christ. Who says that God does not talk to me through the media?)

From there I went across the street to the library. There I picked up and checked out a book I found on science. I do not remember the name of it, but it was so high-profile and deep that it equaled the content of the Stephen Hawking book I had. I went back to the coffee shop to read over it. While I was there, during a spell, to maneuver the cars around the road, for the purpose of learning about how to fight the evils I encountered, I cast a spell on them by moving air and the whims of fallen branches through the air in such a manner that it would change the rate of acceleration by itemizing the gears in the engine. And it worked. As I did it, the car that was on the road decelerated and made a noise in the engine that was evidence of it changing the gears in its nozzle. I went back inside and noticed that the reason I had thought of that was in relation to the scientific element of time travel that many scientists were beginning to think of as discretely possible.

There, I got the idea that Jessica from the casino wanted me to walk around, in a particular direction. That was proof to me of the facility of mental power. The reason I had even though of that without interaction was because she had transmitted the thought to me, and I had received it.

So, I went walking down the road, and got drawn to some stones stacked on top of one another next to the sidewalk. I was drawn there! I went and lifted the stones I was supposed to, and underneath found the stone I was looking for. It was a stone in a perfectly shaped iota. I realized that it was an agent for transporting to different dimensions, or different planets, or even different stars.

To continue in Jessica's direction, I walked farther and was directed to a piece of paper she had thrown down on the ground. It was full of dress material and symbols for payments. I went into Starbucks there to look over it.

As I looked over it, at the same time, I noticed a bicycle outside the café. Then the page became clear to me. It was an itemization of how to separate, or bring together, different ideas that seemed plural but that were similar. For example, I was looking at someone else's bicycle, and the thought of taking it was the same as going into a house that wasn't occupied. A placement of an item, with someone making use of it. And that is what happened later in the day as a result, but I shall get into that in a bit.

First, let me tell you about what I encountered at the Ramada inn down the street, on the bicycle. When I arrived, I found that the front had a lawn on it with trees on it, so I sat down next to the bicycle and thought about how, as I decided to get up and get the bicycle, a man in the café gave me $5.00. He was very kind, and the giving of that money to me at that time was a delineation of the actual effect that having the bicycle was going to do for me finding a place to sleep. Some place besides the bottom of that bridge.

As I lay there, though, I got an urgent sense of evil in my presence. At it, the first place I looked was up in the sky. And there, I saw a hairless face glaring at my direction. It was the face of Satan and Mephistopheles. But I was also told in a solid tone to be cautious and okay, because it came from an Angel. It was an Angel modifying the environment to make it so that I was invisible to the image, instead I looked like grass.

I got up and went inside. The server there inside the hotel was a vibrant female, who tried to get me a room. It was clear from her method of speech that she had seen something in error outside. I brought up the stones I had acquired and tried to get her input on them. She said I should keep them. She was right. Further, she was aware that there were other copies of me in different dimensions. Something new, but also something that I had gotten from that science book in Christa's coffee shop.

From there I rode the bicycle to a restaurant down the road. In the parking lot in front of it, I noticed that it was linearly different than what was expected. It looked like a negative energy field there, and it became plain that the evil ones were planning to put the place under attack. So, I went in to warn them.

The waitresses that came to the table were fantastic. They were in support of God's effort against the sinners of Seattle. I read how some of them had written religious mysteries upon the menu. It described how the city was religiously built.

I thought a lot about what religious ramifications they consisted of. Then it dawned on me to step into the side room, that was a casino and bar, and order a drink and get to know the waitress. I did. I found out that her name was Jezebel, the name of Grace's daughter. And it also occurred to me, almost instantly, that it was a copy of her that had travelled through time. Thus, she had transmitted herself for some reason. I wanted to find out what it was.

As I wondered that question, Jezebel began to talk about how she had travelled through time but did not know how, and at the same time, a woman who I affirmed was an Angel came in and began to play a gambling machine.

I noticed that as she played, she found the formula to my problem-solving ability, and she also, getting lost at the structure of the formulas, began to put in the number 12, over and over again. And I realized at that, that the number 12 was my number. It represented me on a mathematical level.

And I knew, from the movie *Bruce Almighty*, which starred Morgan Freeman, (who becomes extremely relevant in the next chapter), that the number of Angels was the number 7. But I was 12. Why was that?

I said goodbye to Jezebel. The Angel smiled at me. She knew what the answer to the number 12 was, but I had somewhere to go to.

I went that night back to the coffee shop of Christa. There I saw a dog barking at me. I got from him the sign that he was trying to talk me into finding another place to sleep. So, I walked past him and rode into the neighborhood.

There I found a house with a for-sale sign in front. I went to the rear door, and it was unlocked. Inside, it was not put together, so I decided to stay there for the night, because nobody was living there.

That night I read over the science book, and learned about black holes, worm holes, time travel, and other elements of science. It was clear that the elements of it were religious in their foundation. Then I looked on the wall and saw a picture of the Archangel Michael there. He gave me the signal that there were religious figures that were to help me learn, mostly I was interested in learning about religion more and fighting evils. And he told me that it was not going to turn out the way I expected.

And sure enough, to that warning, in the morning some police officers arrived at the house and told me to leave. So, I did.

From there I began to ride through a park. On the other side a police officer stopped me and took the bicycle away from me, saying that it belonged to another man. She told me to go somewhere else. I went back to Starbucks.

There, at Starbucks, I saw a tunnel going under the street and highway. So, I went in there. The bottom was full of water. I walked through it and came out on the other side in a group of blackberry bushes. I had visions of what it meant and tried to get into touch with the Angels on the other side of my webpage access on my phone. One of the messages I got was the knowledge that my mother had been an Angel, named Chrystal, and she had existed inside of Crater Lake, Oregon. That made me an Angel before the existence of Genesis within the Bible. As morning came around, I kept on moving through the blackberries to the river on the other side.

After crossing the river, I came to the hotel I was going to stay at. Walking there, I saw a shifting of light from the sun, next to a room with a woman in there, and I got the signal that she was the Angel of Death. The summary was that I had moved through time, through the underground tunnel, to a place that was safe from the oncoming Armageddon.

I walked over and got a hotel room there.

Then, the next day, I walked over to the bus stop. There I met a man with the same name as me, who was talking about doing all sorts of negative things to people he did not understand. I was under the illusion that he was a copy of me, on a different wavelength.

I went to a different city on the bus. It was a city that had a theater area, where they put on plays. I think it was named Ashland. I tried to go there and found there a demon who was trying to do negative things to people. So, I departed and went to stop him, and saw in front of a closed restaurant a list on the door of a parable of evil doings that the man inside was trying to promote. So I knocked. He answered. I told him to stop. He followed me to the back of the building, threatening me. So I assaulted him. I punched him in the head and threatened to break his chest. He cried out, and a woman showed up and hit me with a backpack. I thanked her and got up and left.

I was arrested and taken to the jail. There, a group of officers came into my cell when I was writing an anti-terror message on the door, and they had the intention to assault me. I thought about the presence of a pistol in my hand and thought about shooting them. That stopped them, with cries. Then I was put into a different cell by myself. There I had visions of how exactly I was going to use spiritual powers and the powers of Angels above to silence and dispel the evils I encountered in Seattle and elsewhere. It worked. The staff got the message, and I am certain they decided to dispel and release me at that note. From there, I went to the Mall. There I ran into a woman who spoke to me about Quantum Theory and Superstring Theory. She brought to my attention that there was something in one of the stores that some criminals wanted to achieve. After that I left.

The next place I went to was a bar down the road from the Mall. There I met the bartender and asked for the recipe and some of one of the drinks. She said there was no drink in there. I got that word and realized that although the place was full of prophets and priests, and possible some Angels, they were not on the same prefix that I was on. There was something wrong with their sense of right and wrong, some of them.

I departed, and down the street I found a trailer that had been ransacked by flame. I went into the trailer park yard and went there. In it I found evidence of what had happened and how it had happened to my real father. He had been possessed by evil spirits and killed by them. That was what happened to him in actuality, not suicide, as I had been told by Paris. I departed.

The list of what happened goes on. If you are deeply interested, then read the full version in the *Cheetah on the Wing* series version number 3. It describes what happened in detail. Know this ... one of the last things that happened was that I found a group of people at the Ramada inn bar that all came from before Genesis was written. All of them did. They were there in preparation for the War God was getting ready to fight. And they were taking care of the precursors to that as I was.

The very last part of that chapter is me thinking deeply about the Angels that I had come into contact with during my lifetime so far. Ariel, Gabriel, Michael, Chrystal, the Angel inside the bar with Jezebel. They all had done something to move me forwards with religious knowledge, in a very holy element of thought and presence. I greatly appreciate them.

I took the Jeep to the airport, and there took an airplane to Seattle. It was broken from the accident I had gotten in on the way to Crater Lake, which I haven't mentioned yet. What had happened was that I had gotten in a wreck on the way to Crater Lake to see Chrystal, and

I had gotten lost in the forest running. From there, days later I was taken to the hospital in Portland, Oregon. I had frostbite in my foot. From there I was taken by Paris to my younger sister's house in Yreka. From there I got my damaged Jeep back and drove it to Klamath Falls, where I was born. There I saw ill images inside of my old grade school. Then I was sent by the police from the VA hospital to Medford, Oregon. And that is where the beginning of this chapter starts.

There was a lot more detail of what had occurred, as put forth in the other book. Religious things are greatly detailed. I didn't have enough room to put it all here.

Now let me tell you about the mission inside of Seattle. In *Cheetah on the Wing 3* it is multiple chapters long. I shall be shortening it greatly here.

The religious war of God in Seattle, Washington.

When I arrived in Seattle on the airplane, I was convinced that God was going to help me bring those evil prison guards and lawless cops that arrested me to justice.

The taxi cab driver, from the airport to downtown Seattle, talked to me about the town. He told me about the dead birds in the city. Then he dropped me off. I almost immediately found the corpse of a dead bird on a bench and realized that it was the dead body of a person who had been subjected to the evils of the area.

I noticed that the architecture of the buildings was

such that it changed and itemized the thoughts of the person witnessing them.

Then I stopped by a store and bought a magazine with some writings from the Archangel Michael in it. It described the evils of the area, and how they were taking over different people. Now, that is what it said, but it was written on the level of a normal story, so one would have to have a higher mentality to read the religious parables of it.

I walked over to the possessed bank that Michael had been talking about. There I saw a vehicle go in with two priests on it, a male and a female, and they were going to come into a fight there. I could read their minds, that they were on a mission. Upon seeing them disappear in there, I went to the parking lot of a coliseum there in the city, and from there was able to look at the outside of the Bank.

I got thoughts about the lighting there and got the summary through mental power that the lights were evidence of the unlawful presentation of forces within the building. I got the summary that they had kidnapped one of the priest's children, and the priests were there on a mission to liberate him.

I came up with a poem about Bananas to help them and recited it for the presence of the story to move to them inside the building. Then they arrived in a truck. They had their kid with them and were discussing what had happened.

That was the beginning of an evil presence within the city of Seattle. It got worse.

As I walked through the city, I thought deeply about how it was that people and their children could become slaves tortured by the evilly possessed demons or agents of the Devil her inside the city. I also thought about what it would take to help them escape that, indifferent scenarios than the one I had noticed.

Then as I walked, I came across a trash bag full of clothes, medicine, and mascara. I realized through mental power that it was evidence of a crime. It existed one way in the dimension that I was in, in a format of clothes and medicine and mascara, and in another dimension, a parallel dimension, it would exist as the dead body that was wearing those clothes. It became apparent to me that the demons had killed one of the central figures of the city buildings, one engaged in construction and presentation of the composite building fabrications, and how they worked, and one that engaged the activities of the people within them. And that person had been seen and killed by a demon or the Devil who wanted control over those things, for the purpose of possessing as many people as possible.

The clothes made it clear that the dead woman was an Archangel in charge of the construction and positive aspects of Seattle.

It became clear then that God wanted me to move through the city and to bring to justice those who were being violated by the forces of evil ... and there were a lot of them.

I went walking through town towards the Seattle Center. On the way, I came across a man at the bus stop, read his mind, and got a message about the Archangel Michael being in a state of becoming present. I thanked him and kept on walking.

The next person I ran into was a homeless man who spoke in a foreign language about the evils that were going on in the area. I kept on walking.

Then the next person I got in touch with spoke English and discussed the evils presence of a person within 7-11 down the street to me. We decided together to go there to stop him.

We went to the 7-11 down the street. The cash register man there was severely negative, and it was plain and clear to us that he was filled full of sin. I cast a spell on the things I had, an episode of scientific prodigy to make him get into a car wreck when he left, and I left. I took off to Seattle Center to think about what had just happened.

There I began to wonder what my relationship was to the Archangel Michael.

I got up after a spell and began to walk farther down the street. I came to a place called the *5 Star Circus, with Beer and Ruminations*. It was a bar, and I got from the conversation of the men outside that there was perhaps a litter of their clothing thrown in the trash; something I could use. I went inside.

Two of the men from outside came in as well, and they sat at a table within earshot of me. They began to talk about how they had seen a car accident with two men in it that had killed them. The dead men were the same evil men that me and the homeless man had approached in 7-11. I began to think about what had happened. Here is the list: 1) created a vehicular level of predestination, 2) who they would be when they got hit, 3) where we would be to prevent a hearing against us, in short, a collection of Time to Now, 4) where we would be through Time afterwards. 1) created a vehicular level of predestination, 2) who they would be when they got hit, 3) where we would be to prevent a hearing against us, in short, a collection of Time to Now, 4) where we would be through Time afterwards. And we verbally separated, through the presence and power of linear terms, the good souls of the evil people to the food we were eating, which they went to on their own because of our descriptions, thus leaving the bad souls to die in the vehicles.

The waitress talked a lot about the negative impacts of the bar. As she talked, I took notice of a man losing at a gambling machine for hours. So, to fix the problem I got a mind-eye view of what the machine was all about and gave the waitress $5 to give that man a drink. And she did. And it worked. He began to win.

From there I got the idea from the Angels to go to the

nearby city of Issaquah. I had been there at the shooting range before the unjustly persecuted criminal charges were brought against me, and from that knowledge I was confident that there was something there that I needed to pay attention to. So, I went. What happened there is seriously religious. The next section shall describe it.

First, let me describe what I had in mind from my experience in the past with religion. I began to remember how one day I had gone to the cliff over the beach in California, next to the ocean. There I had seen a group of birds on one post on the right-hand side. Then I saw them get up and go over next to a carving on the dirt ground. One by one they got up and flew off. They left one there. That one, I got in my mind, was the presence of Satan, after all the other birds, which were Angels, had fought him and left. Then a group of Marine Corp Am-tracks began to move in attack mode down the beach, and the Satanic bird flew away. There was one bird left, sitting on the post on the right-hand side, and I got the sense that the bird was a representation of me.

Thus it became clear to me that it was a message from God that I was to be the last one, with the arms of the Marine Corp in my presence, to fight and do away with the presence of Satan. And I was to be an Angel afterwards who took his presence in a solo place and created a new Universe. How was that supposed to work?

One element I knew of, was that I was on my way

there, by fighting the war of God against evils in the city, as a warrior of Heaven's Army.

Now, let me tell you about the deep presences I got from Issaquah.

There, off the bus in Issaquah, I first noticed the architecture of the hotel near there that was of a nature of invading the space of the customers there.

From there I went to a Coffee Bar down the street and over the freeway bridge. While in there I noticed a lot of spiritual aspects of the writings on one of the newspapers. Then, as I was drinking coffee, a woman came in there and began to speak in severe parables to the other people there, seeking knowledge about them that only an interviewer could get. I got the sense that she was an agent of the Devil or demon possessed. She became aware of my attention, and didn't like it, so she left. I followed her outside a few seconds later, and as I walked outside noticed on the ground the particles of spilled red coloring. And I read it. It was a symbol of her request for an assassination attempt be brought against me.

I found that she had hidden herself inside of a phone store. The door had a sign on it but had no way of opening. She had concealed it, through parallel universe theory, from my dimension. So, I kept on walking, wanting the answer to why I was told to go there.

6 blocks away I noticed a sign that had the signature of the Beast of the Apocalypse on it and noticed his

presence inside of a smoking car. I put out a sign of his presence and he fled. What I got from that was that the woman calling for me to be assassinated at the Coffee Bar was an agent of the Beast, a partaker of evil, and it was sweeping all over the town.

From there I walked to the library. And from there, noticed the religious sign coming to me from the trees upon a hill next to it. So, I went there, deep within the woods of trees, and there saw something you would not believe.

I saw a dual-canopy tree upon the top of the hill. One of the trees were solid, the other one was dead and white. I lay down in front of it, getting the religious semblance of the Jewish religion of the Hebrew Bible there. It was an Angelic symbol of what the location of the religious living and dead would be doing to interact with each other inside of Heaven.

Then I looked down the hill, and saw next a very large, disease ridden tree of very solid construction. Tall, wavy limbs, portions extended like weeds along the bottom halves of the tall widths, and a portion of a bent area on the back that looked like it was about to break. It was the tree of the Beast. How did I know that? Because of the religious ramifications that I was getting from God and his Angels themselves, putting ideas into my mind in conjunction with what I was experiencing. The powers of mental acclimatization are actual. One must experience them personally to get that belief, but once one becomes a believer, it is very hard to change one's mind. That is the actions of the Angels of God.

Along the front of the tall Beast tree, there was a smaller pine, with solid and fragrant branches, flowing along the front of it. That was the symbol of God himself, taking action to disable the Beast. He was smaller, true, but much better built, and flexible, and had the strength to do it right.

Night came, as I lay there, and I began to get a lot of very religious symbols and messages from the trees, the plants, the stars in the sky. Here is what they said ...

First, there was the episode from the dead tree before me, telling me about where it came from. It was a combination of the dead souls of Jews who had died attempting to deprive evils of their powers. They were trying to find a way to unify with the living so they could bring their good deeds forwards in a way that allowed them to take pleasure and satisfaction in the good. I was destined to help them, in a way that I wasn't sure of, yet, but one that the area was bringing to me.

Then, I learned about how people operated when confined within the tree of the Beast. They would not know they were there, at first, then it would become apparent by the evil actions of others within those limbs. They would then seek to separate themselves from the Beast, by separating themselves from the tree and flowing, by branch or vine or leaf, down to the earth, among the plants. Then there, with extreme difficulty, they were to move to the Tree of Remorse, which was the dead tree that I was laying half next to, and there they would either be accepted if they were remorseful enough, or rejected if they were too far along the lines of sin. And if they were accepted, they would be allowed to seek life again though the other living tree.

Then, I started to get images of people concealed within the leaves of the trees. They were people on a religious thoroughfare of action and presence, fighting evils on a bunch of different levels. There were people from all three different religions; some Jewish, some Christian, and some Muslim. Then a light came on from the stars above, and it showed me a picture.

It was of six Angels in a circle of stars, a perfect circle, and in the middle of them, moving out on its own, was a separate star. The last star was the Angelic being of Satan himself, separating himself from the Angels of Heaven. I knew the names of three of the Angels: Michael, Gabriel, and Ariel. I had been in contact with every single one of them in the past.

The sun came up. I was in a religious fervor. I began to summit branches of the forest along the ones that seemed like branches associated to the Beast and moved, through the parallel science of moving air particles against nerves of trees, visions of those Beast branches breaking and moving through the air to the ground. I knew it was one of the powers of Jesus himself.

And at that I got a call from Patton, the man who had

gone to 7-11 with me, and he told me that he had been in touch with Jesus, and they wanted me to tell the believers about what had happened in that forest of Issaquah.

So, I have. Thus, is the portion of this part of this book.

The journey against evils continues.

From Issaquah, I took a bus back to Seattle. There, I found a Diner. Next to it, on the sign there were the sounds I could identify as being sounds of Jesus's speech, as put forth in the language of birds singing.

In the doorway of the Diner, I picked up a flyer about Seattle Museums. From the illustration of a woman statue on the cover of it, and my mental presentation to the Angels, I got a solid idea of how creation comes into effect using the formulas of scientific space and time. The woman actually appeared to become alive on the flyer.

I identified one of the men at the Diner bar as being Adam, from the Bible, Adam, the first man of God's creation. Thus, he was also immortal, the way that Jesus was, I thought.

Could that apply to others? I learned later, in LA, that it did.

After that, I went out walking around. I was thinking at that time about my son. I began to look at the symbols on the ground, and they were of a body. I got in mind that my son was dead, and I was seeing evidence of his body.

I got extremely distressed but kept on walking. It was something I was going to have to deal with.

That ends that chapter within the *Cheetah on the Wing* series volume #3. The chapters on the warfare of God continue, as shall be put here in this chapter in this book.

I went to sleep inside of a building ... and was arrested by the police there. They took me to a mental health clinic. The psychologist there refused to listen to my religious reasoning, and instead thought it hadn't happened ... that it was just a "mental health problem". He was in error. If he had heard the same thing from a priest or an imam or a clergy member in a church, then he would have thought it was "just religion." But because I was in a mental health facility, he instead thought wrongly that it was a "mental health problem."

I began to walk around the place. I met a man named Troy, who I found to be remarkably intelligent and full of humor. He talked about how bulls of a rodeo have a mindset that does not allow a person to ride them for more than 8 seconds - so the way around it was for clowns to put blinding cloths around their heads and make them go blind.

Then Troy and I came across a Russian and a woman named, you guessed it, her name was Jessica, just like the girl at the casino in Medford. And Jessica began to make comments about what it was like to name the bull in a way that would make it go to sleep.

Troy said jokingly, but seriously, that he was going to his room to go to sleep. Jessica joked back with him. I decided to go to my room to rest.

In the shower I came across religious images regarding the soap on the wall, the water, and the frequency of sound there. Then, when I got out of the shower and looked in the mirror, I noticed that my skin looked white and my eyes looked black, and there was a light, like a halo, over my head. At that, I arrived at the conclusion that I had been an Angel before Genesis and I knew it to be true.

Now, my memory of what had happened at the beginning before Genesis, or what had made me transfer from an Angel to a human was not plain at the time, but it became plain, as you shall see in the next chapter of this book, which will explain exactly what had occurred and how I got a mental image of the memory of it.

And then, imagine, I went into the snack room and met a woman named "Angel". She was very soft spoken, and I could tell had problems. Then, as I was getting ready to talk to her, Jessica came in and began to talk to me.

Jessica and I began to talk about Quantum Theory and Relativity, including time travel. She knew a lot about them! Then she describe some special manners of reading sentences that hold multiple ideas, and I realized that what she was talking about was the same thing that I had gotten from reading the Angelic stories from the Archangel Michael and others. It was clear then that she knew how to read Angel-speak.

To that we began to play by putting together the pieces of a puzzle. I realized that it reflected the element of what had occurred with my noticing of the Beast in Issaquah, so I told her to put reflective pieces together on the board, as I projected the concept to her in mind. She read my mind and said that she got exactly what I was talking about and was amazed and dread-filled with the knowledge of it.

From there, Jessica and I went over to another room, where there was a staff member named Karen and Juliet. They were talking about what the treatment there was all about, and they were full of errors. We - Jessica and I - had been sent there by people who wanted to do us wrong. The people who sent Jessica had wanted to use her valid complaint against her, and the staff listened to them! We pointed out that the thing to say wasn't something nice, it was to say: "Fuck you!" to the person making the ill deed. The staff finally listened to us and changed their story into one that was acceptable.

Jessica was like that. She was so intelligent that she could see the finer points behind someone doing something ill against another to bring them, lawlessly, to a mental health facility. And she was able to tell what to do about it. Now, it didn't change the fact that she was there, true, but it did change how she was viewed by the staff members. It changed how she was treated.

After the meeting was over, I went into the other room and got on the computer. I looked at a program called *The*

Complexes of the Universe, which had a lot of pictures of planets, stars, black holes, and other elements of space in it. I was trying to understand the effects of Creation.

After that things got much more intense at the Mental Health Clinic.

I began to notice that Angel was traumatized. Me and the others talked about it. Then, another patient told me about something that got me to thinking about Chrystal, the Angel that I had perceived to be similar to my real mother within the Afterlife, before Genesis occurred. Then I got it in my head a transition thought space and time in a very unreal seeming concept of altered reality, and it became apparent that I was being dragged through time to a hidden or secret place. I awakened shortly after and recovered in the regular time and space.

We were moved to a different ward of the hospital. Then, there I met the female named Rebecca. She told me about how she had interactions with Angels before she was sent there, how she knew of a man who had been to jail, and he had protected her daughter. She gave me a bracelet that had the power to move the sinners thoughtfully to become present and commit their crimes on the streets, from which they would be judged by Angels. That came into play big time in the future, in ways I didn't anticipate at the time. I shall describe those bracelet-found events as this chapter portion about Seattle continues.

After those heavy elements ended, I was released

from the Mental Health Clinic. I found that I had come a long way towards finding a way to resist the evils of the world. My interactions with Jessica and Angel played a large part in that. What I didn't realize was that I was going to become enjoined with parables of them in the near future. Read on, and you will be flabbergasted.

The first hotel that I walked around after getting released from the Mental Health Clinic had the evidence of evil forces there. And looking, I noticed that the Antichrist was there. I kept on walking. It became apparent to me at that time that the evil forces of the city had become aware of what we religious ones were doing inside of that hospital, and they wanted to prevent us from going further.

I walked over next to some trees next to a field with a lot of water and went inside. I found my way through the bushes and plants to a section over the water in a bunch of bushes, and I lay back and thought about the religious aspects of what was happening. It was alarming that the Antichrist was present in the nearby hotel.

As I lay there, I got the images of the foundering of an evil character seeking me out, and got the impression that he was using the knowledge and visions of one of the blinds of a plant vine next to me to see where I was. I put the idea of concealment in my mind and was careful how I was moving so he could not see me.

Then that was past, and dawn started to arise. I

noticed in the sky were great number of birds flying in a particular order. Now, I had noticed before that God was in touch with the animals and birds of the planet, being able to identify through their movement and speech and sounds what it was that they were thinking. Birds had the capacity to learn and do things with the same level as people, they just had a different way of articulating it.

The birds told me, by their song and movement, that the universe had existed before man existed. They knew that at the very beginning, they were in peace, then the dominating negatives of evil demonology came to fruition, and those evil forces began to influence the presence of the good, in a bad way. The good ones then acted, by changing the articulation of the presence of being in such ways as to put a firm harness on the evil forces influencing them. Then the fight of good versus evil began. And that was what brought about the presence of science, government, law, television, and other elements that people take for granted as being normal and actual, when the fact is that they exist only as a way to delineate away from the presence of evils renditions of negativity.

I got up an got a lot of lessons from those birds, as I walked through the field. They told me about how there was a way to sense the evil presence of badness, of how to read over what they were saying on a religious holy basis, how to fight the evils that I came across. They told me about the presence of mind and how it interrupted the forces of evils by plain desire and patience. And I didn't realize it then, but had the idea, that it was going to pay off big time in the near future. It was. My presence against evils became plain in the future, as did the conflict, and I won … at least part.

Upon completion of learning there, I departed to go downtown. As I got there, I went walking near a pier near the waterfront, and ran into a guy who smelled like Sulphur … the chemical of Satan himself. I talked to him, and realized that he was on the side of Angels, but had been drawn to Los Angeles and lived there, and there came under the influence of the evil forces of the area, trying to read, but fight, them. After the conversation was over, I began to walk down by the water.

As I walked, I was being followed by the man. Then, two kids, in a parallel universe, did away with him, sending him to a different aspect of the parallel universe we were in. That was to free him of the negativities of evil that had followed him from LA. I went to the bathroom to wash my hands, and afterwards, started to get a solid input from the man from LA about what was happening to him then. He was being swept along in a dimension of safety that was making him present for the war against the evils of the world. He was given a group of numbers. One of those numbers was the number "0". What "0" was, was a number that had no value and no symbolic unification with other numbers, and what it equaled was secret and special. It was a mystery of numbers, and to have that made it so that the man had severe power over others in the battle against the evils.

From there I went for a long walk through the separate area of town, thinking hard about what had happened. Then night came, and I got drawn to thoughts in the Bible about how it was that Adam was created. And I got the idea in mind that I was being called to a place to investigate. I went down the street, then abruptly turned to the left, into a housing complex. The house was vacant. And flooded. I went in there and began to go through the trash that was on the floor of the room there.

I drew the conclusion that there were certain elements of that environment that played a part in how Adam was created. And I also got the impression of the question of whether I was a member of heaven's Army.

I went to a restaurant down the street. I got some crab there. I thought deeply about how the evil elements of the city had come around. For example, I thought about seeing the Beast of the Apocalypse in Issaquah, and how we had partaken in the trials and tribulations, me and Troy and Jessica and Angel, at the Mental Health Clinic. And I thought, above all that, about how I had been trained by birds in a field to fight against evils of the city. I thanked the waiter and left.

I kept walking, and my feet began to hurt from so much walking. I began to limp. I turned to a blackberry bush off the side of the road and began to read the Bible. There, I got the impression in mind that Jesus was trying to teach me how to walk on water. That was the purpose of the limp as it was raining outside. I didn't learn, and he told me to eat a spider to take in the fluids that would have a mental preservation sense to them. So, I did. And my mind afterwards, as I digested it, awakened, and the thought of how to walk on water became clear to me. But I could not do it, because my mind was interrupted from the spider. That was what I deserved.

I got the sense that the Angels of God wanted me to return to town and do my job, fighting evils. There was something going on there of a very negative precedence. So, I fought them.

As I walked along the waterfront of Seattle again, I came across a homeless man sitting near a bunch of statues he was selling. He was highly religious and told me in sideways terms that there was such a thing as the presence of evils in that city. As he said it, I got the idea to look up at the waves of water reflections on the bridge above us, and I saw in it the image of Satan, glaring at the road. I came to realize that we were fighting him, true, and we were winning.

The efforts of peace and harmony that we had done with the man from LA, and elsewhere, was coming to fruition.

Then I went to a homeless shelter. When I stepped outside, I was met by a presentation of Jesus, who told me to the parable of going out and learning the numbers of Creation. I went out and walked, and as I walked, I came under the serious illusions of what the different numbers meant in relation to how people operated and interacted. I kept on walking, seeing the effects of it, and thinking to people what it meant, and seeing their reactions. I was accurate.

Later I went online and saw a website that explained what each of the meanings of the numbers leading from 1 to 10 all are, and it was the same thing I had gotten from the effects of Jesus.

I went to the college of Seattle then. There I wanted to identify how the students were learning things about religion. I got a lot of answers from watching the students and listening to them. They described some of how their perceptions of Creation occurred, in terms that didn't seem totally related to it, but that could be read on their parallel meanings to be about the effects of Creation.

That night I positioned myself near a tree that I read was of God, and watched the students walking down the pathway near there. A woman came by ... and could not speak right. But her name was Jessica and realized that she was inviting me to experience ambulance to different planets in the galaxy. She was like Krishna, in her presence of righteousness.

Jessica had put forth the mindset of a location deep in the residential area of the city. So I went there, walking tall, and read on flyers on the ground, on trash on the sidewalk, on stencils on the sidewalk and roads, on license plates, how it was that the presence of people in the area were being influenced by evils of the area.

Certain crimes, like events regarding violations of the 10 Commandments, was evident. People were doing them in the presence of evil forces.

I went to the place articulated by Jessica. It was a house with a birdfeeder in the front of the place, and steps. I took notice of the bird feeder, and saw pieces of nutrition in folders of cloth placed in them, and got the idea that they were the spirits of Archangels, like Michael, like I had seen in front of Mesa College in California. Then I noticed that there were some cockroaches running on the stairs. I was getting solid ideas about it from the Angels, in this case, I think it was Gabriel, that a person who died had avenues to be preserved and presented after, in the Hereafter. What was it?

For example, a dead person has a soul that can move not only from person to person, but also to animals, to birds, and to bugs. It can move to trees and bushes and flowers and plants. And the methods of presentation and action are put forth by the actions of the thing that they had put their souls in. And the learning and presentation of that grew as time progressed.

Thus, a dead person could become a cockroach, and learn about people and the universe in ways that were unseen by the average person. And I was told, by the Angel, that cockroaches were some of the most solid creatures that existed.

There were many other aspects of it. I shall not put them all here. But a person who found a way into a cockroach after they died would be able to find salvation in ways that the average person could not. It goes much more in depth than that. I shall describe it in detail in the part about the spiritual warfare in LA.

From there I started to walk down the street and got drawn into a coffee shop. I was thinking hard about what happened after we died and thought about how time operated. As I sat inside of a Starbucks, drinking coffee, I read the paper and came to an article written by Michael. It talked about how the kids of a football team were leaning about things in school. But what it really meant was that they were learning things about time travel. Then I looked outside ... and saw it in action.

The busses and the people walking on the sidewalk were moving through time, years and years in advance. I saw signs on the buses that were of a different shape and description of what was occurring. And the people were in separate groups, and I could see how the evil ones were indirectly trying to influence the good ones into doing or being swept into evil forces.

I got upset and realized at that time that I was so pronounced in my existence against evils that I was going to have to influence, for protection, the good ones. So, I left. I got on a bus, and mentally saw that there was a sacrifice needed to bring about justice from the evils. So, I took out my knife and began to cut off my finger.

I was interrupted by the bus driver, who called the police on me and kicked me off the bus. I began to run and was approached by people who said something religious to me. Then I was arrested and sent to another mental health hospital.

Now I shall, in the next section, tell you about what that was like.

At the second mental hospital, I was met by a staff woman who had the same name as my ex-wife. Her analysis of me was in error, but she said I was "ok".

Then I met some patients. One was named after Jesus's mother: her name was Mary. Another was named Jessica. Another was named Jonathan. They each had different things to say to me.

Elizabeth told me things about how she had existed in a parallel universe and many religious things were happening to her. She was treated differently than one would anticipate. That was because of the evils of the people who were interacting with her. And she acted against them, actions that seemed odd and distant.

I was released soon after and left at the same time as Mary. She told me about finding other people, then left.

I departed by jumping the fence on the west side of the compound and going into the trees there, next to an entrance on the freeway. There I found a homeless hole dug in the ground that had a female homeless patient there, who had a synergistic vial of medicinal fluid of a Gothic nature, called the "Mary Land Potion." It was evidence that Mary had influence in that area. I spent the next few minutes trying to read the mind of the person there. Then the following happened.

I walked down the street to a homeless shelter and was in line outside waiting to find a place to stay. The men outside were talking. Then, I got the idea that there were synergies between what happened in this universe versus what happened in parallel, similar, but different universes. The same people, as a result of that, could be in the same, or similar, places, and see and experience many different things. That was a thought coming from the female of Mary from the hole in the ground.

And then it struck. There was, in my mind's eye only, evidence of a severe earthquake running through the town. It was happening in a parallel universe to ours, but one that affected some of the people there, the sinners, by dragging them, of parts of their negative souls, to destruction. But to those of us who were good, it seemed and looked like no earthquake was even happening. Thus, there were different effects and different evolutions in different dimensions.

At that I wanted knowledge of how the evil doers played. I sought an answer to it.

I went to the Seattle Center, and began to read over what Michael had written. In it were tales of the evils of the demons and the Devil and how it was that people had knowledge of it, how it operated (some of them), and what to do to fix it. It went in synergy with what I had learned from the birds in the field.

Then, I went walking down the seaside of Seattle, and there came across a pier with odd looking pyramids on it. The pyramids contained souls of people who were trying to escape the destruction of the city of Seattle, much more that was going to happen.

I could also tell that some of the souls within the pyramids were trying to escape the injustice of lawbreaking police officers of Seattle. I had come across a lot of them.

It was night, and I got from the pyramid's illustrations on them that many of the souls there consisted of dead people. I went then to catch a bus. While waiting for it, I saw a woman there waiting that looked exactly like Marylyn Monroe. And she was the body of the living dead from the Hereafter, interacting from the leverage of my awareness of the pyramids! She was speaking very intelligently to me.

Then I got drawn to a strip club. From inside I got the plethora in my synapses that there was a uniform present for me at Seattle Center. It was a message from an Angel, I could tell. So, I went over to the Seattle Center, and there, outside under a statue of oblong cylinders of red, found a box of clothes, gloves, medicine, neck braces and ribbons, and a Walkman. I listened to the Walkman. I got from the music and the story in the magazine that there was similar to me, in a parallel universe, an Angel that did descriptions of love for knowledge. Then I began to walk, with the neck brace and ribbons on, waving them in the air for communication with her.

It worked. I got drawn into the coffee shop on the strip, and when I went in there, I was met by a woman named Angelique. She was the Angel I had been interacting with. She discussed colors, and the lights at the theatre across the street. I could tell she wanted me to go there to get a message. It was morning time, and like I had been doing for months now, I hadn't slept a wink. That seems impossible, I know, but it was the full-on effects of the severe religious diatribes I had been sustaining.

Doing what Angelique said, I went to a field on a hill that night next door and watched from there a synapse of lighting across the front of the theatre there. Then, the next day, I went to Seattle Center, on call from Angelique, and there ran into a group of men telling the children there about the science of the light waves. I then realized that a ghost of my father was walking down in the field. As I noticed him, a man above there started to talk to me about how he was manipulating light. That was in tall order, something that nobody but Angels, or fallen Angels, should have the capacity to do. Then I went down below to see my father, but he had left. I got depressed. That man talking about light, I could tell, was a fallen Angel.

The next day I went to Pike's Place Market, and in the square there, I noticed Lucifer standing atop a high room there, looking down. He was trying to draw the people there to become his demons. I came to the realization there that there were people doing a lot of negative things. I used the bracelet given to me by Rebecca to get the summary of where the good ones were. They were out of the area, all in Churches or Mosques. And the reason was because they had witnessed portions of the disaster of the earthquake coming through the town. How did I know?

Because the presence of Jesus came back to me and told me about how the earthquake had functioned. He also told me about the presence of the do-good people involved. He made it clear that there were going to be more disasters as the city was going to fall. I also asked him questions about the Ark of the Covenant, because I was getting the input in the Bible that it was going to have something to do with the future. The chapter after next shall explain what, exactly, is meant to occur in that regards.

Now, the remainder of what happened at the square is interesting. I went inside of a hotel room next to it and read over a sign that described how it was that evildoers within the hotel were going to cast spells of destruction on the area. They were trying to kill the religious people there by making it plain to all. I got kicked out then, by staff, who realized that I was reading the sign correctly. Then I went out onto the street.

There, on the street sidewalk, I saw a woman with flyers saying a lot of things about the programs of the city. Next to her was a man in costume, a costume of green colored reflections that was dancing on the sidewalk, getting donations and charity for them. From the two of them it was clear from their actions and the woman's speeches that she was trying to bring justice against those evil forces seeking to destroy the hotel.

From there I got drawn to an alleyway and went over to it. Next to it was a woman smoking. I asked her was the remedy was against the potential violence and disaster coming. She remarked in an irate fashion, smoking more, and said I knew nothing about what I was talking about. She was an Angel that was attempting to fix the problem and didn't like my interaction with it.

From there I noticed that in the alleyway was a cart with boxes of clothes on it. The clothes were to actors inside of the club whose rear doors were next to me. I looked at the clothing, and it became apparent that they belonged to agents of Lucifer and Mephistopheles, agents of Satan. Thus, it became apparent what side those evil souls aboard the hotel seeking to destroy it were prevalent to. I got in my head a discrete sense of urgency to prevent it, but I didn't know how to. So, getting an idea for help in my head, I summoned mentally the Angels to appear, or to bring someone to help, and I went down the alleyway to a turn-in garage with a radiator box in it.

I took out everything within my pockets, which was a lot, and put them on the radiator box. It was to be delivered to someone helpful as a means to give them power over the evil ones. One of the things there was the bracelet of power that Rebecca had given me. There were also the planet rocks that I had gotten from Medford. In addition, there were a lot of other things, that I cannot remember, like receipts and flyers and forms and coins and a watch and money. As I put them down, a man came walking down the alley, looking my way, and it became plain to me that he was the one to be acting with those products.

And then I departed. That was evidence that I was aware of the second disaster to be coming to Seattle. And I knew that the last one I could tolerate was going to be one more disaster. Then I was going to have to leave to survive the fourth ... which I knew was also going to happen.

Now I shall tell you about that last disaster, how it came about, and the very religious things that happened afterwards, in the Seattle area.

The next day, I began to walk around downtown in a shop area, where I began to read over the stencils that people had been putting on the sidewalk. Then I noticed how there were planes flying across the buildings downtown. It became evident to me that the movement and motions of the people in the city were being dictated on a parallel universe mentality of doing things that brought them to different levels.

Then I walked and came across a psychologist office with a sign of being present on weekdays there. From it I got the idea that she knew about what was going on inside of the field next to me. So, I went over there, jumped over the fence, and saw that they were very large piles of trash and debris from the destroyed buildings that had been there. I went in one of the piles, and found there a book by Ptolemy, the scientist of a very old age. In it he was talking about how it was that people gained the ability to determine what it was that they were going to eat, from day to day. It was very deep.

Later, I would use that Ptolemy book to seek out ideas of a religious nature inside of the restaurants of San Diego. That shall be three chapters away in this book.

I took the book down the street and came to the ideas that the buildings I was looking at were symbols of potential time travel. I thought of how it was that I could go there and do what was necessary for preventing the evils of the city and surviving its destruction. Then I went to a grocery store, and got a flyer, and with it began to put forth the ideas of science of how I would be able to transmit through time to do it. The idea I got at that time was a stringent realization that there were copies of myself in parallel dimensions that were able to transmit to me ideas about what they were experiencing. And that concept came in to play large in my understanding of the next disaster to come ... which shall be described in the section after the next section.

I went back to Pikes Place Market that night. This is what happened there.

Next to Pikes Place Market, that night I went to a fountain down some stairs there. Late that night, around 3:00AM, I came into realization that there was a man there. I introduced myself. His name was Jeff Holder. He was very intelligent. We began to talk about Quantum Theory and time travel and multiple dimensions. Science and catastrophes and how the city was ill. Then he told me that it was my job to fix it.

He had a higher idea of what was occurring. I came to know that later that morning, as I went to the Greyhound Station to get a bus ticket out of there.

When I was there at the Greyhound Station, it was closed at that time, and I went into a closed access room and read a sign on the wall with a picture of what was about to occur. The ramifications of it were intense. Then I went outside, and the mysteries started to happen.

What I saw outside was evidence of destruction of the city on a level of parallel universes separate from ours. Some of the people there were to be destroyed, but to others, the good ones, it was not going to become evident. I shall not put all the numbers here but know this: there are a set of numbers that dictate everything in science and the universe on levels that are highly religious. I saw the events of those numbers happening. The sky split into 5 different dimensions. There were collisions of cars along posts on the ground. There were airplane crashes into the buildings. There was the number of the parallel universes awakening. Now, each of those things did not happen in my time, but there was the visual evidence, on a level of near-perception, color, and style, that they were occurring. It was the way that the parallel universe effects were having a presence in our universe.

That was a deep and serious disaster that killed a lot of people. And I noticed that it was the third disaster to come across the city. I realized that I would not survive the fourth one. The fourth dimension, as put forth in the website article about numbers, is the dimension of time moving forwards. There is a past, a present, and a future in the fourth dimension. That left no room to escape the effects of a disaster. So, I took actions to leave.

This is now about my departure from Seattle.

I have mentioned Jesus being reincarnated in this time multiple times. Is that believable, you might ask? Or is this author just "mentally ill?" Let me answer that for you.

Today, in December 2016, as I was writing this part of this book, I asked the Bible the question, "am I accurate in what my experiences were with seeing the reincarnation of Jesus?" So, I turned it to a random page, and this is the part I turned to: *John 19, 38; 20;* and *21*. It is about the Burial of Jesus, the Resurrection, and the Epilogue.

In other words, what is the chance that I could randomly turn to a page about Jesus being resurrected when I was asking about his resurrection? There is none.

That part is actual. Jesus exists as a living person today. It is a fact.

And that also plays a large part into what I am about to tell you. I came into contact with Jessica again. And I got the semblance that, in another life, she was, and is, my sister.

So, to access the truth to that, I asked the Bible, "is Jessica my sister?" And here is what it said: *Leviticus 16, 13*: "There in the Lord's presence he will put the incense on the burning coals so that a cloud of incense will rise over the Ark's cover – the place of atonement – that rests on the Ark of the Covenant. If he follows these instructions, he will not die ... He must sprinkle blood seven times with his finger in front of the atonement cover."

What does it mean? As I shall put later, in the chapter after next, I was told by Angels to go, when I die, to the Ark of the Covenant. And thus, this element of the Bible states that when I am there, I am to use the symbol of the number 7 to awaken Jessica in the levitation of an Angel. That is what the number 7 represents ... Angels before Creation.

Now, what occurred next? I went down the street of Seattle to a place that was a market, and there tried to get a taxi, but I had no money. So, I went and ordered a beverage from a store by there and walked out on the street. A man then tried to rob me for money, and another man came up and rescued me. The man's name was Black. I recognized him and realized that he was someone I had known in a different life. He paid for a taxi to take us down near the airport, outside of Seattle.

At the hotel we went to, I noticed that there was pornography on the television, and that it was deeply in line with how God had created Eve, Adam's wife at the beginning. So, I watched it.

Later, Black and I went for a walk to a restaurant. On the way back, he noticed a truck driving on the road and got the driver's attention. "That is my friend Jessica, and her friend Angel!" He said it with joy. They came to the hotel room.

Jessica showed interest in my finances, because she wanted me to be able to pay for the hotel room. We went to the bank and tried to withdraw money, but it wouldn't go through. So, she went in and talked to them about it, and they gave me money then!

Then, back at the hotel, Angel took me outside and asked me if I had a car. She was telling me that there was a way to get me one, which I found out about later.

Jessica was remarkably fantastic. I told her a little bit about the religious adventure I had in Seattle, and she gave me a head's up about how certain things people did can affect one's health. I was very thankful for the fact that she had helped me get money to pay for the hotel room. I noticed and read Jessica's tattoo, and talked to her about how her others in the past had sent me messages on the street.

Upon completion, she said that she and Angel and

Black needed to leave. I told her that I wanted to talk to her again in the future. She agreed.

From there, after they left, I went to a different part of town. There, at the Mall, I saw a damaged episode of the evils of Seattle saying all sorts of mentally disheveled evils about random things. He was severely stricken. In addition, I also found other flyers put out by a copy of Jessica, and it told me about the present tense of things. They brought to my attention that there was something evil going on inside of Los Angeles, the City of Angels. That was what the man by the water that I had come across and rescued had been through. He had taken a flyer of picture of evil forces and demons ... from those he had seen there.

So, I decided to go to LA, to move further, homeless, and not sleeping at all, on the religious mission for God that I was on against the forces of evil.

And there turned out to be a lot more to it than that. I shall put how in the next chapter.

CHAPTER 9

WARFARE FOR GOD IN THE CITY OF ANGELS

This chapter shall be about the religious war against evils for God Almighty. It is about how it occurred in Los Angeles, also known as the City of Angels.

When I got off the Greyhound Bus, the first thing that happened was that I walked across a man on the lawn of a building who looked injured. He wasn't. He was faking to get someone else in trouble. He called the police on me for talking to him and they took me to a mental health facility.

There I met two patients, one named Hubver and the other M, the same name as my son, and they were talking a lot about religion. Hubver was Muslim.

I also met a man named Steadfast, who was an agent of the Devil himself.

There was also a man named Jammer, who was mentally ill and disabled, who said a lot of things about going to a graveyard and getting the ideas of the dead there. That meant a lot in the future, because I wound up, as I shall put in this chapter, going to a graveyard and getting a lot of head's up about my life and people in it there.

One day I addressed Steadfast's shirt illustrations, because he thought it had a much higher religious power than it was supposed to have. I shut him down. That was also what M and Hubver had been attempting to do.

Another patient, named Steve, came up to me and began to talk about the mysteries of sea life and what occurs at the presence of the beginning of time.

I went into another room, with nothing in it but a fan and a medical bed and tried to fluctuate between religious thoughts about numbers and my situation and what Steve had said. I had memories there of the time I had spent in California previously at the beach, where I had come under the communication by the birds that I was to be one of the last people left on this earth, and that I was to fight Satan almost barehanded and beat him, thus departing and going on my own to create my own universe. A tall order.

Then I went out near the television. There I continued to think of the numbers, and my mission there in LA. I got from that a message that I was going to be taking to the graveyard later, I just didn't know it at that time.

I was then released.

The next place that I went to was amazing. It was the LA campus of Citrus College.

School on board the college campus was getting ready to start. My timing was good. There were a lot of students there on the campus.

As I sat there, thinking about the campus and the programs available, a female student came forwards and was talking to other students about the campus and how the programs were. One student said her name, and her name was, you guessed it, it was Jessica.

And what she didn't realize - that I was attune to - was that many of the students she was talking to were living dead. They had been swept there from Seattle after the disasters and were taking part in the war against evils.

Then I went to the main office and met there a man named Ambrez. He was Asian. We became friends and he offered to help me study and buy me food. I took him up on the offer. I realized that he was one of the dead from Seattle, and wondered how he got there to LA.

I then met a girl named Hera who I could tell had powers like those of the highest Angels of Heaven.

That night I went walking down the sidewalk outside of campus. I stopped near a wall and got on my computer, looking online. I found an article about how, in Florida, there was a disaster of things like bugs and disease moving through the city. It was the same place that the man named Michael that was a scientist that I had been in touch with online before had lived. I was sure that the same sorts of disasters could come to LA.

From there I went to a Coffee Shop and Diner restaurant down the street. There I listened to some men talk about the effects of the college, and I tried to put together a mathematical formula for the preservation of Florida.

Then morning came around. That was the first day and night at Citrus College.

The next morning, on campus, I went and had lunch bought for me by Ambrez.

Then I went and talked to a military person about the presence of the dead there. My questions were indirect. I also got information about the library there. He was very kind and interested in my success.

There was a fountain outside on the way to the library. On the way I stopped by an empty classroom, and inside got some paperclips. I then went to the fountain for the purpose of putting the paperclips on the sign covered ledge next to it, for the purpose of equating students to come along in sight and presence of mind that there were a lot of living dead students, that they hadn't noticed before (because the other students were dead), but that played a huge part of their presences there.

I noticed Jessica at that time walking around talking to students again, but I was busy, so I couldn't talk to her.

Outside the library, on the wall there was a mosaic of a stencil and artwork representing God and his Angels. I read over it and got an idea about what presences of Creation there were present, before, during, and after time existed.

In the library, I found a book about King Arthur. It was also about the Ark of the Covenant, and I got from it that I was supposed to take part in the Ark manifesto.

Then I departed the library.

On the way out I noticed that on a hill next to the school, a tall hill, there was a cross built. A cross, like the cross that Jesus had been crucified on. That plays a big part in things in this chapter later.

I went back to the Coffee Shop and Diner, and there wrote on a piece of paper the following: *"Come out all ye, forthwith! Take on the readiness of a scribe, and write down my message! The question is, do you know what this is about? Or do you seek the answer from within? What is your nature of determination? Seeing, spelling, or both? You are a ready soldier, man … bring us the gluten-free synapsis!"* At the same time, a couple of fat people at the table next to me began to say a lot of arrogant things about the menu. And to that, I presented something like magical thought to it, and suddenly in reaction to my thoughts, water started to gush out of valves on the street hundreds of feet upwards. I was aware that it was the Ark of the Covenant speaking to me for the first time!

That ended the second day and night on board the Citrus College campus.

The next morning, I arrived at the campus early. On the way there, I had been thinking about numbers and the presence of the water at the Coffee Shop and Diner, and what the numbers had to do with Angels that were within my actual family ... people like Jessica ... or copies of her. Then, when I got on campus, I felt drawn to pay a lot of attention to the cross on the hill.

To make it plain, I began to feel like I was being crucified. My hands raised up and shook, my head was lurched backwards, and I began to feel like I was dying. Then, deep in concentration, I thought about what Jesus had done in that same situation and came up with the idea that he used it to find the power to resurrect himself. And at that thought, suddenly, the errors stopped. I was free.

It was plain to me that there were also evil forces seeking to come aboard the campus and take up arms against the students. I pushed forth the mental power of preservation, with lessons from Seattle there.

I decided that school was not going to work in session. So, I began to walk down the street. I came to a graveyard and went inside. There I got notice of and sat down next to a gravesite with the same name as a doctor at the VA that I had seen, getting her input through the grave about what my treatment meant.

I also, later, got an input on how Paris had been born and existed in repeated episodes before she had killed my real mother and had abused me as a kid. I also found an urn with my grandfather on my dad's sides name on it, and from it, for purification, I drank some water from it and thought about how he had performed as a grandparent.

I stayed there until dark. Then I went walking down the street, through a neighborhood on a side street. On the way I ran into a couple of people and asked them about directions to a grocery store. They told me a direction to go down the street. I could tell there was a lot more to it than that. They could sense who I was.

I walked their direction, and down the street came to a house marked in the number 666, the number of the Beast of the Apocalypse. I realized that he was taking over possession of many of the people there, and that was where the threat to Citrus College was coming from.

I turned right and walked down the road. I came across a park with a large tree in it. I recognized the strong spiritual power of the tree in that it was alive like a person was alive and had the power of speech through the wind. I spoke to it and got an input on how the kids were facing drama from evils, how to fight the evils, and what methods of presentation could be used. I thanked him and went on.

Then I ran into a man named Dave. He told me a

lot of things about the houses and the religious people within. He asked me about the house numbered 666. We went to the train station to take it to downtown LA. There I told him about how the first Indian Jones movie had a scene at the end involving the Ark of the Covenant, which involved Angels and the killing of a lot of negative Nazi soldiers. I told him that I was beginning to think that I was going to have something to do with that.

While we were waiting, a cleaner train came by driven by the Archangel Michael, and it was surveying the grounds of the warzone for the presences and cleanup of the evil forces there. We got a lot of information that we couldn't process at the time from it, but it was there, waiting for us to use, as you shall see with the rest of this chapter. Keep in mind that everything miraculous that happens was in part a portion of the effort brought forwards by Michael.

Then we caught the train to LA.

There in downtown LA, I got the summary that the Ark was somehow present within my hand. And as I walked, I saw an angry, demon possessed cat making growling noises at me in a parking lot. I chased it off, then walked across the street to the place the cat was trying to keep me from. It was a Chinese garden of shops and tantric signs.

In the front, I read over a sign of Chinese handwriting. I got from it a message about what I was supposed to do about the Ark. Then I went into a building to speak to a Chinese man there about the Ark, trying to put it in his possession. I did and left.

As I walked, I came to a part of the road that was away from most buildings, except a fire station next to a field. In the grassy knoll I came across the headstone of a Jewish gravesite sign. On it was evidence of the fact that there were man souls present in the rocks of the cliff that was across the street. So, I put forth a mental spell there to release them for the presence of goodness to fight the evils in the town. I could tell from the message that I had gotten from the man from LA that I had met on the seaside in Seattle, that we had saved, that there was a deep presence of evils there, and we would need all the help we could get.

I went far down the street. It was getting night. I came to a building with what looked like a Mobius strip sidewalk around the front. I began to walk along it, getting the sensation that there were a lot of good and evil souls fighting within the city, how it was presented with signs, litter, and flyers, and how the good and evil ones were operating. A Mobius strip is an odd piece of cloth, that has two different sides on it that are joined together making one level on two sides of coin. That was what the presence of good there was supposed to be. sometimes seeming good, while doing things strange but unseen, or the opposite, strange and different, but seeming totally normal. That was how I was to present myself there.

That shall play a large part into how things went, as you will see.

As I walked, I got the sense that many of the buildings had signs of a religious nature on them.

Then as I walked, I came across a doll in the street, and realized that it came from a girl named Emily. Emily, I had the sense, was a relative of mine. I wondered if she and Jessica knew each other.

I realized that I needed a hotel room to stay in. I looked on the ground and found an ID card there and took it. I went then to the Reprograph Hotel, and got a room on the false ID.

There in the room I got to thinking a lot about the warfare to be fought. What was in error there in LA, what did the signs on the buildings outside the windows say, what did the presence of Hollywood and the TV say about it? And then I started to watch a movie on television. It was a deep movie about how a group of men had found within a tunnel the presence of alien life and intelligence, and they developed special powers as a result. At the end, they begin to fight, and the main one gets killed. Now, that was more than just a movie. It was a message from the Angels about how the mentality of religious propagations moves and interacts. It is not just alien, it is deeply religious, and operates in ways that the average person doesn't think is possible.

The next day was remarkably busy. I started out

getting something to drink from a cart in a square next to the street. Then I got the sense that there were demons in the area. Then I got drawn to a Fire Station, and on the walls saw evidence of the demonic activities, through the past and present, starting fires, and a noise alerted me to the outside. I had been transmitting that knowledge through ESP to other interested people in the area. I went outside.

There I saw some tape on the road. A film crew had blocked off part of the sidewalk and were performing anti-demon activities there, making it look like they were filming a movie.

That night I went back to the Reprograph Hotel. Next to it was a theatre with a movie in it about a girl named Emily. I went and watched it. Emily became possessed by demons and had a very difficult time with her parents but was freed at the end. It made me wonder if I was going to face the same challenges.

The next day I went walking around town. I saw two men at different times with carts of bells and ice cream on them. At the same time, during one of them, I came across a picture painted on the wall of a Mexican soldier who looked like a troll with huge aspects of colored blackness lines along his scalp in the shape of hairs, and it was a pictured symbol of the signs of demon worship and presence, and how to disable and rupture those demons. Then I kept going, and the next thing I saw was a murderer within a car doing something near a store door with a card in his hand, probably the address of the victim. Then I kept going, and the next thing I saw was a group of pipes behind a window on a wall, with levers and fonts and noise coming from them. They were signs of what it looked like when a person was demon possessed, with excessive noise coming from their mouths, leverage on their ears from the pressure, flexing of the necks, and oddity in the head spaces. The picture they put forth was horrible. It was a sign from the people who worked in the city about the evils they faced.

That night as I was walking, I came across an elderly woman named Jessica. Jessica told me about her place of work, that was a building that had a lot of errant characters in it, doing the wrong things. I could tell she was talking about the same building that I had been thinking about her being in, and the structure was such that it portrayed a lot of different things to different people in different ways. There was sin inside of that building, and the captain of the business was one that was playing a large part in the possession of the city, and Jessica was one of the main players to stop him.

The next day, I went downtown, and saw a picture from the movie I had watched on TV. It was a Bus that had turned wrong on the road and had hit three cars. I could tell there was an element of motions and science that occurred that was not seen there, but that had happened in a parallel dimension.

From there I went back to the hotel and decided to go out somewhere else the next day.

This next portion of the story is really intense.

The next day, I went to the far edge of the city. There was a street fair going on in the neighborhood, with tall, elegant signs and stores with products like clothing, fashionable toys, animals, parts of machinery, purses, trinkets, you name it. I went before an African shop and looked at the clothes there. Then I went to another story, and was looking at the trinkets there, and a young girl, who looked just like the picture I had seen of Emily, pointed out to me a trinket of a Unicorn with a horn on it. I bought it.

What I didn't know at the time was that it had a special power to it, and it helped me win the war against the evils in that city. That will become present at the end of this chapter.

From there, I began to walk to the side of town, through an area that looked like everything there had been destroyed. There was no traffic on the road, the shops looked like they were closed, some destroyed, and there was nothing to view inside of the windows to the stores.

As I walked, a tall, elderly woman came up to me. She said her name was Laura. We talked for a long time as we walked through the battered neighborhood of broken shops. She told me about her adventures at a young age, and it became plain that she was an adventurer. She was also feeding the cats there. And she was homeless.

At the end of the street, we came to the first business in session in the area. It was a grocery store called Coopers. I had never heard of anything like that before. We went in and Laura bought some cat food, and me a drink.

We then kept walking. It got dark, and she was feeding the cats of the neighborhood. The cats were living under people's cars and other parts of their parking lots and yards. As we talked, it became plain that one of the people she talked to was a knowledgeable woman who knew a lot about mentalities, and it was clear that she had ESP. She put in my mind the solution to my problem with realizations of a religious mindset, and suggested I get brain surgery. So, I agreed, and felt her open my mind with her mind and place in there a set of ideas that paid stringent heed to what was necessary. What it meant will become prevalent in the next couple sections here.

Laura and I went over to where there were a lot of black men next to a fence, and she talked to them. They were really solid and friendly. They hadn't always been like that, I could tell, they had used to have problems with the evils, but they said that it had changed deeply when they became aware that there were people that were going to be coming through there and killing the cats.

Next to them were a group of people all dancing on the sidewalk. We went over there, and they gave us some cake to eat. Then we went walking to another part down the street.

We stopped in front of a store for a break and to eat the cake. While we were there, I noticed a woman standing a whole block away on the sidewalk, dressed all in a black robe with dark hair and likely dark eyes. She was looking at me and Laura intensely. I read her mind, and very briefly got the summary of who she was. She was the Angel of Death. And she was very interested in what we were going to do. And I got the sensation, very briefly, that she was on our side for God's Holy War. Very briefly, and she sensed it. At that, she turned abruptly and walked away around the corner.

We got up and walked again. This time, I noticed on the ground what looked like stars. And as I looked, she got the attention of another man who was walking, and he gave her shoes. I came under the summary that I was then, at that time, seeing the element of numbers and space in the stars on the ground, and it was a partaker of the knowledge of the Ark of the Covenant. It had been sent there as a message and protection by the Chinese worker who I had given the Ark to earlier.

Thus, it was all coming together. That number game plays a huge part, as you shall see in the next section.

From there, Laura and I went down the street, looking for a place to sleep. We started to sit down on the sidewalk next to a man guarding the parking lot of a hotel, but he started to speak Japanese to us, telling us we couldn't sleep there. At the same time, a man came walking by us, and apologized if he got lost. I could tell from that that we were on the edge of time and space in a manner that had never been explored by anyone on this planet, and he was about to depart what was known and go explore something new. I put him on a level of mental protection, and he disappeared. He showed up about five minutes later. By then, I had, at random, spoken in Japanese-sounding lingo about how we were protectors, and he needed to help us. He told us to go across the street. So, we did.

Across the street, Laura put out a blanket and went to sleep on the sidewalk. I turned on the music on my phone and spent all night long not sleeping and listening to Metric play songs. The songs were about the religious effects of the numbers I had seen on the stars on the street.

The next day, as we walked, Laura brought to my attention how a homeless woman living there on the street had stolen from her and asked me to go get it back. I went to her camp site, and she got irate and struck me hard in the face with a stick. I left, doing nothing.

We ended our meeting that day, Laura went on her way elsewhere. We said we were to keep in touch.

This next section talks about the very serious ramifications of the war against evils, and how we pervaded what was expected to do something very articulate.

I went downtown LA the next day. In my English class, I had read a story about the Lejolion Hotel, and went there. Inside there was articulate water fountains and elevators of a high status there. I looked at the water, flowing through ponds, and it became plan that they were operating on a frequency similar to what the solid actions of multiple people were, all moving and buying and eating things, and the movement of the water was an articulation of what occurred within the lives of the average person.

I had no money, so I left.

Outside, there were a bunch of teenage and older kid bicyclers and skateboarders. I read their minds with ESP and realized that they were thinking about the founders of thought and existence in a way that allowed them to create puzzles from their new knowledge.

I got a sense of urgent understanding from that. It grew in thoughts to a new level of comprehension, one that was growing steadily as seconds passed. We were right next to a museum, with steps on the outside in the front of it. I immediately went over there and noticed that on every step were written code words from books and poems, many of a religious nature. I took up the pen that I had in my waistband and used it on the only blank step there was, and carved in it a series of rhythmic and numerical drawings and letters that equated exactly to the odd and seemingly foreign, to most unseen people, ideas regarding the scientific new message of equality and perseverance and creation that I had gotten from the skateboarders.

And that was not all. As soon as I finished writing, I immediately had the idea of the deeper meaning of what the writings meant, and at the same exact time, a staff member moved at the top of the stairs and started to yell counselling at me. "Do you know what that means, what I wrote there?" I yelled it aggressively. "It is the solution to all your problems! It is the key to the 10 Commandments! How do you like those apples, YOU FUCK?" And with that, I walked off, with the highest mental articulation of the deeper thoughts I was having.

In my mind, I immediately began to flow fast a wide variety of numbers and letters, on a level of the highest code, unified by theories of Quantum Physics and time travel, architecture and mechanical engineering. The thoughts were so fast that it was nearly impossible to keep up with them. Then, suddenly, I felt finished, and at the same time, I began to see a full-on image before me.

It was of the inside of a huge Mosque, with a giant tower filled with writings of religious nature that was unseen and unwritable except by a person with the most stringent character and reserves. And I saw who it was. It was a presentation of the world class constructed bug that I had seen inside of Seattle, when I was learning about parallel universes and the means behind them. It was a cockroach that was colored brightly and that was in control of all the writings on the walls! And not only that, but it was a highly religious creature, with a solid input from God himself, and would itemize those who sought information from the tower, and if they were right, if they were holy, and if they were respectable ... not necessarily intelligent, but able to transmit their needs and wants through thoughts to the bug, then they would get information on some of the creates secrets of Creation and science and existence that have ever occurred.

And the cockroach was aware that it was my creation and reserved a small portion for my availability. That comes in later, near the end of this chapter, when one is told the ways and means that I won the War in LA against the evils there.

From that deep revelation, I began to walk. As I walked, I began to get ideas from the parable of Creation that I had made that I didn't necessarily agree with. One of them was a level of the evils within the city of LA. Another was the abuse and near-death experiences I had endured through my whole life, which I got the symbol of the fact that they were confounds of evil. I walked a long time, departing Los Angeles and refusing to fight the evils there anymore. I had too many problems overall, and it was atrocious. I couldn't get out of my mind that my grandparents on my dad's side had told me at about the age of 5 that Paris had killed my real mother when I was born. I knew that she had talked my father into committing suicide. And then there came into my head a fresh idea ... one I hadn't had yet. What was it?

First, let me tell you that it was a very long ways away, near Culver City, to the west, near the ocean, away from LA. The idea came to me in a flash. I was not a child of an American mother. I was created by an Angel named Chrystal. And I had a real mother, here, on earth. Her name was Morgan. And then I saw immediately upon the idea what you wouldn't believe.

It was my real mother, Morgan, walking the way I was walking, in front of me, and she was getting approached by two kids of hers, one a boy, and the other a girl. They loved their mother and were treated very well by her, giving and getting hugs. Then the idea hit me hard ... the boy was a plural universe copy of me that had arrived in my universe under different conditions as a result of the great Mosque tower I had put at the museum.

And the girl was Jessica, my copy's sister.

I was more amazed than I have ever been in my life. But the kid was pleased, and a safe copy of myself, so I left the communication alone, and kept on walking, thinking hard about a solution.

Now, you may be wondering if this is accurate. Is Jessica, Morgan, Emily, and Chrystal my real family, one kept away from me by a murderous woman who kept me from them? Did they exist? I asked that of the Qur'an, at a random page, in December 2016 as I was writing this. The Qur'an said: "Thus, there is such a thing as Angels. There is such a thing as Priests, witches, immortals, the Beast of the Apocalypse, and even, as put forth in the Qur'an, *Surah 76, 6 – 16*, even my visions of my real family are accurate. I have the names of Jessica, Emily, Morgan, and Chrystal listed as relatives of a religious foundation.

Part 15 - 16 states: "And amongst them will be passed round vessels of silver and goblets of crystal – crystal clear, made of silver: they will determine the measure thereof (according to their wishes)." Thus, the Qur'an is verifying my rendition of being related to an Angel named Chrystal, and thus, my memory of the other relatives is accurate!"

Then I encountered Jessica, in actuality, again. But first, there was the input of the negativities of the evil ones left. Let me describe that first, in the next section.

From seeing Morgan and little Mitchell and little Jessica, I kept walking, thinking of them. Then I saw on the side of the road a limousine with a man getting out of it. Up until then I had been yelling aloud at the power lines about the evils I had encountered and the strangeness I had encountered with the Ark of the Covenant in my hands, the colors and stars I had encountered with Laura on the ground, and the full-on parable of scientific and religious oneness I had created and encountered within the museum downtown. The man out of the limo was trying to ascertain exactly what it was that was making the electricity shoot out of the powerlines with noise and shaking. That person was, unknown to him, was me.

What I didn't understand at the time, was that my syllables and sayings upon the power cords was being ascertained to other priests and Angels fighting the evils of the city. It played a large part, as I shall put near the end of this chapter.

The man outside of the limo was evil, I could tell, but was lost as to why he was failing.

I kept on walking, into the area of Culver City. It was a downtown area with a fountain and a statue of a lion. A man approached me there, and gave me his camera, asking for a picture. I could tell that he wanted a picture of himself next to the lion statue to pervade his ascension into control there. He was a sinner and in error. I took the picture, and instead of focusing on him, focused on the lion. It had serious spiritual power that nobody but the kids that played on the fountain beneath it could ascertain. But it was there, and the lion was sending me signals of success. I didn't know why at the time.

I found out soon, as you shall see.

I got called along the road to walk down a side road to the side of a lake there. What were the chances of getting called to such a remote place, that was out-of-sight? There was none. I was brought there by Angels wanting me to understand the next level of evolution. I sat on a dock and began to think about what was being said to me.

And then I saw it. The people at the far end of the beach were very much facing the proclivities of religious presences and had to make decisions that they were confused about. Something had happened to severely change the essences of their lives.

Then I looked up at the hotel across the street and got from it the message that it had been visited by aliens. Aliens from a different planet, from outer space. Did they exist? My senses told me in plain terms that the science fiction books and Hollywood movies that were about aliens and the idea of aliens was based on actuality.

So, I went to the hotel and sat down in the room on the bottom, next to a break room with fancy seats and a bar. There were two waitresses working at the bar. And one of their names, as I heard the other waitress call her, was Jessica.

Now, I witnessed the other waitress steal money from Jessica, and say a lot of negative things to her. It dawned on me that Jessica was facing the actuality of knowledge of the possible presence of aliens there.

Then I left. I got called strenuously to go down the street from the direction that I had come from, Culver City, and on the way came to a Bar by the road with a woman sitting in front, smoking a cigarette. I got called to her. I felt like I knew her.

"Can I have a cigarette? You would not believe this, but I just found aliens. And I just found out why the electric cables are buzzing so loud." I was profound. "Who are you?"

"Here you go." She gave me a cigarette. "My name is Jessica."

She told me that she worked in the bar, that she knew about aliens, that there was errancies in the cars going down the street, and then, get this, she said items that described in unequal terms that she was from the future, that she was being treated unjustly by the staff of the Bar, and then she called her friend Dave and talked to him about the "magical events" behind the negative things she was encountering. And then it dawned on me that she may have known about the special creation I had made at the museum downtown, and then part of her argument to Dave was that a lot of the negative things were going to cease.

Then she mentioned walking home. I got the drift that she wanted me to go and talk to her, but as we walked across the street, I turned my hand in the other direction and walked that way, to something different.

I came across that different thing the next day. But the rest of that day, because it was early, like 1:00 in the morning, was a day of victory against the evils. Let me describe in the next section how it went.

Keep in mind, I was homeless at that time. If you ever see a homeless person doing things like this, you can either think they are mentally ill, or that they are on a religious mission for God. I was the latter. Here is what happened.

I kept walking, a very long way, and finally made it to Venice Beach, next to the ocean. There I got very tired – I hadn't slept for months at a time, for religiously found reasons, if you can believe that. I want on the beach that night and found board and lay on it next to the water.

In my pocket was drawn to my attention a necklace of beads. It had one round circular bead that was thin, one medium sized, and one long one. It got drawn to my attention that the small one was a bead of Jehovah, the medium bead was a Christian one for God, and the long bead was Muslim one for Allah. Most people would not notice or agree with that, that all three of those words of the Holy One are all different names to the same being. The different religions are written slightly different to be itemized to the different mindsets of a lot of Holy, but different, people. The necklace was sent to me by Emily, as a rendition of what was actually occurring, so that I could understand all three of those elements of meaning. Why?

As shall be explained in the next chapter, I have been told by God's Angels that after I die, I am to go aboard the Ark of the Covenant, and operate on mystical powers on Judgement Day, judging people by ESP to either Heaven or Hell. And to do that appropriately, I must understand the rules and graciousness or lividity of the Holiest being, all versions of him, so that I can do justice at the end of times.

I watched the horizon, the sky, and the clouds, On one side, there was a theme park on a pier. On the other side, I could see airplanes flying in mystical reverences along the sky. Their pattern, I could tell, were of the

makings and movements of Angels before Judgement
Day. And then I saw a woman walking in the water, ankle
deep, and looking for fish, or urchins, or stars. Stars! She
was an Angel showing me how the Heavens of Creation
operated, by action, not words! And the spinning wheel
of the theme park put forth a rising and lowering of color
that reflected the higher and lower elements of everyday
life, the causes and effects of it, as we were designed to
have on a daily basis.

What I saw there was so elegant that it moves on a
level of extremely high understanding of what occurred at
the beginning of time here, on earth.

I got up and walked over by the path along the beach.
There I ran into a small group of people who were highly
religious. They appreciated what I had seen. One of them
was named Peter Parker, the hero from my favorite comic,
Spiderman. He gave me a whole draft loaf of bread and
told me that the next day I could go to a homeless stand
there on the beach and get some free food. I thanked him.

Then I walked past the theme park pier. On the other
side, I saw a washing hovel with a hose and a shower
outside, and next to it were some lost kid's clothes. I
could tell that they had been delivered by Emily for use
in the mission against the evils. So, I took them. Then, as
I walked to the north, the beach got overrun by the road,
and I looked and saw, you would not believe this, but it
was a group of foxes walking on the road going down a
side road to the east.

They were the preserved elements of humankind evolved into animals. As you will see in the San Diego chapter, it later became apparent that there is such a thing as immortals. Immortal people who do not die. And some of them, with their lengthy evolution, learn how to become like animals. And that is where the foxes came from. They knew in depth about where I was going, and why. Why is going to follow, soon, in this section.

I walked up the street and had premonitions of many things that had happened. I was being drawn there for reasons I did not know, at that time. I walked past a school that was in session at that time – it was morning – and I wanted to see and visit to see if Emily was there. But I then came across a trail moving through a hill of rocks and bushes and stones. So, I walked up it a longways.

Up at the top, I came across two very large rocks that looked like the types used by people to climb on. I went over there to them, off the trail, and then noticed, wholesale, that they were speaking to me.

"You have won," they said. "You have won."

Getting the summary of events, mentally, I took the little unicorn statue given to me at the street fair by Emily and knit it to the taller of the rocks. Then I walked over to the other rock and saw in it a tunnel going from the inland side to the southern, LA downtown facing side. I put the clothes I had along the bottom and went laying down inside of it, looking at LA.

The city itself was clear and bright, in ways that I

have never seen it clean before. It became plain to me then that the thoughts of the Mosque and tower by the museum was present to many of the good people of the city, to many priests and imams and Angels and others seeking justice, gave them many of the ideas of how to defeat the evils of the city, and they had put it into action and had done so with victory. So had the Chinese, with their copy of the Ark of the Covenant, they had learned a lot of details on how to tell me, through experience, how it operated. And they put it into power, with doing what I was to do when I die and clearing the sins and evils of the city with it.

I didn't know this, but Hollywood also experienced that positive outlook. That is why the movies that have come out since then have been so good.

Eventually, I got up and walked to the top of the hill. There I found a neighborhood of extremely professional and precisely manufactured homes with great decorations and plentiful plants and trees in the yards and expertly made walls, windows, and doors. I could tell it was a very high-class portion of Hollywood or Beverly Hills.

I started to walk down the street there. At the bottom of the hill, I came to a restaurant, and went inside because my feet hurt, and I wanted to sit down. Then while I was there someone called the police on me. They showed up in a police car and put me in the back.

The driver saw that I was homeless and drove me back into Culver City to a homeless shelter, that had no entries in it. So, he gave me twenty dollars, which was extremely nice of him, the best I have been treated by police ever, and told me to get something to eat and go ahead and sleep on the street.

I walked to a fast food restaurant and ordered some food there. Then, when I was eating, a man came in and said we had to go. I didn't know him, but I could tell, he somehow knew me.

His name was Jakutis. He was friend with a female named Gabrielle. Now, the name Gabriel is the name of one of the Archangels of Heaven, on the same level as the Archangel Michael or Ariel. And I was certain that, because of the victory against evils I had taken part in, that she was there to help me find the next mission. Me meeting the Archangel Gabrielle after a victory in LA was like me meeting Angel after the victory in Seattle.

We went to a hotel room next door.

In it, Jakutis turned on the television and told me that he had lived in Marysville, which had witches and warlocks in it. Gabrielle went to sleep then. Jakutis and I stayed awake and had a long talk that night. We talked about how there were 12 different witches and warlocks in Marysville – 12, which is *my* perceived number at Creation – and how they engaged in a lot of evils there. At the same time, the program on TV had a telecaster talking to an actor named Michael about the sins of the nation. To that I mentioned that I knew Jesus up-front, in this time, and Jakutis said it was good and amazing. As I said it, it became plain that Jesus was talking to Gabrielle in her sleep, because she made a face as I said it.

I walked over and gave Gabrielle a kiss, and Jakutis tried to shove me through the window. Then I talked to him and he understood. We went outside at around 3:00 AM in the night for a walk.

On the walk we talked about many highly religious things. I shall not explain all them here. They are inside the book *Cheetah on the Wing 3*.

The next section is about what happened to bring about the next chapter. You would expect me to face victory after my victorious presence during the Wars against evils within Seattle and LA. But what happened next is actually atrocious. The next chapter shall describe the basics of it.

To get there, though, let me describe what my thoughts were. I was thinking that although I had won a portion of the war, many errant things had happened to me in the past. For example, I thought about how my grandparents on my dad's side, when I was around 5 or 7 years old, told me about how Paris had killed my real mother and taken over me, and would kill me if I said anything bad about her. That was why I went my whole childhood, my teenage years, and part of my adulthood not saying anything about her serious abuses to me. I tried to forget them. And it turned into PTSD. Severe PTSD.

Then I got to thinking about how she had attempted to kill my father, and how she had talked him, I knew this for a fact, into committing suicide when I was in prison. And then a month later she tried to talk me into committing suicide, and I tried twice to hang myself. And I remembered how she had tried to make me fail high school, when I am a genius, by forcing me by abuse to 5 different high schools in 3 years. Then there were the injustices she did during my prison sentence. And then, afterwards, she abused me some more, told me the lie that Krishna was a terrorist – which she is not – and that she had "gotten word of that" from the Attorney General's office. Her abuse gets far worse, which I shall tell you about in the last few chapters of this book.

As a summary of that, I came under the impression that she was a victim of being possessed by a demon or the Devil or Satan himself, and given my justice inside of Seattle and LA, I decided to go up to Yreka and save her.

A discreet mistake. But I tried. It was the right thing to do. The next chapter shall talk about how she lied to the justice system there, assaulted me, and had me sent to prison over lies when I had done nothing but try to defend myself. She tried to put me in jail, when I was innocent, with her lies, for 7 years. This next chapter is that story.

CHAPTER 10

FALSE IMPRISONMENT IN 2012

I flew into Yreka, northern California, to be close enough to save Paris from possession by evils. I had help. One of the women at the airport in LA had, I could detect, because it was mentally told to me, ESP. She read my mind, and recognized that I was on a new mission, and said she would transmit ideas of correction to me from the place she was going to be in. Thus, we had mental imaging system in place when it was time to get on the airplane.

When I was picked up by Paris, she immediately began to talk in an abusively negative tone to me. I could tell by identifying it to be exactly the same way she had talked to me when she was abusing me as a child and a teenager and an adult. I reacted to it by thinking about what nature the city of Yreka was in, what it was like to be possessed by witches and warlocks, or the devil, and how the people interacted to that.

I got in the thoughts that there were some people who had different approaches to things, that were positive, but not understood by Paris. I got the idea to present, through mental power and communication, different ways of putting different paths and methods to people who sought good, while confusing the evil ones, with messages that were strange but highly religious.

We went to a grocery store. On the way I identified a homeless person that we stopped next to, and I told him about, in strange terms, the secrets I had put in the code. Paris did not understand, but he did. He thanked me.

I was immediately having an effect on Paris, who said lost remarks on how she was getting some of the ideas I was placing in her head about how to be saved, and then the conflict of it being against what was already in her head; and what was already in her head was the curse of Satan.

Then we went from there to Paris's apartment, a very small place of two floors with no furniture in it hardly at all except for one folding chair. She had a television with a video player that she watched movies on. She would not give me a tour of the house. My room was upstairs, and empty. There were blankets in there on the floor, and no bed. I left and went to the nearest restaurant to eat.

And things progressed, downwards.

The restaurant was called The Bear. As I sat down, I had thoughts brought on by the book I had gotten from Michael online that was called *The Prognosis of Beginning*, and those thoughts were, "could a person could bring forth elements of Mythology?"

I opened the book and saw that the waitress, Susan, was remarkable. Turning to a random page, I came up with a couple sentences that said that the concept of myths and Legends existing was real. I was brought to the awareness that there was such a thing as parallel universes next to ours, that have different sets of rules and creatures, and one of those rules was the existence of fabled creatures like unicorns and trolls.

The book was highly scientific. The introduction was about how aliens had invaded a planet and destroyed everything on it, the buildings and the people. Then the chapters continued, and once was about how a man found a broken alien spacecraft, went inside, and found incapacitated aliens that were evil that had been part of the invading force against his old planet. As I read it, I thought about what Jessica had said in LA about time travel, about aliens, about the behavior of people and aliens in transitions of different times, and what those legends meant.

I got the sense that some of the staff of the Bear were creatures of mythology. To that I noticed that one of the cooks, Aubrey, was over 6 foot 4 inches tall, was not a human. He was a troll of very high character.

I had some pie, ordering it from Susan with the words to get her ideas about the mythology concept. Then it came and I had it. I wanted to find a way to bring myself closer to my real family. That plays in a large part in the rest of this chapter and the next chapter.

It was getting dark, so I went back to Paris's house.

At Paris's house, she introduced me to the video player and her movies. They were all mythology or survival movies. Then she went to sleep.

I went up to my room and saw there was no furniture there. I had clothes in the closet, though. They had come from the damaged Jeep that Paris had gotten. Let me describe where it came from, for a moment.

On the way up past Paris's house in Yreka, at the beginning of the war of God, before I got to Medford, I was drawn by the full-on physical presence of God and the religious seizures I had in the Jeep as I was driving. The thought of my real existence occurring before Genesis by an Angel named Chrystal became plain to me, and the concept that at the beginning of earth-time she existed at the Oregon place called Crater Lake became a theory. So, I was going there, but on the way, I was having the mental projection of a negative soul inside of the prison concept years before and I got in a wreck. It damaged the front of the Jeep a lot. I ran away into the woods, which had snow on the ground, and almost died there a few days later of hypothermia.

The journey was highly religious, and in it I found out that I was, for one, Jewish, and for another, an element of God himself, who had steered the wrong way.

I was rescued by a Marine sheriff, who sent me to the hospital in Portland, Oregon. There I was cured, and released to Paris, who took me to Yreka, to my sister's house and there I saw evidence that the both of them were agents of Satan.

Paris got my broken Jeep and brought it to me at the house. I took it to my home town in Oregon, Klamath Falls, and got sent there from the VA hospital to Medford. And that is where this story starts.

Now, that night at Paris's house, I went and read some of the book I had and noticed in it that it mentioned unicorns again. That got me to wondering if it was true.

The next day I found out.

I came across, in the back yard, two different neighbors. One was an artist named Leverse, the other named Taylor. They began talking about movies about aliens on earth, and the other about zombies, and as they talked, I got the heavy perception of the picture of a real unicorn moving through the sky atop the image of a comet flying by the clouds.

And the unicorn projected to my mind that night how to correct the problems of the witches and warlocks of the area.

To that things took a heavy turn roundabout the next morning. Mythical and mysterious. Let me describe how.

The next morning it became plain that Paris was trying to do me harm. It was because of the call to her by the demonic possessing agents of Hell that she was swaying to.

I went outside and began to walk. I came in a far neighborhood across a man on the street and had an interesting conversation with him. Then I went down the street to the town's cemetery.

At the cemetery I found a gravesite with the same name on it as that of my father, who had been talked into suicide by Paris. I picked up the cross on it for the purpose of finding a way to save his soul. Then I walked back towards the Bear.

The next place I came to was a car dealer, who told her client, in a way that I could hear, how to move the religious solution of the cross to positive means.

Then I walked over to a fenced yard of tractors and rocks before Carl's Junior. In it I got drawn to a couple of small rocks that I could tall had the same methods or special existence as the rocks I had found inside of Medford. I picked them up and took them with me.

Then I went to Carl's Junior. There, I found a woman that was a copy of Morgan, my real mother, in the age of her 30's. I went over to her and asked her if she wanted to see the rocks I had. She said "okay," and I told her the correct location ... that they were from France. Now, that will play in big time in the further part of this chapter ... France. She agreed to take them.

At the same time, I saw a man there that I had seen inside of Medford named Carl. He was a special man who knew about the higher ruminations of religious disorder and the spacing between Angels and the presence of solutions to problems on a realistic nature. That is what he had been doing when I encountered him in Medford. There, though, he was present for my mission, but did not want to talk about it, so I left him alone.

I then listened on my phone to a song by the band Tool, that said a lot about what was going on.

From there I went over to the Bear restaurant, across the street. I wanted to move farther along understanding what had been told to me by Jessica.

At the Bear, I began to write a story about the dead in the Hereafter. Incidentally, it was the precursor to the 5th *Cheetah on the Wing* books. (It was later called *Movement to the Hereafter* ... this book!)

While I was there, Paris came in and tried to sit next to me. I told her to leave. She did, saying a bunch of negative comments. Then I immediately departed, and walked to the park down the street, feeling threatened.

On the way I thought about numbers and got the summary of how to reduce my visible size by changing my numbers to a very small one. Then, when I arrived at the park, I was walking by the water, and I saw a woman that looked like Paris by a small child girl that I recognized but couldn't place where. Then, as I walked, it occurred to me, the girl was a unicorn in a human body.

I walked over to a part of the park that was a field near trees and lay down. Under one of the trees I could see the outline of an actual unicorn hiding in the bushes. It was real, and amazing. My theory of mythology in the 9th dimension, in parallel universes, was correct!

Then the copy of Paris showed up with the girl near a car, and Paris said a lot of negative things to her that I could tell she was trying to escape from.

From there I began to walk a longways away from town. At a bar at the edge of town, I got the impression from what people were saying that they anticipated me helping them get leniency on their religious effects. I kept on walking, beginning to walk down the freeway.

A cop car stopped by the freeway and told me to get off it. So, I walked down the side road, to a very large field next to an artistic house. It was night time.

The house had on the front of it a sign that had pictures of birds on it. I could tell from that that they were likely relatives of mine on a religious basis. So, I lay down and looked at the stars to get their word. This is what I saw. In the sky above, the path of the stars made the words "JAEL-COPE". That meant that I was to find a way to cope with Jael. Now, I could tell that the name Jael was the name of one of the Angels on board the Ark of the Covenant, and I was to find a way to work with him. The message on that will become apparent later in this chapter.

There was also a flexing curve in the stars, going up and down the horizon in a greater and lesser than function of showing the different paths of fortune I could take in the War of God against evils. I listened to them and made a choice. The next chapter shall articulate exactly what that choice will amount to, I think.

The next morning, I went to a restaurant and inside saw a kid that looked and spoke exactly as one of my friends in grade school had. I spoke to him. Then, I got up and asked the waitress to tell me about things related to time travel, because I didn't know if it was happening to me. She didn't know.

That night I went to a different park near town. There was a restroom there, with a locking door on it. I went up to it, and thinking of the code, put in the code ALPH, and it worked. I went inside and lay down on the floor. Looking at the ceiling, I got in mind pictures of mystical properties of special, hidden planets, of Godly souls finding presence among ships to take them there, and I realized that there was the differences of different dimensions present in those ideas, and they were to actual places that had not been seen of discussed yet.

After hours there, I got up and walked down the street next to a car cleaning area. Under the roof of one of the towers was a van. It was closed. I got the mental image, from dreams within, that Jessica was inside of it. I waved a message that she could see next to the window and I left.

I walked back to Paris's house and lay on the front floor. It was about 4:00 in the morning. I had deep visions of the presences of unicorns in the universe. Then Paris came downstairs and started to yell at me. She tried to give me some money. Now, before I had departed on the mission for God, in Temecula I had been across a poor person with special abilities who told me that someone stingy had tried to give him money, and he said if someone tried to do that for the wrong reason, to kill them. And Paris had done it for the wrong reason.

So, I got up and walked to the front door, getting ready to leave without the money. Then I felt a painful strike on the back of my head. I turned immediately, on instinct, and pushed her against the wall and told her to stop, I was leaving. Then I saw on the ground next to me a frying pan. She had assaulted me by hitting me in the back of the head with it.

I left, walking towards the Bear. On the way, a police car pulled up next to me, and the officer came over to arrest me for assault. I tried to tell him to take a picture of the back of my bleeding head ... which was bleeding out of the strict area that she hit me ... and that despicable officer refused to do it. He arrested me for a crime that was nothing more than self-defense that hurt nobody.

The jail effect was atrocious. I have written about it in detail in *Cheetah on the Wing 4*. I shall only describe the summary of my deep visions I had there here.

In jail, I got an attorney named Lael Kayfetz. That is her actual name, it is on the jail records. She is an outstanding attorney. While I was inside the jail, she came to visit and told me that Paris had been trying to talk the prosecutor into putting me in prison for 7 years. 7 years ... for self-defense! She did not agree and fought hard to bring me justice.

During the first hearing, the Judge Langford was asking the arresting police officer questions about what the arrest was about, and that officer was lying. He refused to even say anything about my request that he take pictures of the head injury I had from Paris's assault. So, I started to yell about his lies to the judge. The judge had me kicked out of the courtroom.

Now, the jail staff were told by Paris that I was mentally ill, so they kept me in a cell downstairs by the main desk by myself.

Many things religious and evil happened there. I shall not go into them all. But I had dreams and visions of what was happening and what was to occur.

One of the visions was of Morgan Freeman, who is an

actor of the *Through the Wormhole* series. He was present in helping me find a way to a foreign planet in the future. It actually existed.

And upon it were dragons. Now, the summary of dragons actually exist as per legend and the effects of parallel universes in known and accepted science today. They are members of the 9th dimension of mythology.

I had visions of the fact that I was an Angel before the beginning of Genesis in the Bible. During that time we came under the presence of evil forces moving through the universe, destroying us, and we drew conclusions about it that made it actual, and the name we gave to it was Cobra, the enemy of the hero GI Joe. And there was a time-space bi-locality as well. What was on TV about GI Joe occurred in the 1950's. Thus, the scientific idea of the concept that time can move backwards, or that people can time travel to both the future and the past is actual.

Then, as the battle was rapidly moving forwards, it stopped. I woke up looking at the Eiffel Tower in France. That was where I had gotten the idea to tell Moran about France. It was the beginning of the creation of people on earth and their presence against the evils of the universe.

Then I got drawn to a place next to a stream, looking at a mirror. In it was an image of myself, and I was young, about 5 years old. Then I noticed the image of the copy moving differently than I was, and something negative caught my attention. I turned, and behind me was an enemy soldier holding a gun against my head, pulling the trigger and shooting me.

And then I woke up as a person, having been born.

I have a scar and a lump on the back of my head that, until then, I didn't know how I got it. I know now. I was shot there by Cobra when I was still an Angel.

There were other parts of the vision. Part of it was moving with Jessica through space and time through the stars to one of those foreign and special planets. There were two of them in our galaxy.

I woke up then. I was taken back to court and the judge sent me then to Napa Mental Health Clinic, across the mountain and next to the ocean.

Now I shall tell you, very briefly, about what Napa was like.

That Napa Mental Health Clinic is a much better place than jail. We, as patients, were seen by doctors, were taught art and music and had access to the library there with books. The place where we lived was in a group of rooms locked by doors, true, but it was large, with hallways between rooms that we could walk in, phones we could use, televisions we could watch, and radios we were played from time to time.

During one of my meetings with the doctors there, I told them that I had PTSD and needed treatment. They gave me none. But I think they told that to Judge

Langford, and he used that knowledge during my sentencing hearing.

There were a lot of religious things going on there. Many of the patients had a religious mindset and talked about those sorts of things a lot. They did not belong in prison. Most of them were disabled and treated unfairly.

I was there for about six months. I found that some of the staff were demons, some of the Devil, and some others were Angels.

I shall not put what else it was like here, besides the fact that I was able to talk to Krishna on the phone a lot there, and she was extremely helpful.

Then I was sent back to Yreka jail for sentencing.

Krishna was present in the courtroom for my final sentencing hearing, 9 months after I was arrested, unjustly. The judge was Judge Langford. He had gotten word about the PTSD from the staff of the Napa Mental Health Clinic, I am sure, because he said that, for one, I should never have been sent to jail in the first place. Not in 2012, and not in 2005. Instead, he said I should have been sent to a hospital. He was right, and just. So, he put me on probation for three years, and a no-contact order between me and Paris for three years ... to protect me from Paris, not the other way around.

She violated that severely at the end of 2013, as you shall see in the chapter after next.

Because I had PTSD, and because I had been abused so badly as a child and a teenager by Paris, I had it in mind that the judge would do the same thing she did, which was use my words against me. I had been told by my grandparents when I was 5 or 7 that she had killed my real mother, and if I spoke badly about her, then she would kill me to. That lasted a long time, because I did not say anything bad about her literally for 40 years. Not until now. Now I know better. But then, in 2012, I plead guilty so the Judge would not say anything bad about me, and I did it when I was innocent.

Now let me tell you about the leader to the chapter after the next one. This is ESP and time travel in action.

After the sentencing hearing, Krishna took me to a hotel in Yreka to stay for a night. There, in the room, I had my computer. For a reason that I didn't understand at the time, but I do understand now, I asked the question: "what is going to happen to me when I die?"

Let me tell you where that idea came from. It was not a memory of when I had almost died in the past. It was a precursor to what was going to happen, given to me by the Angels of God, like the Archangel Gabriel, in preparation for memory of what was going to occur, before it happened. Science predicts that that is how time actually operates, for those who do not believe it. What was the answer?

The answer was that I was going to be sent to God's

Garden, in the Hereafter, and I was going to be visited by three Angels. Two with visions of the future, and one the Angel of Death. The two future Angels told me about how my duty upon death was to go aboard the Ark of the Covenant, embody mystical power, and enjoin my ESP to judging people based on their sins or holiness to be sent, on Judgement Day, to either Hell or Heaven. And then afterwards, I was to fight Satan on my own, and upon glory, create my own universe for the people with me.

A very tall order. I forgot about it at that time, for literally nearly two years. The following two chapters will explain why.

From there we went back to Krishna's house in Temecula. There I had a lot of religious visions. And it led to me going to fight God's war in my military home town of San Diego, which led to Phoenix, Arizona.

And that led into being a victim of attempted vehicular homicide. And that is what this book is mostly about.

Read on.

CHAPTER 11

WARFARE FOR GOD AGAINST EVILS 3

Now, upon the end of my unjust and unreasonable sentence for a crime I did not commit, for the second time, I went back to Temecula with Krishna and began a full-on mentally religious diatribe against the evils there. It was very profound and played a large part into my travelling on God's Crusade against evils within San Diego. I live in Temecula and have lived here for 7 years now. I am going to leave that part of this book blank. If you want details, feel free to read *Cheetah on the Wing 4*. It also contains details about the rest of this chapter, at its end.

So, let me talk about the religious mission within San Diego. This will startle and bedazzle you.

I started out in Temecula. There I went to a pizza store and called on my cell phone for a taxi.

The man driving the taxi was a gentleman named Muhammed. As I spoke to him, it became clear that he was a child of Allah, the Muslim element of the one God. He started talking to me about immortals, about death, and about the very high religious capabilities of people who seemed, on the surface and only the surface, down and out homeless. Now, I had gotten the input on the possibility of immortal in the area from the mental projections in Temecula at a Breakfast Diner by a disabled veteran, and at a doughnut shop by other veterans of the military.

Then he started to talk about 911. I got from him ideas that were accurate about it that I didn't know about before then.

I asked him to stop by my ex-wife's old house at that, so I could drop a document about my religious mission within San Diego. I dropped it off at the door of a stranger's house, an elegant story written in code for their perusal and influence on a spiritual level. As I did, I had memories of what had happened on 911 when I was in the Marines at that house.

I had rescued my son's blanket from a grill in the parking lot, where my ex-wife had meanly thrown it down in the gutter. Then I drove down the street to the gas station. I went in and the cashier was watching the TV with much imperious attention.

I looked at the TV, and on it was a picture of one of the World Trade Towers, in smoke, and an airplane crashing into a second one.

"What the hell is that?" I asked.

"Holy shit … it is terrorists, man … terrorists!" he said.

I got gas and drove to the base of Camp Pendleton for our drill with Force Recon then. The gate was on very high alert. They let me in and told me that for a time I would not be able to leave.

Out training was interrupted, and we were put on deployment notice to Afghanistan, during a new war, to leave months early.

I have covered what happened during that deployment in parts in the last chapter.

Now, the input of 911 goes much more into unexpected detail. The taxi driver dropped me off downtown San Diego near the CityCoffee Bar.

I went inside and ordered a coffee. Then I noticed a man sitting by the window at a computer that I recognized from Seattle. It was Lucifer! Looking at his computer, and attempting to use ESP on him, I got the idea that he was seeking to find the victims of 911 on a spiritual basis, so he could trap them and drag them to Hell, forever.

Getting notice from other customers, I could tell that

some of them could mentally read my character, knew about the war participation, and wanted me to go to Balboa Park in the city to solve some unspoken problem there.

On a sign outside on a stand chair for the bus was a picture of Michael. So, I knew he knew about the Lucifer effect, and was likely to intervene. I found that out later.

At the time, I wanted to go explore Balboa Park. I began to walk downtown, through the Old Town area. As I did, I got in mind the ideas of what my real relatives were doing, Morgan form LA and Yreka, Jessica from all the places, Emily and her statues, and then I suddenly got it in my head to think about the woman I met inside the mental institute of Seattle. Her name was Elizabeth. She was special.

As I thought it, I felt a call to go into a downtown restaurant and bar. I sat down at the bar and talked to the waitress. Her name, I found out, was Elizabeth. I started to wonder how it was that she got me the ideas of her.

Soon I found out, through Angelic projections identified through seemingly random projections as being instituted by the Archangel Michael and the Archangel Gabriel. And it told me many things. One of them, I interpreted, was that Elizabeth was an agent of the Archangel Michael, and was very high classed.

The commercial on TV, as I ordered some Crab, was about how certain cars were immortal. On the Gilligan Show that was on, then, I got the sense that immortals exist. During the program the character Michael told about how they were to go fishing and pull the fish to the surface to eat. That was a message of what he wanted me to do, to find the evils with lures and drag them to the surface, and when they got there, to correct them. A parable. The next commercial showed that many immortals were dying and did not know why.

Now pay attention to that, because death is what happened to me in the next chapter.

To that, I was finished eating, and Elizabeth said something that was in indirect invitation for me to join her team in Michael and Gabriel's fight against the evils of the world. I took her up on it.

Then I left, planning on coming back and going further.

My goal at that time was to find out what was going on with the city. So, I started to walk down towards the water on Broadway Avenue. This is what happened. It is very interesting. And magical.

Down Broadway avenue, right before it got to the water, I came to cross a set of train tracks near a building that was a reception area for passengers. On the way, next to the tracks, I spotted a man who seemed disabled. I stopped and talked to him.

He spoke to me in strange and mysterious terms. I realized that he was a veteran of the military. He was older, in his 50's, and then talked about car insurance. As he did, my eyes were drawn to the sky, where they saw the word GEICO imprinted in clouds and mist from the airplanes flying there. It was so deep and profound that it seemed impossible. I knew that Richard, which was his name, had done it mentally. I wondered if he was an Angel, a deep veteran of wars, or immortal.

We got up and walked over to the field and sidewalk and stands on the beach next to the Midway ship. The Midway was a combat ship from 1947. There were many people around the table there, who I was introduced to. Branoll, Kefer – who was Muslim - Chael, Heidi, Brandon, and, you guessed it, Michael. They talked about the secret mysteries of the ship being made on a spiritual basis to be able to fly and defend the country against the unseen, like aliens and the Hereafter.

I went with Richard to a local small coffee shop next to the water. On the way he said a lot of very intelligent things about his analysis of the people. And he impressed them by speaking out to them. One man was so impressed he gave Richard some money.

As we sat down, Richard started to talk to another customer about the magics of the Midway, service, and time travel. I got from him that time-travel actually existed. Then he went into secret detail about how the veterans of the war-stricken Midway aircraft carrier are using time-travel and seemingly magical abilities (which were actually valid science on a level of the future far beyond the current ability to understand it ... thus making it seem "magical" today,) to make the craft fly, and they are preparing it for operation within the Hereafter.

We began to walk back to the Midway. On the way, I come across a very relevant, vocally profound and mysterious woman in punk rock clothing that identifies miracles with the Midway, and where I have been. I agreed to meet her later. She said she was leaving, and she left quickly.

We got back to the Midway, and Kefer and Richard say there is no place to sleep there, so they left. I went back downtown.

And I found there a deep element and agent of the process of Creation that you would not believe.

I come across Paul down at the end of Gaslamp Quarter by the tracks and a power box. We talk about the magic of Creation in relation to how a train crash can look the same as a model of a train crashing. In Creation that could happen in different places at the same time, as they are noticed. Then he asked about my son. I didn't know. I had seen parts of his supposedly dead body in Seattle. The man was Paul, who, I think, in the Bible is a disciple of Jesus, one of his acolytes.

What Paul was doing was magic, as soon became pronounced. After our conversation I left and began to walk down the sidewalk, and on the way saw a 20-year older copy of my son.

It was very pronounced. I wondered if he knew who I was. I could tell he was thinking hard. He went to meet a female at the train station, and I got the sense that he wanted to assault me. So, I changed his mind by projecting images of karate to him. Then I left, thinking hard about the definite interactions with Angels and him, the apparent time travel he seemed to have gone through. I began to think about what his performance would be under the auspices of Michael or Gabriel. And I thought about him joining me after death on the Ark of the Covenant.

Above all that I thought about the mystery of Creation that Paul had brought around.

How was the Ark, and where was it?

As I lay down in the dark on the sidewalk, I thought hard about the divinity I was getting of, well, everything in the universe. It was all components, in actions and deeds of one of two things: Creation, and warfare against evils. Everything fit within those two categories.

That was heavy. And thus, the title of *Cheetah on the Wing 4: Creation and Warfare: Choose.*

The next morning, in the north part of Gaslamp quarter, I met a homeless man. He would not accept any money from me, saying he got his from visitors. He said he lost his legs in a bomb in Vietnam. He illustrated obstacles for religious men on the street had to meet.

Then I walked back over to the restaurant that Elizabeth worked at. Across the street I got called over to the World Market. I went inside and browsed. As I did, I immediately began to think of Jessica. Then the shop employee came over and introduced herself as, you guessed it, her name was Jessica.

I know you may not believe in ESP. It exists. This is proof. How else would I get the idea of her name with no indication but mental power from her?

I immediately began to ask Jessica questions about the products, that were actually variables of my questions about her opinion of me being unified with my real, religious family, and what avenues, on the level of Angelic justice, would she take towards bringing about either Creation, or warfare against evils. She answered that she would do whatever worked, and her answer about the relative issue was one that I interpreted to be a "yes, definitely!"

What that meant will come up at the end of this chapter.

I departed, and walked to the north, called again. I found on the other side, outside of the Gaslamp Quarter, another Breakfast Diner. I went in there. And sure enough, the waitress was a varied copy of Jessica. I got coffee there and left.

Down the street I saw signs on the license plates of cars and tall building windows, that indicated the sign on a license plate that read EATMSSG. MSSG was a code for Marine Service Support Group, and then I looked up at the building, and in it I saw a reflection in the window of Lucifer! He was the very same person who had been at the CityCoffee Bar doing plots against the victims of 911!

I wondered at that the interaction of the Archangels Michael and Gabriel, and mentally projected the concept of Jessica and Elizabeth to them, in preparation to the assault that was going to come.

I also began to question what was going on with the immortals of the area. With the question of the immortals in mind, I entered the area of the Midway ship.

I looked across the street from the Midway and saw the Naval Center building. I saw signs there that some of the staff were on call to do the bidding of Lucifer.

By the Midway, I went over to Michael, and asked him about people from the Naval Center visiting the Midway. Michael didn't want to talk about it. Richard came over and talked me into going back with him to the Coffee Shop. When we got there, Richard began to speak on open terms about Lucifer doing evil things like making slaves. I asked him about the proclivities of the dead, thinking about how they had moved from the destruction of Seattle to LA, and to Yreka jail. I was interested in what it had to do with the immortals, who were for some reason dying now.

The question I had to Richard was, what are the veterans going to do at Lucifer's footstep? The answer was, "They will fight."

Upon that, the conversation ended, and I went back downtown.

From there I walked over to the Gaslamp Quarter, thinking of my son and his presence in the fight against Lucifer and Satan. I had the sense that he was doing good at it.

I got drawn into a hat shop. I went in and got a message from the waitress there of how they were seeking the actual location of the fallen Angel of Satan to defeat him. Not in plain terms, mark you, but in understandable parallel terms.

I departed, and the cashier said: "God bless you!" As I walked, I came across other people who were seeking the actual location of Satan to defeat him. I mentally read them and saw that they were trying hard. I was glad.

So, I walked over to the Breakfast Diner, and got some coffee.

I realized there that the people I had witnessed before had driven Lucifer away. The people sitting at the table said it had happened, not in plain terms, and it became evident that they were demon-possessed individuals who had taken a part in that dissention, because they had wanted revenge for what Lucifer had done.

The waitresses name was Jessica. She gave me counsel about the damage that was going on in the city with apartments. Then, showing that she knew about my justice against Lucifer, she said "thank you." I thanked her back, got up, and left.

From there, I went back to Gaslamp Quarter by the train tracks and saw Paul again.

The next section shall talk about the becoming elements of people that I came into contact with and how they were creating miracles.

With Paul, we began to talk about him having the idea of my son. Then Paul started to talk about science in a way that drew my attention to the idea of unicorns. Then I asked him about immortals finding their way to Paradise, and he gave me a mythological answer. Deep inside, I thought it applied to the concept put forth by Steven Hawking about the possibility of parallel universes having mythological creatures.

Then it dawned on me that, perhaps, he was issuing Creation of unicorns in a way that would bring them here, in some form or another.

From there I headed north.

I was still in a part of Gaslamp Quarter when I met a man that was homeless inside a sports jacket. I was honest with him and asked him about the immortals and the unicorns. He did not respond, saying he didn't think about those things.

I knew though that he knew more, he just wasn't saying.

I rested there, not falling asleep that night. The next morning, I went over to the Midway, to Elizabeth's restaurant, and to Gaslamp Quarter, seeking evidence of the immortals, the dead, and other priests, or religious figures in the areas.

I got called over to the mall. I went there and went to the Coffee Shop in it. There I listened to a man that I could tell was a Jewish Priest on his phone talking about the evils that were happening within the city. He talked somewhat, in an indirect manner, about what had happened during 911 and the effects of the souls on it. He stated that many things had changed, since a variable related in meaning to Lucifer had been defeated.

As I sat there, I got the picture in mind of being called to another restaurant downtown, so I went there next.

At the new restaurant, I sat outside next to the train tracks station and ordered from the waitress an iced tea. Then I got her name, and, you guessed it, she was another version of Jessica. She mentioned something in the line of, I got the idea, that she was seeking the actual location of Satan to defeat him.

I looked down the tracks and got a signal from Michael that he was on the case, and then I saw a car approaching to cross the tracks a long-ways away, and it got in a wreck. Then I noticed on the walkway to the train another man running, and I could tell it was Satan trying to preserve himself. Then a train came and there was a large noise. The man was out of sight, but it was clear that he had been hit and killed by the train.

So it was that, against the largest fallen Angel there is, we were successful and defeated him. Mission accomplished!

I went back to the Midway and talked to Richard there. We discussed such things as time travel, immortals, death, and unicorns. I began to wonder as we spoke what the elements of each of those things was. Regarding death, there was an input there of a theory that people after death would still be active in the Hereafter. That really became evident to me in the next chapter.

After the lengthy conversation was over, I departed.

I went back to Elizabeth's Restaurant, and there sat next to a very attractive woman. As she spoke, she confirmed that she was, indeed, a unicorn in a human body. Thus, it was a complete conglomeration of the theory that mythological creatures actually existed in Steven Hawking's theory of parallel universes and multiple dimensions in the 9th number.

She was quite articulate in the theory that people, like priests, the immortals, the dead, the religious, were all of a frame of mind to be saved by profound elements of unicorn influence. I realized that she had been brought to this realm by the magically scientific Creation of Paul the other day.

I complimented her and left.

I went back to Paul's area of the Gaslamp Quarter and met him.

From our conversation, I pointed out that he had, one, brought my son through time to meet us, and two, he had brought a mythological uniform here in this time and a human body to interact with me and Elizabeth. Then he began to talk about a third thing, that had something to do with the current place and the four dimensions of space and time. I left to find out what he was talking about.

That night I walked way down the street, outside of the Gaslamp Quarter to a place where I felt I was being called by Emily. Now, I had in mind how I had met Emily, on the doll within LA. Then I saw the movie about her and demonic possession. Then she gave me the direction to the trophy of the unicorn, which, incidentally, was in some way her telling me about Paul's episode of Creation of one. Then she was mentally present upon the victory against evils of LA and told me about some of the special things we had done to bring it about.

I was at a Mexican car shop there next to the freeway. The cars were not being predictable, so I began to walk down the freeway. I came to a bridge over it and climbed up it. On the other side, within the fence, I rested, and thought about Emily. That early morning, I found a sign on the ground about a church down one of the nearby streets. So, I got up that morning and went there.

There, at the street, I found the church, and there, in the parking lot, I drafted a sign on the note and left it for Emily upon the top of a fence. Then I started to walk down the street.

I passed by the Library, across a fence across a field between us, and saw in there some evidence of fallen heroes who were seeking a remedy for their death experience. It was in signs along trash and parts of clothes in the field. As I looked, some people walking on the other side of the street started to talk about it. At the same time, a bus appeared, spitting out pollution and smoke from its bumper.

It was driven by Beelzebub, a fallen Angel of Hell that was trying to take over the position of the fallen pair of Satan and Lucifer in the city, by attempting to possess and engulf as many people as he could. He wanted to hit people with the bus.

He drove on, and I went and communicated with the very disturbed members of the bus stop.

Then I walked back to Elizabeth's Restaurant, seeking a solution.

It was closed. I called Krishna on the phone and told her how much I loved her. I let her know that I was a Priest now, and I was working for God, and couldn't come back yet. "I'm still homeless," I told her. She let me know how much she loved me and wanted me to be safe.

I thanked her and thought that it was starting to look like we were actually going to be saving a lot of people.

It was Halloween. I saw many people in costumes saying erroneous things to each other, making fun of each other's makeup and clothes, and being generally distraught. I went over next to the CityCoffee Shop, which was right next to a steakhouse and a Horror Show going on inside a city museum building. I saw there my old friend Black, the man who had helped me escape Seattle when it was being destroyed in multiple dimensions. He sat blank, staring at the people in costumes getting ready to go in the building.

I tried to talk to him and failed. He awakened in me memories of Jessica and Angel who had also saved me. He was deep in misery from the mental irregularities of the people in costumes. I offered him some money and told him to go ahead and get something to eat. Then, distressed, I departed.

That night, I went to Elizabeth's work. There she told me to sit next to the fence looking across the street. As I sat there, I got the attention of a woman dressed like a nun across the street. I went over and started to talk to her.

She had my same opinion that there was something evil to be seen with so many people wearing costumes and saying so many negative things about each other.

Then I walked over to meet Paul. To that he directed

me to go eat at a grocery store there. I left, wanting to see what he was talking about.

And, go figure, at the grocery store I met a resurrected copy of Jesus Christ. Jesus mentioned an indication to a name I knew. That name was the call sign I had in 29 Palms in the Marines. It was the term "Phoenix 1". Phoenix ... was there a place called that, somewhere? Why was he telling me that?

I went over to the Midway to visit with Richard. He had a lot of negative things to say about the people there, impeding with the Creation of a flying ship. As he spoke, the punk rock girl came up and began speaking riddles to me.

Me and the punk rock girl began to walk uptown. She was talking about warfare, and as she spoke, I could hear gunfire coming from the Midway. It was loud and rowdy. We walked, and she said riddles about the immortals and legends, all having to do with warfare. I could tell by the way she was speaking that her words were having an effect on the very real war that was being fought upon the Midway.

We came to a 7-11 and I felt I was drawn in. There was a sense of evil being done there. I left her outside and went in.

There I got a beverage and saw and read a man there who was wholly evil, who was trying to get the people there to begin to kill others. I went to the counter, said something counter to what he was trying to accomplish, the register cashier agreed with me, and said things that were disabling the evil man from doing evil. He was angry about it and said a lot of hateful things but could do nothing.

When I left, the punk rock girl had left.

The next day I went back to the Midway, and Richard said he wanted to go uptown that time.

We went uptown, a long, long ways from the Midway to a residential area on a hill. There we sat down at a table in front of a small grocery store. Richard stated talk about a lot of evils, trying to get my impressions. On the way, I noticed a car drive by with a license plate with numbers 666 on it, it was of the Beast of the Apocalypse. Then a woman walked by to go in the store, and I could tell she was an agent fighting against the evils. Following her was a man who I identified as an assassin that was seeking to kill her. He was also a threat to us.

I began to get Richard's opinion on the gunfire on the Midway I had heard the day previously. He got defensive and started to walk. As we walked, a car stopped next to us and a man got out, talking about religious ways to find a solution to the evils of the city. I could tell he was a reincarnation of my son, at an older age. He began to speak about the mental presence of multi-dimensional personalities. Then, as he spoke about others doing things in a magic-seeming sense to help, I saw a man walking rapidly next to us.

He was seeking to assault me. As he drew up his arm, my son said something in defense, and the man vanished immediately!

I was amazed at the image of him vanishing. And at the same time, I got the thought that I wanted to go downtown to search for Emily.

I went to a location between where Elizabeth was working, and I had visited Paul and got drawn into a place called the *Rohan Steak and Fixer's* Restaurant. I went in there to eat.

The table I sat at was right next to some men talking about the difficulties they had to face in the city. They brought up the idea of time travel. They also brought up the concept of interactions with family members that were helping them out. And as they did, my young, twenty-something attractive waitress came by and took my order, with the proclivity of one who was extremely intelligent and knew a lot about the menu. And her name was Emily.

As we talked, Emily showed an extreme knowledge of me that was unexpected. She said "What are you, some sort of Priest or an Angel? Hahaha! That makes me laugh so hard ... a man who is being made into an Angel who spends his life broke and bringing Hell into the scenario. Go figure!" For her to know that I was both a priest and had been an Angel was remarkable.

As I talked to her, it became clear to me to go to Phoenix. There I was to be united with my real family on a holy level.

I ate a great steak meal, told Emily I would see her later, thinking hard about transiting to Phoenix, which I recognized as a place, I just didn't know where. I thought it was next to 29 Palms, California. I had no idea that it was in the next state over, in Arizona. More about that later.

I walked there to the water area, down southwest of Gaslamp Quarter. There, the odd happened.

I went to the waterside in a field next to a sidewalk next to the water, and watched the people migrating there. I had the sense that half of them were immortal but were now facing death.

I got up after a spell and went to a restaurant by the water. I got food and a drink. I had the sense that the staff were putting chemicals or poison in the drinks. Then a woman with two young boys, about 5 years old, sat next to me. One boy started to say many things that were atrocious. I got the sense that he was trying to talk staff there into assaulting me, so I left.

As I walked on the sidewalk by the water, right after, I came across the reason for the child's errors. I saw walking a bearded version of Satan himself. Satan, who had been destroyed by us, had found some way to come back, but was trapped for the time within a human body, and he was aware of possible casualties from all of us. Did I attack him? No. I did not want him to have the ability to call justice on me for any reason. So, I kept walking.

I came across a field downtown and went there to

talk to a man and his girlfriend there. He said a lot of negative things about the police and citizens of the area, then made an excuse to leave. I got from him, reading his mind, that he somehow knew of what the person who was thinking of assaulting Emily in the near future looked like. And I got the image.

I kept walking, looking hard and reading minds of walkers steadily. They were all thinking the same thing, about a show they had seen on television about a man assaulting a young girl and getting let go free afterwards. I could tell from them that they were seeing the picture of the man. Then, I suddenly got a deep image of the man himself who was going to assault Emily. And as I did, I heard a loud noise behind me.

It was him. I immediately turned and punched him so hard I almost knocked him out. He fell. I kept walking fast now.

I was arrested by the police, who refused to listen to me tell them about how I had only defended myself against a man who was coming in to assault me, which he was doing. The officers were possessed by demons.

The inmates in the jail were just as bad, for the most part.

The inmate in the cell that I was put in had a lot of books. He immediately began to talk to me about the negativities of the inmates and how they broke the rules. He was also against the police and guards. I got a book and began to read it, getting input from it about the religious war we were fighting.

Then the guards, out of cruelty, put me in a different cell with a racist skinhead who thought he was a World War 2 veteran: *which he wasn't.* He immediately started to say a bunch of negative things to me. I took a stance to hit him and he quieted down. The guards at the door saw it and moved me to another cell.

Then, the next day, I got called to a room upstairs, next to some counters with social workers working there. One called me over. I immediately started to yell at him, telling him about how the man I struck was going to rape a family member, so I hit him to stop him. I was abrupt. He listened, and agreed that I was, in fact, innocent, and said I was going to be released the next day.

I went downstairs and waited.

That night I decided to go to Phoenix immediately, to find a way to be near my real family. They were partakers of the beginning of Creation, agents of Angels of Heaven, and warriors for God against evils. They were on the same profile as I was, that of a Priest. Emily, Jessica, Morgan, and Chrystal, all of them were going to find me there. I knew it.

So, I got on a Greyhound bus and departed.

The rest of this chapter is about what highly religious ramifications of being, the effects of good versus evil, and the behavior of Angels. And it ends with disaster ... but I will get to that at the end of this chapter.

When I departed the bus in Phoenix, Arizona, I immediately got out and, looking around at the very tall buildings of the downtown area, it became plain to me at that time that Phoenix was not anywhere near 29 -Palms, California. Not at all.

The passengers at the Greyhound station were speaking in errors and hateful diatribe to each other. Some of them were trying to plant verbal traps out there that would negatively affect the mind of the listener and make them confused and lost in the city. I could tell they were getting their power, many of them, from possession by the Devil.

I went outside the station to the smoking area. There I got the sense that many of the people were also demon-possessed. I got in mind the idea of thinking about how subliminal thought operated, and how it was, on the surface, confusing, but to a religious priest, like myself, there is a method of thinking that makes it more reasonable and actuated. I had gone there, with my trials so severe as to be nearly unspeakable. Being in prison when innocent for almost 6 years. Fighting a war for God with the homeless and troubled immortals for two years. That was just 8 years of serious trials.

I noticed out there that there were special elements of trash and knots and bruises in the paint on the walls and sidewalk that said a lot about how the mental projections of people out there were interacting with them.

I went back inside, and there began to listen to a

couple of people talking about religion. They were talking about the Hereafter and the effects it had on people who went there and who had read and was influenced by the Bible. After a while, I asked to speak to them. They said it was okay.

First, I told them how I was a student of Quantum Theory and Relativity. To that I mentioned that, per those rules, disciples of Jesus would not be able to go to Heaven directly. They would have to work to save a lot of people first.

The female didn't believe me, so I told her about a formula, a rhythm of numbers given to me online by a man named Michael, a scientist. It was six numbers, that, if subtracted one from the next 5 times, would leave remaining a combination of two editions of the number 12. That was the religious number of all Creation, as I put it. And if one did math along all the numbers, they would all be changed to equal the number 7. I explained that the number 7 was, per the Bible, the initial number of Angels.

The woman noticed that Michael was the name of one of God's Archangels, and she was amazed at what I had said to her about the numbers of Creation.

From there I walked down the street to 711, got something to drink, then went back to the bus station. The people there were disturbed. I left.

I walked far down the street, looking at the signs of the people on the buildings, the signs and addresses and numbers, and it was giving me clues as to how the people of the area were struggling. I went down a side road and came across a food truck. I stopped and got a pastry. What I said to the driver was a religious question about the wherewithals of the people, and he answered in respect.

The next place that I got called to was a Mexican restaurant down the street. I went there and ordered tacos and sat down inside.

Each of the customers were talking about the wrongs they had to endure. I drew from them that the city was filled with priests, messengers, reverends, Angels, and believers who were each fighting the evils there, and the evils were trying to drag them from God's Garden to Hell. Then I heard two women talking about elements like the demonic Mephistopheles, and it became plain they were of an evil presence. They were talking about how damnation was activated.

One of those evil women recognized that I was reading her mind and said something really negative to me. I got up and left.

I walked down the side street to a church. I sat in front of it and thought. There was virtually no traffic down that road. I stayed there until the sun started to go down. As I thought there, I got to thinking about many facets of how I could bring forwards miracles of Creation to success. I got up and kept walking, now it was getting dark.

As I walked, I came to the realization that a lot of the people there saw me as a danger. It was due to the fallen

Angel, like the ones that Jessica, Michael, Elizabeth, and I had faced, using forces against us and trying to infuse us and people we were interacting with, with evils. They had been doing it for years, thus the reason why I had been abused my whole life and sent to prison twice for charges I was innocent of.

I also realized that I was protected by Angels. And as I realized that I noticed a scarecrow statue in a yard. It was designed to be present if a person died and possess their souls and rag them to Hell with it's magic. I could tell that it was itemized to have contact with everyone who drove down that part of the road. Pure evil.

I kept walking. Across the road I saw a medical center with a special sign on the front. The words on it were itemizations of people who were having spiritual problems and going there to seek a solution. As I looked, I saw a man getting arrested across the street by the police. I could tell from mind reading that he was innocent of what they were vocally accusing him of, and he was one of the patients of the medical center across the street.

The thoughts I had of that issue, of the interaction of the scarecrow, and the police arresting that innocent patient, was to think solidly about how to interact with the severe PTSD I had, and to equate the activities of healing of military corpsman for me if I wound up in that situation again.

That paid off big time, as you will see in the next chapter.

I went back to the Greyhound station first.

The first thing that happened was that I wanted to get my ticket changed. It was to go back to California, and I wanted to go somewhere else. The woman working at the counter started to ignore me at first, but I got into her face and corrected her. Hating me, she gave me another ticket.

Then I went over to the videogames and saw one playing on the precipice of telling the player venues to take of preservation to Heaven. Not in clear, plain, terms, but it was what I drew from it.

Then I got up and had my attention drawn to another passenger. His name was Rufus. He stated that he was really interested in me coming to his town in Missouri. He had a deep story of events happening there.

I told him then about how the term "Phoenix" was to an ancient mythological bird that had the ability to come back to life after being killed, and that there was proof that there were people who could do the same thing in San Diego. He was amazed.

From his stories, I decided that I wanted to go out into Phoenix and identify the characters on the streets.

That was where the adventure really began.

I took the bus to the airport. There, at the bus stop, I found a bag of clothes with a jacket in it. Then I went and sat down at the ground level, outside next to the road in front. I watched the cars with signs on them coming by, and they were telling me about the altered parallel dimensions and the fabrics of them throughout that city.

As I sat there, a security guard came up and told me to leave and go inside. So, I did.

I went to the ticket counter and tried to change my bus ticket to an airplane ticket. The cashier would have nothing of it. I asked her about the zombie-like customers, and if they had anything to do with it. She had no idea what I was talking about, so she said, but in actuality she understood exactly what I meant.

I left, and as the sun was coming up, walked a couple of miles back into downtown Phoenix.

The first place I came to on my way to downtown was a hotel with pictures of Jesus in it. Next to it was a gas station. I went in. Inside, the cashier was an embodiment of Emily, and looking at the newspaper I saw an article that appeared to have been written by the Archangel Gabriel. It was about aliens from other planets influencing the artwork on the buildings in the city.

Emily showed with her remarks to me that she was trying to protect me. She told me about the details of the city and things to pay attention to. I thanked her and left.

As I walked towards the city, I came across a bicycle with a rude sign on it. As I looked at it, a rude man came up and began to say a lot of negative things to me. He wanted my money. I told him I had none. I got from him that he was a demon-possessed assassin that wanted to kill me, if I was unable to defend myself. I left.

As I walked, the song on the phone radio came on called *Hotel California*, by the Eagles. It is about people getting sucked into a hotel run by Satan and trapped there, doing evils. That is what that rude fellow was going through. It became clear to me that the evil forces were getting my location and seeking to do something negative to me.

As I walked, I kept looking behind me to see if that rude fellow was following me. I turned down a side street and began to walk through an alleyway. Then I turned right again and went back towards a church on the main street. The church had signs on it about the ability to see in other's things that were either sinful or holy, something that only Priests or Angels had the capability of doing.

A man and a group of well-dressed kids came up to me and said some very illuminating religious commentaries. I was appreciative.

And then I reached the downtown Phoenix area, to be covered in the next few sections.

I stood outside of a grocery store before it opened and looked at the cars and drivers. The drivers were operating on a subliminal frequency of hidden thoughts. I could tell from some of them that there were Creation abilities in the town, on many different levels.

Then the grocery store opened, and I went in. I went and found a magazine that talked about how different people had different perceptions of God, who could appear as a human, but it was on a level that nobody could understand. The cashier also said things about Creation for the record. I left and went out the back.

The back door was on a large patio that was part of many different stores. I looked across the street and saw a painting of a man with letters and words on it that was describing on a level the different elements of magic within the city. I walked over to the porch of the coffee shop there, and met a man reading a book.

I began to talk to him. The man first got introduced to the idea that I had seen something on the statue that was no longer visible. He explained how some things disappear without reconciliation. Then he began to talk a lot about being an author. He was an author himself. I addressed it in terms of Quantum Theory, and he began to identify it in terms of the space and behavior of space aliens and doing time travel. A very intense conversation.

Then I began to walk down the sidewalk. On it I saw a bunch of stenciled footsteps marked on it. Then I saw a bizarre expression on a driver in a vehicle near me, looking at me with a strange, curious, and disturbed look on his face. And then it occurred to me … I was being submitted to the magic of the city by being near those stenciled footprints, and people were seeing me as a Sasquatch.

It got night, and I kept on walking. I came across a parking structure that had the precipice of a gigantic flying starship. There was a lot of invisible proof of alien vehicles there, locked in the yard. I thought about what Jessica had told me about alien beings within LA.

I looked up at a tall, multi-storied building, and saw in it, art that was an indicator of an evil man doing things when he was expected to protect others and was failing. It was evidence of the occupation of aliens from outer space there.

Then I kept walking and came across a bar by the rock star Alice Cooper. It was also a restaurant. There was inside of it a high level of Angelic messages.

I walked back downtown that night and saw along the building walls artistic tesla signs with forms and computer animated colors. They talked about the presence of aliens within their commercials. As I walked, I came across a man that late night. I began to talk to him.

He described the many ways that the city was full of evil. He discussed how he was at a bar and witnessed a fight between a large group of people. He also described his difficulties with a woman he met. Then he mentioned how there were a lot of fallen Angels there.

I listened to him, identified myself as an artist that was seeking illustrations of the same sort of ideas, and then, the conversation ended, and I left.

I stayed at the bus station until dawn. Again, that was yet another night that I didn't sleep.

That morning, I looked at the instruction sign on the bus and saw that it had coded in it articles about the presences of people there, and how some of them were seeking a way to Heaven.

I went on board the bus. The man I started to talk to discussed a lot about God and his Angels, about the churches, and about how to find a way to Heaven. He described a certain building down the street as being interesting on the subject. I departed.

I began to walk out of the city.

On the way, I looked at many cars and drivers, and identified that many of them were evil. I also saw a vehicle with passengers that were lost that resembled my real family. Then I came to a church far out and went in there.

On the ground floor there was a room with a coffin in it and a lot of art on the walls. There were a lot of people in there. I looked at one of the papers, and saw it was a picture of Jesus and his disciples. The other pictures gave me messages about the sensations of the senses and food. A man came up to me and said good things about the pictures and told me to keep them in mind.

Upon reflection, the messages I was getting there were items related to the aspect of what I was to be learning in this life in preparation for going aboard the Ark of the Covenant, and bringing justice and saving or damnation to those they, whichever they are, applied to.

I departed and walked down the street. The next place I came to was a bus stop.

The man there had a beard and drew my attention. He mentioned the elements of how certain places there had magic about them and spoke about Angels. I gave him 15 pages of my notes to read, and he told me to go down the street to the Indian Park and rest there. I could tell he wanted me to do more there. It was a place of magic.

I went down the street to the Indian Park. In it, there was a field over stones of plants and bushes. I went there and lay down on the rocks. There, I got drawn headlong into reflections of ideas regarding Angels, and, as I drifted into a state near, but not quite in, sleep, I began to have discrete and bright images of meeting an Angel there. She was appearing in my dreams, with strong ESP and mental proclivity.

The Angel told me about finding Paradise and said there was much more to it than that. She was on fire, and set me on fire, but it was not painful, it was Bright Existence.

I got up and walked at the end of her message. Then dark fell, and I found a statue by the road of an Angel by a field of grass. I lay down before her and got another set of messages from her. They were about the multiple dimensions, and how those dimensions were going to play a part in my success in the area.

What I didn't realize was that those two Angels were the same Angels that I had been told about online when I asked the question "what is going to happen to me when I die?" immediately after release from the unjust jail sentence in Yreka. What I didn't know at the time was that those two Angels had been sent to me through a particle of time-space levity that allows one to transmit from the future ... what was going to happen to me ... which was death ... to the past ... which is where I *got the message of what was going to happen in the future.*

The next chapter shall discuss exactly what I was told by those Angels when I was killed and sent to the Hereafter and God's Garden by the Angel of Death.

It reflects what is discussed and similar to the book *Proof of Heaven: A Neuroscientist's Journey to the Afterlife.* It is a true story about what could be seen as some as a medical miracle. I was a victim of severe brain hemorrhaging, which could have, and did, kill me. But I recovered so profoundly that a year later I was able to become a new author and write five different books. And my mental capabilities have maintained sound. I still have the IQ of a genius, as my books shall indicate.

The next chapter is the next to last chapter of this book. It is about my presence in the Hereafter. It is highly Angelic and Godly. I hope you enjoy and learn a discrete lesson from it.

I was a victim of attempted vehicular homicide, that killed me. And I survived to tell the tale about it. It was a miracle. Imagine that.

Read on.

,

CHAPTER 12

SURVIVING AND TREATMENT OF HOMICIDE

This chapter of the story is very difficult to write. It is about what happened after the religious war I was on, and what the evil forces did against me.

It is about how I was the victim of attempted vehicular homicide. I faced severe injuries and was put in the hospital for 11 months after. And I have never recovered all the way.

It happened on November 29 and 30th, 2013. In November 2016, recovering from the severe PTSD and severe cerebral hemorrhaging I had as a result, I purchased a book from Barnes and Noble about the Hereafter. The reason was because, when I was in a coma from the assaults, I have a memory of dying. And when I died, I was surrounded by three Angels who told me what to do about it. Now, I was not sure if my memory was accurate, because it was so foreign and amazing, but the book I got, called *Proof of Heaven: A Neuroscientist's Journey into the Afterlife*, told a story about how a man faced a strange coma for 7 days from meningitis, and there, even though his brain was supposed to be dead, he had images of Angels and God in ways that prove that the Hereafter exists.

He was only in a coma for 7 days. I was in a coma for two months. He was only in the hospital for two weeks. I was in the hospital for almost a whole year. What happened to him was, as he said, a miracle of medicine. What happened to me was far more profound.

The Hereafter does exist. This is my story of my interactions with it.

First off, let me describe something relevant here.

The memories I have of Paris and Downlow and my ex-wife have been told to be false by Downlow to Krishna, right after the event. She said she was in Africa. There is no proof of that that I know of.

But I do know this: I have discrete, substantial memories of them being present at the coffee shop where I have memory of being killed. My memory is the source of nightmares. It is always the same. That is something that would not happen if it was made up. So, it is real.

There are two reasons why I know it is real. One, I have just asked the book *90 Minutes in Heaven*, which I haven't read, on a "random" page (meaning a page brought on by my subliminal mind and ESP), "is my memory accurate?" and my finger was on the following sentence:

"You're the first person I've met who understands what it's like to live with pain twenty-four hours a day."

If that doesn't mean that it is definitely accurate, then I don't know what is. And that was a question I asked of God Himself. And it is what he wanted me to put here for you to read.

Second, I have also begun to study parallel universes right now. I am writing a book about them. The fact of parallel universes and multiple dimensions is that they can occur based on the thoughts of a person, and the itemization of the perceived elements therein can occur to the soul of the person in the parallel universe. Thus, I know that they had had the illusion of being present during the murder, that they had requested it, at least in their minds, and they had communication with the partakers of that crime against me.

What I have written here is what my memories say happened. And it did. In either this universe, in actuality, or in a parallel universe, in thought - they happened.

Let me start where it started.

The record from the police, but is lacking from my

memory, is that they had come to the Phoenix airport to find me, due to the mission person's complaint that Krishna had filed. The officer had been on the phone with Krishna, who told him that I was a disabled veteran with head trauma who was seeking care with medications from the VA hospital. So, she asked him to take me there and get me some help. He agreed.

He took me to the VA hospital. They refused to give me my medications. They also refused to treat me. I remember, though, getting sent to go talk to a doctor or nurse or staff member, and he told me that if I wanted a place to stay, then I would be able to find one from some people inside a coffee shop down the road.

So, I left the VA and walked there.

On the way, I was having serious mental images of strife and conflict coming. There were signs as stencils on the sidewalk, signs on the doors, license plates, and mental images of deep conflict.

I got to the coffee shop and went inside. As I entered, I looked to the left, and saw at a table there were the presences of Paris and Downlow. I could sense immediately that they were up to evils. So, I tried to ignore them, and ordered a coffee.

Then I turned to the right, having my attention drawn by a woman crying "do him! Do him!" over and over again. The woman was my ex-wife, the woman who had filed false charges against me in 2005. As she cried it out, two off-duty cops next to her, if my memory is right one of them was wearing an NRA shirt, drew a jimmy out and struck me on the head and skull with it extremely hard.

They caused severe brain hemorrhaging with the breaks they put into my face, nose, and scalp with that assault. And they knocked me unconscious.

Now, a year after the assault, I remember seeing my face in the mirror. I have six L shaped scars from the breaks along my face. Two are on my lip, one on my nose, and three between my eyes and along the front of my skull. I have records from the Saint Joseph's Hospital in Phoenix of there being breaks to my face and skull and nose in those locations.

What I have of memory after that, of the event, is different and separate from what actually happened. Let me explain why.

For one, from the strikes, I immediately began to develop brain hemorrhaging. That is an influx of blood and moisture to the tissues of the brain. That causes pain, errant thoughts, and ideas that are a proclivity to suspicious and paranoia. Now, at that was going on, I was facing the realization that, for one, I was dying from an unjust assault, that it had been by off-duty police officers illegally, that it had been asked by people of my so-called family, and I had PTSD from being abused as a child that affected how I perceived what was going on. Let me describe how.

First, I was told by my father's parents, my

grandparents, when I was about three years old, that Paris had killed my real mother at birth, and if I said anything negative about her, she would kill me to. Then, that very same year, I was taken to go see the first movie of the *Star Wars* series, in 1977, at a very young age of three years old, by my father. The Jedi of the movie had profound mental ESP powers. After the movie was over, my father, who was a genius, told me about how ESP actually exists, how the Force exists, and how the main characters of the *Star Wars* movie were influenced by Angels from Heaven. Now, let me tell you about where I got confirmation of the ESP, then the presence of Angels.

The concept of ESP was something that I got in contact with during the extremely religious ceremonies during solitary confinement, in 2008 and 2009. The counsellor of the unit, his name was Mitchell, came to me alone in the breakroom one day with a magazine, and he said that he had his attention drawn to the concept of a J-shaped hook for fishing, that had certain features on it. Then he turned to a random page in the magazine, immediately, and his finger was directly over a picture of a J-shaped hook with the exact same features that he had been talking about. He was surprised, because, as he told me then, he had never opened up that magazine and had no idea of what the pictures were in it.

His ability to turn to that page at random, was proof that he was somehow able to read over what was in that magazine without having ever looked into it. Those are the ESP powers of Angels. Plus, he had read my mind in the proclivity of my religious experiences and was testing my knowledge about ESP to see if I understood it. And it was clear that that was his first time doing that, because ESP was something he had just learned and had questions about.

Now let me tell you about the Angels. In 2011 for a year, and 2013 for a year, I was homeless, as put here, and on a religious mission for God. As I defeated the evils of different cities, I was visited by Angels. One of them was named Angel. The other was named Gabriel, an Archangel. And another was an Angelic relative that I have named Emily.

And before I survived the attempted murder, the very same day it occurred, I was visited in dreams by two Angels. And they were two of the three same Angels that came to me when I died inside of God's Garden. I will get to that shortly.

Now let me tell you about the full memories I have of the event after I was attacked and my face and skull and nose broken, and I was, for a spell, unconscious.

From my unconsciousness inside the coffee shop, I awakened with severe cerebral hemorrhaging going on. My PTSD, because I was a victim of attempted murder, who was dying, was also profound. It altered my memories of what was going on, with me trying as I did when I was abused by Paris to try to change my mental reaction away from reality to ideas of a mythological proportion. When I was being sexually abused by her when I was 12, right around then I had watched the TV show Mitchell and the Argonauts, and the legend of those things happening replaced my memory during the same time I was being abused. That is what some of PTSD does to its victim.

As the vehicle I was in drove, I had in mind the presence of the environment, and I had in mind that I was walking, not being kidnapped, as was actually happening. I saw on the road a bridge with a sign over the edge, and we took a right there. Then we went to a multistory building. We parked in a parking lot there where I was able to see trees and bushes across the lawn and the building across the street.

There, I had severe PTSD issues of envisioning help coming from my kids, my son and the adopted kids I have. I was there for a long time. Then my memory of leaving there is blank.

I faced so severe brain hemorrhaging that it impeded my memory and mental capabilities for over a full year. This shall describe how. Because of that, I had a hard time identifying and remembering what had happened. At the end of 2015, though, I was writing *Cheetah on the Wing 4*, and as I wrote the end, I started to remember everything that happened, as far as my memory would remember. And I remember the actual hit-and-run that I survived.

The morning of 30 November 2013, very early, still night, I was taken to the road in front of the VA hospital in, what I remember, was either an SUV or a van. I was taken out and put in front. Then it hit me from stationary, hard, forcing me face-first down on the ground beneath it. I have a memory of being stationary for a few seconds. Then it accelerated rapidly, with the tires squealing and kicking up smoke, and ran me over hard, breaking my C5 spinal cord, both legs three times, and my right knee.

The men who attempted to murder me probably thought I was dead, so they left after that, leaving me there as dead.

I think about that a lot. Paris is, as far as I know, guilty of attempted murder on three different occasions. My ex-wife, if my memory is accurate, asked the guilty party to kill me. And Downlow, per my memory, was there as well, and she had said many lies to the Oregon state police about me trying to turn them against me. If I am correct, then they are all three guilty of requesting the worst crime of them all ... attempted murder.

The Bible itself has listed in its 10 Commandments that murder is the worse crime of them all.

I was picked up around 5:00 in the morning on the road in front of the VA hospital, found by a trucker who mistook my dying carcass as some mail on the road and he stopped. After I recovered, in early 2015 I saw a Phoenix Times webpage news article that had a picture of me in the hospital, near death, bleeding all over from my face and scalp, with a strong bandage on my head, a chest tube in my throat, and a strong neck brace on from the break in my neck. The picture was atrocious.

I have no memory of the coma, but this one. I died there, in the Saint Joseph's Hospital, in the coma. I have a distinctly vivid memory of getting led, by, as my mind told me, an unspeaking Angel of Death, to God's Garden. There, I was met by the same two Angels that I had been in touch with in Phoenix the day prior. One told me that after I died, I was to go on board the Ark of the Covenant. There, I was to be put in the mental presence of ESP and allowed to read the minds of the living and the dead, on Judgement Day. I was to identify who did during their lives things that were Holy, and give them the avenue to Heaven, or to identify if they did sins, and if they did, sentence them to Hell. And afterwards, I was to be made into God's son, the way Jesus Christ was, and be placed in charge of constructing my own universe using my intelligence and Holy presence.

The other Angel addressed what I had experienced during my time at the ocean cliffs by Camp Pendleton. I had been drawn to a message from the birds, that they were copies of Angels, for the most part, going next to a glyph on the cliff by the beach and fighting Satan there. One by one they flew away. Then, at the end, there was only one bird left there, a representation of Satan. At the same time, a group of Marine Corps combat Am-tracks drove down the beach, and I could tell they were with me, as I stepped forwards and drove Satan away, that were there to help me, as the last Priest standing, to defeat

Satan. Then I was to fly over to the next pole, by myself, and create my own version of a new, parallel universe there with the keepers of justice and holy religious rudiments among the people.

Now let me describe other ways that I see that they are guilty of the attempted murder.

First, while I was in the coma, Paris, Downlow, and my younger sister (over the telephone) tried to make me a do-not-resuscitate ... leaving me to die. Krishna was there and heard about it, and told them certainly to keep me alive, and they listened to Krishna.

Then Paris called the nursing board at the VA hospital where Krishna worked in San Diego and told them the lie that Krishna had asked for the doctors to make me a do-not-resuscitate.

Then, in around May 2014, Paris took a false set of paperwork from the courthouse saying she was my conservator – when she wasn't – and committed fraud with it to the Social Security Administration, stealing $4400.00 of my funds. She was probably doing it for the money that I was in the Phoenix Times paper as suing the VA for $15 million dollars for. At the same time, Paris violated the no-contact order put forth by Judge Langford in Yreka in 2012. She violated it by coming in 2014 to the Loma Linda, California VA hospital that I was sent to, and when she was there she went and said a lot of negative lies about me to the doctors, nurses, and social workers there. The social worker, that was a very solid character, told me at the end of that day that they had kicked Paris out of there for her lies. The next time she came there, I told her that I remembered how she had attempted to murder my father in 1988, how she had talked him into committing suicide in 2007, how she had told my teachers that I was crazy and almost made me quit high school as a kid, and that she deserved felony prosecution for it. I told her to leave. I do not remember hearing from her again after that.

The reason I didn't hear from her again is probably because she is afraid that I will seek justice for her attempted murders. And I am.

Now let me tell you about the total sum of the injuries I have as a result of the attempted homicide.

At Saint Joseph's Hospital, they identified these following injuries. There were 6 spots, three fingers apart each on my face, nose, and scalp where I had been hit with a jimmy, and had my face, nose, and skull broken. I also had a broken C5 spine, a broken right knee, a break in my left leg, two breaks in my right leg, and, not on the record, but probably a break on my right big toe. It healed crooked.

During my recovery, I was placed in a cane, a disabled walker, and Krishna bought me a mobile, electric scooter for walking the dog and wheeling me to the park daily. Krishna is remarkable. She spent over $1000.00 on the scooter alone. The reason I have all those is because I am now disabled with permanent leg, knee, and right foot damage. It hurts to walk, every time, and my right leg hurts nonstop on the damaged right side from the time I awaken to the time I go to sleep. When I put my finger on the right side of my right leg, from the knee all the way to the ankle, it hurts. It buzzes. And my right foot was also injured, because I feel friction along the upper level of the bottom of it constantly. And it is difficult to walk on that leg. It is off-balance, and when I walk without the cane … I run the risk of falling. The reason is because, due to the irregular healing of the breaks, it limps and stumbles when I try to drive it forwards. It lands in an irregular fashion, making my right foot impact the ground in an irregular manner, making a bruised, loud noisy slam every single time. My footstep is flat now.

My right knee cracks every time I walk now.

There are other errors. One of them is the fact that, since my nose hasn't healed right from the break, it constantly runs. I have to clean it with a napkin at least three times per day, putting it up my nose and drawing clear the excess fluid that it has in it.

Another thing is that, from the C5 spine fracture and broken nose, I have severe coughing every single day now. I cough up phlegm and have to spit it out into a cup, repeatedly, every single day.

And yet another thing is my vision. Since the attempted homicide, the television has been blurry, the computer screen is blurry, making it difficult to write, and my ears sometimes crack. I have been intermediately on glasses of different frequencies and focus for the eye problems. Sometimes it is really bad, other times my eyes are normal. I think it is due to the skull fracture I had right between my eyes that is causing my eyes to malfunction.

And yet another thing, resulting from the breaks to my tongue and nose areas, is the sensitivity it has done to my teeth. I have "L" shaped scars on my top lip and nostril, from where they were broken with a jimmy, and I think the healing process was irregular and makes my teeth hurt every time I eat something hot. It is painful, uncomfortable, and it sucks. To have my teeth ache every time I drink coffee when I have no cavities defies common sense.

Another big problem that has occurred is that I have been diagnosed as having cancer and diabetes. The doctor of the cancer thinks it comes from my exposure to the sun in the military. The thing is that the dead skin symptoms of it are along my face, nose, skull, and chest … the same places very near where I was broken. I was diagnosed as having a precursor to actual cancer in the Loma Linda VA hospital, sometime in 2014, sometime after I awakened and became cognizant in July 2014.

Then, in October 2016, I was on a cruise to Canada for vacation with Krishna, and the first day I came under severe diabetic ketoacidosis. I was sent immediately to the hospital in Halifax, Canada. I almost died from the ketoacidosis, which put me in a near-coma. During that episode, I was severely dehydrated, in part due to my rapid vomiting every time I drank a fluid. The reason was because I was on the medicine olanzapine, which is the anti-psychotic medicine they put me on due to the brain hemorrhaging I faced. It was severe. It caused me to put on 90 pounds of weight, it was what was causing me to vomit drinking, it was what was causing me to drink way too much water, and it was what caused the near-fatal ketoacidosis.

After the diabetes episode in Canada, I went and sought treatment as an inpatient at the Loma Linda VA Hospital. Right afterwards, my foot hurt so badly that I was home and began to cry, asking Krishna for some Tylenol to heal it.

When I was in the hospital right after the attempted homicide, I was put on so many medicines it would blow your mind. And it is now 2016 ... three years after the episode, and I am still on tons of medicines.

After the diabetes was taken to the hospitals, Krishna was ambivalent to a doctor to remove me immediately from the forced recipe of olanzapine. She explained to him that she had asked, not one doctor, not two doctors, but three different doctors to remove me from it. And all of them refused and forced me to stay on it. The unruly fact is, by doing that, those doctors almost killed me.

Now, one of the major ailments I had, that actually

did kill me, was the severe brain hemorrhaging. Let me describe what effects it had for a whole year, in the next section.

When writing this, I looked up the term "brain hemorrhage" online. This is what it said.

"WebMD site: A <u>brain hemorrhage</u> is a type of <u>stroke</u>. It's caused by an <u>artery</u> in the <u>brain</u> bursting and causing localized bleeding in the surrounding tissues. This bleeding kills <u>brain</u> cells." "What Causes Bleeding in the Brain? There are several risk factors and causes of brain hemorrhages. The most common include: Head trauma . Injury is the most common cause of bleeding in the brain for those younger than age 50." "If you exhibit any of the following symptoms, you may have a brain hemorrhage. This is a life-threatening condition, and you should call 911 or go to an emergency room immediately. The symptoms include:"

(The following portion has a circle icon before the webpage portion, followed by my itemization of what occurred surrounded by parenthesis spacing icons … like these: ().)

- A sudden severe headache: (in Loma Linda VA, from July 2014 to September 2014)

- Seizures with no previous history of seizures: (on recovery in Loma Linda, in the psychiatric ward room, while I was also having severe PTSD illusions of negative things happening to me, seeing the room move irregularly, as a result of my recovery from the brain hemorrhaging.)

- Weakness in an arm or leg: (in Loma Linda and constantly afterwards. There were leg errancies even on the disabled walkers and canes.)

- Nausea or vomiting: (A result of the poisoning from the olanzapine I was put on. Also, the ketoacidosis that almost killed me.)

- Decreased alertness; lethargy: (Loma Linda. It caused a very hard time reading and writing.)

- Changes in vision: (I had blurring to the television, intermediate glasses of different frequencies, and blurring of computer screen intermediately.)

- Tingling or numbness: (I felt it in my arms and right leg, during and after Loma Linda.)

- Difficulty speaking or understanding speech: (For 6 months after coma, Krishna told me that my speech after the coma, for 6 months, was highly irregular, incomprehensible, and confusing. Barely spoken.)

- Difficulty swallowing: (Loma Linda, eating there and some after, including the special snacks that Krishna brought to me in the VA.)

- Difficulty writing or reading: (For a long time

after, for about a year, then wrote 5 books … the *Cheetah on the Wing* series books 1 – 4, and the *Movement to the Hereafter* book.)

- Loss of fine motor skills, such as hand tremors: (There was shaking after Loma Linda.)

- Loss of coordination: (I had, and still have, difficulty walking.)

- Loss of balance: (I have right leg errors, imbalance in my right knee and foot, and my hip turns out-of-bar sometimes.)

- An abnormal sense of taste: (After awareness in July 2014, hardly any taste left and no smell whatsoever. That error has been consistent since the last three years.)

- Loss of consciousness: (Have no memory from most of November 30, 2013 to July 2014. May have gotten consciousness on recovery in Loma Linda.)

The web page also said: "How well a patient responds to a brain hemorrhage depends on the size of the hemorrhage and the amount of swelling. Some patients recover completely. Possible complications include stroke, loss of brain function, or side effects from medications or treatments. Death is possible and may quickly occur despite prompt medical treatment."

That hemorrhaging killed me. I have a memory of dying in the coma and getting sent to Heaven in the Hereafter.

When I was in the coma in the Joseph Hospital, Krishna came to Phoenix to see me. She went to a business by the VA there to see the video of me getting run over by the car. The business refused to give it to her, telling her they could not release it to the public. As far as I know, the police did not review it. I have no memory of the Phoenix police speaking to me at all.

In November 2016, I told Krishna's brother M about the refusal of the police to find the culprit on the video. He said they should have gotten permission to release it from a judge. They did not. They were in error, and did it, and the police probably did it, because they were trying to defend the off-duty police officers that attempted to murder me.

I was told by Krishna in 2016 that when I was in the coma, I was asleep the whole time and did not open my eyes. After the coma I was irate, saying crazy things, was unspoken and when I spoke it was slurred, and I did not sleep right. I said to Krishna that Paris was a witch, and that Downlow was Paris and Downlow together, which was an indicator of how Paris had made Downlow just as abusive. In 2015, Downlow sent me an email that said that we had talked about a lot of things politely, then she started to saw a lot of things irate. I think the reason was because she was defending Paris's lawless activities.

My errant speech was due to the brain hemorrhages.

I remember becoming aware and conscious in July 2014. I was in the psychological ward inside of the VA hospital in Loma Linda. The part I was in had locked doors separating it from the rest of the hospital. The part I was in, a hallway that, at the end, had stenciled on it the military POW (Prisoner of War) flag, with pictures of warriors within an enemy concentration camp surrounded by wired gun towers. I had from it immediately the impression and belief that I was a prisoner of war in a concentration camp. The reason was because of my PTSD from being a murder victim, from being sent lawlessly to prison for literally 5 ½ years, and for being abused in high school for 3 whole years.

I remember being out in the scaled-out yard, talking to a psychologist about why I was there, and I told him that I had been sent there by Satan. I still believe that. Paris is an element of Satan. So are all the people responsible for murdering me.

A few weeks later, they sent me to an open ward within the hospital.

Up until then, I had no contact with Krishna. I did not have her phone number and could not remember it. Then, one day, I went outside of my unit across the hospital to the Starbucks within. There, drinking coffee, I saw

Krishna come on board the hospital. I flagged her down and told her how much I loved her and really appreciated her. She agreed to come and visit me a lot after that.

During her visits, Krishna brought me plenty of remarkable food to eat. It was much better than the food served at the VA. She also brought me paper and a computer to write on, getting the input that it would be good for me to be able to write books about what had happened.

Writing was extremely hard. I read over what I wrote in 2014, and it was literally very intelligent, very religious, and very insane. It wasn't until 2015 before I had come around enough to begin to write the *Cheetah on the Wing* series. It was so heavy in mind that I finished all four books in just 1 year.

I had extreme difficulty walking. The staff gave me a walker, and I would spend large parts of every day attempting to walk down the hallways. It was extremely difficult. It was hard to get on the walker in the first place; I would have to move myself along the bed to get in position, which was difficult. Then, when I got the walker, I would take it very slowly out into the hallway, and start to walk, slowly, step by clumsy step, forwards. I had to rest in between each step. And it hurt.

One day, the nurses gave me a machine for my leg, that had a lever on it that stretched and bended the leg according to the frequency. At the same time, I was going to physical therapy there. In it, they would do things like have me lift weights on bars or move my hand through a machine at a certain pace or solve puzzles on draft cards. They worked a lot on having me practice walking next to hand-bars on a walkway, trying to get the steps normal. They also worked hard on my mobility on the walker. For parts of it, I would have to take a wheelchair there, when my leg was acting up.

I also had a leg brace, which I no longer wear.

When I was released, I went to the SSA with Krishna to find out why they were taking so much of my money. They told me that Paris had gone in there with false conservatorship papers, committed fraud and stole $4400.00 of my money. They said they would get it back.

They refunded me later.

Then I went to court over the conservatorship hearings. At the end of the first hearing, Downlow told me near the elevator that she had taken good care of me living with her when I was in the military. I pointed out the fact that she had actually kicked me out and made me homeless. She started to retaliate, and Krishna got irate and began to say a lot of negative things to her. Then we left.

Downlow the next hearing tried to get Krishna convicted for attempting to fight her. She failed.

She ultimately lost the hearing, when, at the deposition, I pointed out that she had tried to have the staff let me die at the Saint Joseph's Hospital. They made

Krishna the conservator. And she has been extremely positive with helping me out financially.

Now let me tell you about the lawsuit I have against the VA of Phoenix for their refusal to help me and sanctioning me as a victim to attempted homicide.

The lawsuit I have filed against that VA for what they did to me, and their refusal to help me, is for $16 million dollars. I hope it works. I died from what they did. I deserve to be paid, and treated, for that.

Since my release from the VA hospital in Loma Linda, I have been doing physical therapy at Healthpointe medical group. The physical therapist has been extremely helpful, with helping me find better means of mobility with my damaged leg.

This next, and last, chapter talks in detail about the many severe negative things that have been unlawfully done to me, what justice I deserve, and how Krishna is the most excellent and Heaven-deserving person you could imagine. And it finishes with the religious desires of God himself and what he has told me about the future.

It is deep, and distressing. Please enjoy it.

LAST CHAPTER

This is the last chapter. It shall be a total summary of all the evil things I have had to face since birth. It is heavy. Most people would not have been able to survive these things.

First, a list of what this chapter sections are all about. 1) the severe PTSD I have and where I got it, 2) the diagnosis I have of schizophrenia and where it came from, 3) the rough effects of Solitary Confinement, 4) the illegal activities of the police against me in 2005, 2012, and 2013, 5) the 18 illegal activities of the prison guards in Washington State, 6) the illegal activities of Paris, Downlow, and my ex-wife (the names have been changed for avoiding lawsuit for this book), 7) the positive aspects of Krishna, 8) my current study of religion and the Torah on Nook, 9) the Bible and Qur'an's version of after-death, per ESP.

Each section shall be separated from the next listed section by a straight line and numbered in order.

---

1)

I plead guilty in 2005 because I had severe PTSD and wanted to kill myself in prison. I had severe PTSD at the time from the extreme abuse that I had sustained as a kid, as a teenager, and as an adult from Paris. In addition, I also had gotten in the week before knowledge that my son was being abused by the so-called victim, my ex-wife, because the arresting police had refused to listen to me tell about my ex-wife's lawlessness and told lies and felonies against me to the judge, because people in the jail had told me about how the prison guards violated the law, because my so-called mother Paris was saying abusive things to me still, and because during my High School years, to escape justice for her attempted murder against my father, Paris forced me into 5 different high Schools, telling them I was mentally ill when in fact I am a genius. Those things all together gave me PTSD, as did my lawyer, Victoria Smith, saying that she had been intimidated by police and would not protect me at all. That created such severe PTSD that, at that hearing before the court, I plead guilty when the fact was that I was innocent.

I plead guilty in 2012 to the false charges put against me by Paris because I was reacting to the PTSD that I had from the abuse of Paris. I had been told as a 3-year-old by my dad's grandparents that Paris had killed my real mother, and if I spoke badly about her she would kill me too. I believed them, so all the way, until presently, in 2016, I refused to say the truth about her stringent abuses and lawbreaking. I was worried that Judge Langford would hold it against me. So, I plead guilty, when I was innocent. I was wrong about Langford. He then said I should have never gone to jail in 2012, or to prison in 2005. The reason he said that, I think, was because I had told the doctors at the Napa Mental Health Facility that they had sent me to that I had PTSD, and he probably realized that was the only reason I plead guilty when I was innocent.

Here is what I want to do in-regards-to those unjust, PTSD inspired guilty pleas. I want the ACLU to clear my record because I was innocent on both counts, both in March 2005 and 2012. I want my voting rights recovered, and my firearms license reinstated. In 2013 I was a victim of attempted homicide. If I had a firearm on me, that would not have happened. It would have saved my life. And the only reason they took away my firearms rights in Washington State was because of the lies that officer McNulty and Detective Pfaff fraudulently and with perjury and malicious prosecution told the judge. The reason I even drew my weapon on my ex-wife in the first place was because she was making the same exact motion that the targets that we had been shooting at for anti-terror exercises in the last three days had done. Even more, I did exactly as I had been trained to do for 11 years-worth of anti-terror exercises in the Special Operations Capable Unit Force Reconnaissance. If you have any doubts about that, then know this, our training in firearms combat is far more strict-and-thorough than any other military unit in the world. It is more detailed and challenging than the police's, and even the SWAT. I had the right and the duty to draw my weapon on her. She looked exactly like she was drawing a weapon on me, and I had one second to act and be prepared to shoot her in defense. One second. That is not enough time to think, to step, to move, to do anything other than present your weapon and be prepared to fire. It was a mistake, but an understandable one. I should not have been charged, with felony perjury and felony malicious prosecution, for something I had a right to do.

To go further with the errors in not letting me vote, this last election I would have voted for Hillary Clinton. She lost. Here is what the newspaper says about it. The article online is titled: *U.S. Judge Rejects Jill Stein's Bid for Pennsylvania Recount*. It states: "While there is no evidence of large-scale voting machine hacking, U.S. intelligence agencies have concluded that Russia targeted Clinton in a series of cyberattacks on Democratic Party groups. Trump has questioned those reports. He has been determined by the CIA and the FBI to have taken part in those illegal, warfare-induced hacks. He even sent a Twitter about

Russia hacking democratic emails. Trump knew and participated in their evils. U.S. presidential elections are determined not by the overall national popular vote but by the Electoral College, which awards votes based on the outcome in each state. Trump, who won a projected 306 Electoral College votes to Clinton's 232, is set to take office on Jan. 20. Clinton won the popular vote by more than 2.6 million ballots nationwide, according to the latest count." Trump is corrupt. He has said a lot of negative things about Muslims, and I, an honorably discharged Special Operations Capable USMC Veteran is not only a Muslim myself, but have had my life saved by the Muslim I live with repeatedly. Who the fuck does that lawless, crazy fool Trump think he is? He should not even be president! He didn't win the popular vote! Russia interfered, lawlessly! Yet I have no right to vote over false charges that I was innocent of? What the fuck is these people's problems?

And think about it, there has been on CNN this year multiple articles about protests and violence against the police in revenge for those police killing with firearms unarmed and innocent black men. And the disgusting courts have been letting those homicidal officers go. What the police have done to me is no different. It is evil. They have put me in prison with their lies and refused to protect me three different times for literally almost 7 years! I deserve justice against them, Goddammit!

Now let me tell you where the PTSD came from.

It actually began at youth. I was abused as a child. I was told by my father's parents that Paris had killed my real mother at birth and had taken over me, and if I said anything bad about her, she would kill me too. So, I didn't say anything about how she abused me until this year, 2016. Leading up to that, in 1988, when I was in 9th grade, she came to the house in Klamath Falls, Oregon, and packed us in the car and took us to Concord, California. On the way she told me about how she had gotten in a fight with my father, gotten in the car, and tried to run him over. I told her that was attempted homicide, and she got angry at me. Then, because she hates men, she forced me in a total of 5 different high schools in three years, abusing me the whole time. She was telling the instructors that I was "mentally ill." In actuality, I am a genius. I joined the USMC in 1992, and when I joined Force Reconnaissance in 1998. I was given an IQ test by the company psychologist, and I got 142 points correct. The psychologist told me that I was a genius with a score higher than almost everyone in that very elite, world-class best unit in the military. Thus, one should recognize that when they see the severe problems I had with the PTSD, and how severe that makes the abuse I sustained from Paris was.

Now let me tell you about the military aspect of the PTSD, which is where it really started to show up.

In 1999, when I was on my first Force Reconnaissance deployment (my third deployment overall), the Gunnery Sergeant, Mr. John Bell, told us how 7 members of 5th platoon, 1st Force Recon Company, died on a helicopter in the ocean after a crash on board the USNS Pecos. It was a training evolution on board the same vessel that we had trained on, and about a year and two months later, after the deaths, we went there to train again. It was horrible. We kept taking about what we would do if the helicopter we were on went down and crashed, what actions we would take to survive. But we knew the truth … there was nothing we could do in a crash but pray and hope to swim. We still spent the whole time on the aircraft going through emergency procedures.

Let me explain the details of this PTSD for you. It affected me seriously in the Marines. The next deployment we went on with Force Recon, on the ship outside of Kenya I broke my foot wrestling and talked the doctor into placing it in position and saying the lie that I was okay. I should have been sent home. Instead I went ashore and trained with a broken foot for anti-terror missions in Somalia. The reason I kept training was because we were on a Combat Zone deployment, and my PTSD was such that I could not allow a member of my platoon to come under fire without support.

Then we got called to Afghanistan, and on the way to Pakistan on the ocean side, I was told to run up the ramp multiple times to prove that I was okay to go into combat. I did, with a broken foot. Again, it was the

PTSD talking. I should have gotten sent home. Instead I was seen as "mission ready".

There is another form of PTSD that is known to arise from men and women in Combat Zones. I was, and I developed PTSD as a result.

Then, in 2007, I was serving an unjust prison sentence in Clallam Bay Correction Center, Washington State, and I started to show severe PTSD symptoms. They were because I had asked Paris to get my father's phone number so I could call him. A week later Downlow called me and told me that he had committed suicide. I thought that Paris had told him to do that, and I was right. How do I know? For one, I showed severe PTSD as a result, and second, because she came to visit me in unlawful Solitary Confinement in Monroe Correction Center, which they had sent me to for treatment for the PTSD, and Paris tried to talk me into committing suicide there in the prison. And I did. I tried to hang myself twice.

Now I shall go further with it. In both 2011 and 2013, I was on a religious war for God Himself against the evils of the places I had been. I was homeless at the time. Now, during that two years I was placed by the police for wrong reasons inside of mental health facilities. And not once did they do anything any of those times to cure me of PTSD, or solitary confinement.

Let me go even more into detail. In 2012 I was unjustly lied about to the police by Paris, who was trying to put me in prison over lies for 7 years. I got sent to

Napa Valley Mental Health Facility waiting for trial. I told those doctors that I had PTSD and needed help, and they did nothing for me. No treatment, no medicine, no counselling, nothing to cure it. But they told the Judge, who, at sentencing was Judge Langford, and he told me that I should not have been sent to jail in 2012, and I should not have been sent to prison in 2005. I should have been sent to a hospital. So, he was told by the doctors that I had PTSD. He still took my plea of guilty when I was innocent.

Of note, I want to tell you about one of the episodes that occurred in one of the Mental Hospitals the police took me to in either LA or San Diego. When I was released from the unlawful jail sentence I had in Yreka in 2012, I had a message sent to me by God's Angels about how they were going to take me to God's Garden when I died ... which I have memory of one year later, in 2013. Either right before that or right after, I was in that Mental Health Hospital, and there got the song on my phone, called *Hell*, by the Squirrel Nut Zippers. It went:

"In the Afterlife,
You will be headed for some serious strife,
First you make the scene all day,
But tomorrow there'll be Hell to pay!"

The song was a summary of what I was to face at the very end of time, on Judgement Day, at the end. I have been slated to, alone, to fight and defeat Satan at the end of time. And I had an image of winning. That is going to happen in either Hell, or near the borders of Hell. And when it is over, I have been slated by God to go and create in a parallel universe my own universe, from nothing. The summary of those visions and events has articulated the PTSD I have, by making my visions even more religious for preparation of that.

Let me give you a list of the places that failed to treat my PTSD. Four hospitals in Seattle, LA, and San Diego. Napa Valley. Joseph's Hospital in Phoenix, Arizona for the PTSD and severe brain hemorrhaging I had from the attempted homicide I survived. The Loma Linda VA Hospital in California, for the same thing. And the San Diego VA for failing to treat me for the solitary confinement when it almost killed me there from the hunger-strike I was on. Franky put, I HAVE HAD PTSD FROM THE MILITARY FOR AT LEAST 17 YEARS, AND NOT ONCE, *NOT ONCE HAVE I BEEN TREATED BY ANYONE!*

Goddammit! It is becoming serious now. More than ever! We went to go see Hacksaw Ridge the other day, a war movie, and it was so realistic and so upsetting that I wept the entire time, thinking over and over and over again about how those 7 Marines died on the helo. Fuck, man, I am in a coffee shop and I am crying right now just writing this. Fuck! I have been crying on and off writing this whole story, because it is so atrocious that it would have killed almost anyone that has had to go though it!

---

2)

The diagnosis of schizophrenia and where it came from.

First off, I have been diagnosed as having schizophrenia from the San Diego VA in 2009 after I was released from solitary confinement in prison. Let me explain the errors, really quick here. For one, Paris was present during my time there. Paris had accused my father of being schizophrenic severely during his parenthood. I never once saw any signs of it. And Paris was so abusive to her second husband, the father of my younger sister, that he refused to see her for years all the way until she was old enough to graduate from High School. Now, I have no doubt that Paris had told the VA while I was there that I was schizophrenic. *I was not.* What I was showing was proof of the permanent mental disability that is a part of the unhuman aspects of solitary confinement, which I was in unlawfully for a year and a half.

Second, solitary confinement has the effects as put on the online newspaper titled *The Horrible Psychology of Solitary Confinement*. It tells, in accurate detail, what the symptoms of it are. If you read it, you will see in plain terms how a person with permanent disability due to solitary confinement can be misunderstood as having schizophrenia. They seem the same. They are not.

Finally, I am a genius with intelligent that is higher than virtually everyone in this country. It is probably as high as geniuses like Stephen Hawking. When I speak what I know to psychologists, I am probably a lot smarter than they are, mathematically, so the things I talk about they may very well not understand. And instead of itemizing themselves as ignorant, which they are, they instead listen to my abusive so-called mother and think I'm schizophrenic ... which I am not. Let me give you an example.

I read a lot of Michio Kaku, the man who invested the very divine Superstring Theory. One of the theories of that, that educated scientists think is very plausible, is the concept of time travel. When wormholes are invented, which many scientists think will happen, then a person is ruled to be able to travel either forwards in time, to the future, as expected, or ever to the past, which seems surreal, but it is identified as factual by scientists of today's high-tech age.

Another thing I have discussed that psychologists have dismissed as "mental illness" is the scientifically acceptable concept – see the TV program by Steven Hawking supporting it – that there exist such things as parallel universes that flow next to ours but have different rules. And by those rules, then in a parallel universe, the proclivity to such "mythological beasts" – like unicorns, for example – actually exist. They are real, in a parallel universe with some ... not all ... just some of our rules.

So, I have bene diagnosed wrongly as schizophrenic. I am a victim of lawless solitary confinement. Read the article and you will see it makes sense.

---

3)

The rough effect of solitary confinement.

Solitary confinement is being placed in a single person prison cell for literally 23 out of 24 hours per day. The staff offered me no PTSD support and even told me I was lying when I told them the mental problems I was having. Those fucks. And they refused to bring me my legal papers, my college books, my property, or even store items. I was left to nothing but a Bible and a Qur'an to read as other mentally disturbed criminal inmates said all sorts of crazy things through the walls and doors, every day, all day, and night long. It was obtrusive and gave one, eventually, disturbing and crazy thoughts. Criminal thoughts. Evil thoughts. Anything to get rid of the noise and abuse one had to live though. And I had to deal with that every single day, without any break, nonstop for a whole year and a half.

The reason they put me there was because the prison guard, on the way to Monroe, pulled over to a gas station restroom for me to urinate, and while I was next to the toilet, he threatened to assault me for no reason. So, I did what a PTSD victim does when he has Special Operations Capable training and is threatened with illegal violence, and I turned around and shoved him against the wall. I got knocked over and his partner pointed a pistol at me, threatening to kill me.

Those despicable officers at Monroe told the lie that I had tried to escape, so they unlawfully, for a lie, put me in solitary confinement. And when I was in there, having severe mental problems from the extreme PTSD, they fabricated lies on documents to keep me there even longer. At the end of my sentence, they had me see a psychologist that tried to get me to tell him about me inventing fights with innocent people, and even criminals, to force me to stay there even longer.

I despise the prison staff in Washington State. I have a list in this book of how they violated the law 18 different ways against me in the nearly 5 years I was there. And the solitary confinement is torture. That is a violation of the 8th Constitutional Amendment. The judge that put me there, Kessler, violated my 8th constitutional right on three different counts. That torture caused mental damage that had so far lasted 12 years straight. He deserves a prison sentence for that for at LEAST that long.

---

4)

The illegal activities of the police against me in 2005, 2012, and 2013.

Here is a copy of what is written on page 33 of this book. It states:

"It gets even worse than that. Let me describe what lies Officer McNulty and Detective Pfaff conducted against me, with their letter of felony lies, felony perjury and felony malicious prosecution they conducted against me.

Pfaff wrote a *Certification for Determination of Probable Cause* against me to Judge Kessler. In it she wrote the lie: "(My ex-wife's name) was shoved to the floor." The fact was that if I had done that, I would have taken my hand off the pistol against what I had learned through strenuous anti-terror exercises in Force Recon. She also wrote the lie: "Mitchell took a few fast steps towards (my ex-wife's name), grabbed her by the hair and slammed her against the French Doors." Again, that did not happen! A person has only one second to respond to the concept of someone drawing a weapon on them. There is no time to take a few fast steps anywhere, and again, we were trained to never, ever take a hand off the weapon and grab someone by the hair. That is totally in error.

The fact that those officers would make such novice, stupid mistakes with their taking on of what actually occurred is proof of their total ignorance and incapability to fight a firefight with anyone. They did the same stupid mistakes as done by cops talked about on CNN in 2016, who were from police behaving like those of Cleveland, Chicago, Baton Rouge, Ferguson, who killed innocent, unarmed black men by gunshot. And they were found innocent in the courtrooms even when proven guilty. That is the same sort of stupid error that those despicable officers, McNulty and Pfaff, did, by lying and maliciously prosecuting me to the judge."

That came after I had, on the night of arrest in March 2005, I had called my ex-wife and Officer McNulty answered the phone. I told him about how my ex-wife had committed crimes against me, how she had her fiancée list himself wrongly as my son's father while illegally restricting me from his documents at his daycare, and how she had gone before the Sergeant Major of Force Recon during my deployment and tried to get me fired for a "high profile assault" that had never happened. I told McNulty that it had never happened, and I was not kicked out.

McNulty and Pfaff instead chose to listen to my ex-wife's lies and wrote the perjury on the letter to the judge that I "had been kicked out of my Force Recon unit for a High-Profile Assault against (my ex-wife)." It was a flat out lie!

Let me describe the rest of the lies and lawbreaking that occurred at that first hearing, on around 22 March, a week after I bailed out. This will blow your mind that the justice system would do this to an innocent veteran of Special Operations Capable Force Recon.

About three 8th Constitutional Amendment violations by Judge Kessler. They are:

1) he raised bail so high after I had bailed out that I couldn't afford it. I had bailed out after I was arrested for

$150,000, all the money I had. He raised it to $500,000, beyond my ability to pay. It was in violation of the 8th Constitutional Amendment, which reads: it "prohibits the <u>federal government</u> from imposing <u>excessive bail</u> ..." He deserves to be sued for millions of dollars for that.

2) January 2007 at Clallam Bay, my ex-wife gets DCS or DSHS to violate prison rules on sending them my money, they take 100% of it illegally. I complained and they ignored me. I wrote to the King County Prosecutor about it and he did nothing. Then Clallam Bay stole library books from my cell in 2007 and tried to steal from me by forcing me to pay $1140 for one book. That is also a violation of the 8th Amendment. I had no money literally from January 2007 to September 2009. The 8th Constitutional Amendment states: it prohibits "excessive fines ..."

3) I was lawlessly put into solitary confinement in 2007, which is torture and a violation of the 8th Constitutional Amendment, which prohibits "cruel and unusual punishment." In *Furman v. Georgia*, <u>408 U.S. 238</u> (1972), <u>Justice Brennan</u> wrote, "There are, then, four principles by which we may determine whether a particular punishment is 'cruel and unusual'." ""The "essential predicate" is "that a punishment must not by its severity be degrading to human dignity," especially <u>torture</u>."" I was in there for a year and a half. It gave me permanent head trauma and brain injury that has been significant all the way to 2017. That is 12 years-worth of

trauma from the three violations of my 8th Constitutional Amendment right. What I experienced, and what is put forth in the online article *The Horrible Psychology of Solitary Confinement*, is that it is, in fact, severe torture.

Kessler deserves to be: 1) sued for millions of dollars for the fiscal injuries, 2) fined for the bail injury, which is $500,000 when I had to forfeit literally $150,000 paid, 3) a prison sentence for the torture at least as long as the damage he has caused me ... 12 years, 4) in addition, a prison sentence as long as mine was, because he did those violations per the lawless orders of the prosecutor Scott A. Marlow, and Seattle Detective Pfaff and Seattle Officer McNulty, 5) in addition, a prison sentence as long as mine for me pleading guilty to a violation of my PTSD from military injuries, because I was suicidal from the abuse I had been getting from the justice system, and 6) when I was arrested, I was a member of the protection agency in war zones called Triple Canopy. The payment was $105,000.00 per year. Because I was unlawfully arrested and given severe mental disability from being tortured in the prisons, I faced mental disability and no ability to work for them, or at all, for 12 years. That, at $105,000.00 per year, plus the $150,000.00 bail money I lost to their illegal ruling, cost me about $1,500,000.00. That is one million, five hundred thousand dollars. Kessler, and each and every single justice system official who broke the laws against me during that time owe me that ... each one of them does. ACLU, I want you to get it from them.

Oh note, right before the fiscal assault against me taking all my funds in January 2007, I had participated in a court hearing with my ex-wife on the phone in the courtroom of Judge Steven Gonzales. Gonzales listened to my ex-wife's lies about me holding her at gunpoint for, she said, 10 minutes, when the fact was that I had only done it literally for about a minute and a half, then apologized. Gonzales wrote a bunch of lies at the end of his statement, refusing to let me visit my son or have any remedies. And then, about a week later, DCS steals all my funds illegally from the prison? That was at my ex-wife's lawless request, that they listened to, and Gonzales probably took part in it. If he did, Gonzales deserves to be fired and sued for violating my 8th Constitutional Amendment right. He deserves to be fired anyways, for holding my ex-wife's lies against me and refusing to let me see my son.

My attorney Victoria Smith violated me by going to Kessler's hearing and doing nothing to defend me. She went there when they violate my right to attend the hearing and kept me out while she attended. Then she forced me to plead guilty when I was innocent, saying I would get a 15-year sentence with her refusal to protect me. Why? Because she said that Kessler and the Seattle police had intimidated her. She got fired from the BAR in 2012 for failure to protect clients. She deserves a sentence as long as Kessler's.

The prosecutor Scott A. Marlow deserves a prison sentence for his refusal to obey the law. He used my legitimate complaint against my ex-wife's and Small Face's Lynn Ingraham's lawlessness against me, instead of bringing me justice for it. And he lied on the record, stating that there was no way for me to bring a pistol on the aircraft, when that was exactly the way I got it there! He was trying to fabricate a reason to try me farther. It was his lawless request to increase bail beyond my 8th Constitutional Amendment, that Kessler listened to.

Lawsuit against Lynn Ingraham. Small Faces violated their own policy by refusing to give me my son's records. They concealed my ex-wife's lawless request to put her fiancé as my son's father on his records, when I had identified myself as his father. Then, after I was getting my son, Ingraham went on top of the stairs and said some feisty things to me, I don't remember what, but they were highly negative. If I remember right, she wanted me to stay there during the day at the daycare because she thought I was abusive, my ex-wife's lie. Then, after I was arrested, Ingraham wrote a false statement about the day of the event, March 17, that said that I had tried to "kidnap my son" by putting him in the car without signing him out. She gave those lies to the court. I think it was her revenge about me telling little M about how the teachers were evil and I was sorry my ex-wife was abusing him, and I was going to kill myself. The effects of her letter to the court was shown to me by Victoria Smith after the first hearing, so she probably got it from Kessler, and Kessler probably used it as justification to take my son away from me forever. And because of those abuses, I have not seen my son for the last 12 years. That was when I was never abusive, and I didn't even spank him except for one time when he was 5 during the whole 5-years I had him. I want Lynn Ingraham sued for literally hundreds of thousands of dollars, at a minimum. She deserves to be fired forever. And if what she wrote was breaking the law, then she deserves prison.

I was placed in prison for almost 5 years when I was innocent. Upon release, I have been able to see the proof that they were lying. It is in my military records. I received two good conduct awards that I would not have received if I had been kicked out of that unit, or any unit, for that matter. I also received my separation papers that illustrate that I was at Force Recon required courses during the time they said I was kicked out, which would not have happened. And my fitness report for 2002 states plainly that I was seen as one of the most excellent Marines in the Force Recon Company at that time. If I had been kicked out, would I have received that? Absolutely not! And if I had violated any other things put forth in the lies by Pfaff and McNulty, then I would have gotten kicked out of the Anti-Terrorist course, not given a stellar fitness report by the commander of the company that said I was one of the best Marines around.

McNulty and Pfaff committed felony perjury and felony malicious prosecution against me, when I was innocent. Judge Kessler violated my 8th Constitutional

Right on three different counts. The prosecutor rejected my actual complaint on the phone about my ex-wife's lawlessness, and he used it against me! What the fuck is his problem? Every single one of those mentioned that unlawfully sent me to prison to be tortured by violating my rights deserves to be sent to prison for the next 12 fucking years ... minimum!

The lawlessness of the Seattle police goes into even more detail than that. I found out, online, reading the article called ar15.com website, *Kerlikowske in the news again*, stated the following:

The same day as my unfortunate lawful accident, March 17, 2005, Seattle police officer Penelope Fulmer threatened to kill and fired her weapon at a lawful, unarmed homeless man. That was nothing other than attempted murder. She lied to the internal investigator on the issue, who could tell she was lying, and said it was accidental. It was not. Then, Chief Kerlikowske heard her and sentenced her to only 15 days without pay for it. 15 days without pay for attempted murder. The court let her go free without charges.

Now compare that to me thinking a woman was drawing a weapon on me, and me, with only one second to react, did what I had trained to do in an anti-terror Special Operations Capable unit for more than four years straight, and spent one second drawing my pistol on her, prepared to defend myself. One second. I fired no shots and apologized. And their officers lied on their Determination of Probable Cause letter to the judge to commit felony perjury and felony malicious prosecution against me. They did that to threaten to send me to prison, when I was innocent, for 15 years.

And they let a lying, homicidal cop go free with only a 15 day suspension.

I am thinking that McNulty and Pfaff both probably had a head's up of what Fulmer had done, and Kerlikowske probably told them to file false charges against me to distract from justice against her. What the fuck is those Seattle police's problems?

Now let me tell you about the idiot police officer that put me in prison in 2012 for 9 months when I was innocent.

What happened was that Paris started to yell at me in the living room one morning. She tried to forcibly give me money that I didn't want. I got up to avoid her and began to walk to the front door to leave. She got angry and hit me hard in the back of the head with a frying pan, making me bleed from the wound. I immediately did what I was trained to do, and in self-defense pushed her against the wall and told her to stop because I was leaving. Then I left.

She called the cops on me telling them lies. When the cop arrived to arrest me, I told him I was innocent and wanted him to take a proof of that photo of my bleeding head. He refused. Then, later, in court before

Judge Langford, he lied about what had happened. I don't remember how, but I do remember that he refused to say I wanted proof of my innocence in a photo ... and my head WAS bleeding ... and I immediately got pissed off and started to yell at him. Judge Langford had me kicked out of the courtroom for that.

I went to prison for 9 months and, because of the PTSD, plead guilty when I was innocent of a crime I didn't commit.

ACLU, I want you to take this before Judge Langford at the Yreka courtroom and make it clear to him why I have severe PTSD, and why they need to find me innocent and replace my record with innocence. And they can do it for the Seattle justice system as well. Why? Because I want you to put, at a minimum, McNulty, Pfaff, Kessler, and Scott the prosecutor in prison for their lawlessness against me for 12 years, minimum. If they get recovered inside of prison for that long, and start to act holy, then I may forgive them. If they do not, and go free with their crimes, then when I die, know this ... I have been told by God to go aboard the Ark of the Covenant when I die, and when I'm in the Hereafter, to use my knowledge of ESP to read the minds of the souls of the people. And if you do not get punishment, then know this ... I have been selected by God himself to send your asses, or their asses, to Hell, to burn, FOREVER. SO ... CHOOSE.

Now, let me tell you about the worst effect. In 2013, I was a victim of attempted homicide. What happened, per my memory, is that my ex-wife, Paris, and Downlow went to Phoenix, Arizona when I was there at the VA. They requested that two off-duty cops assault and attempt to kill me. I was severely injured and placed in the hospital for 11 months. Two of those months I was in a coma. And I have a memory of dying in that coma. When I died, I was taken in the Hereafter to God's Garden, and was met by two Angels of the future and one Angel of Death. They told me about how I was to go, when I die, aboard the Ark of the Covenant and judge people with ESP to have earned either Heaven or Hell. That is their judgement for Judgement Day.

Krishna, when I was in a coma, went to businesses near the VA when I was dropped near death out of a truck or van and asked them to view their videotapes. The tapes likely have proof of who did it. They didn't concede to that, saying they could not release those videos to the public. Now, what they should have said was that they needed a judge's order to do it. Instead, they avoided the issue. And I have no memory of the police of Phoenix asking me anything about who did it. Why? Because they probably know who did it, and don't want off-duty police officers to be found guilty of attempted murder!

What the fuck is your problem, Phoenix police? I risked my life to defend you for 11 years! I fought a war for God homeless to protect you against evils for two fucking years! I risked my life for you! And what do you do? You protect the biggest sin of them all held against me from being held accountable for it? WHAT IS YOUR FUCKING PROBLEM, PHOENIX POLICE! WHAT THE HELL IS YOUR PROBLEM?

I have been gifted by God to find out who is responsible for that. And I will. And rest assured, I will be sending them to Hell for what they did to me. The same goes for Paris, Downlow, and my ex-wife. They are all going to Hell for killing me. Killing me twice. I also almost died in October 2016 from the diabetic ketoacidosis that I went through from it. They are going to pay the price for that.

The very last chapter of this book is about my Movement to the Hereafter with three of God's Angels.

---

5)

The illegal activities of the Washington State prison guards and staff members.

I have listed a full 18 item summary of their lawlessness in this book. They are coupled here.

1. Destroyed or stole my legal papers repeatedly,

2. Found me guilty of infractions that their staff created for the purpose of unlawfully punishing innocent men, and I complained about it to the runner of the prison, who showed up as I was about to be transferred

to Clallam Bay, and she said nothing to me: she very likely lied to the officers while she was ignoring me and sentencing me for an infraction I didn't do. That is one incident of multiple happenings,

3. Threatened me,

4. Tried to force me – a Genius with an IQ of 142 questions right – into going to GED class, when I have a High School diploma, then refusing to allow me to do college work,

5. Forcing me into classes that were obstructive of me moving forwards with my education,

6. Took my property with legal papers, art materials for my son, letter writing ability; they took it away from me and never gave it back ... which is illegal; and I had no funds and no way to replace any of those products for literally two and a half years. I was unable to even get a snack. That had not happened to any other inmate, and the inmates who saw it happening said "those officers have given you a "Death Sentence"". The people who did it were either DCS or DSHS at my abusive ex-wife's request.

7. I complained to the Authorities of Property about the loss of my property, and those vindictive fools tried to lie to me and tell me that no such property existed,

8. With no college books in my possession and no money after the stealing of my property, I began to get books from the library. Then one day the staff put me into solitary confinement based on what members of

the gangs were doing (a flat out lie), and while I was there, the officers went into my cell and took all of my library books. They did not give the library books back, no matter how much I complained. Then I went to the library and tried to check out a book, and they didn't give me a book ... they gave me a bill, that said I owed them $1140.00 for one of the books that, like the other books, wasn't returned. What does that prove? It proves that the staff were working together to steal library books and force funds from me that they were not entitled to. The bill was illegal, and they deserve to get sentenced for what they did ... stealing my library books, taking away my ability to read and go to college, and falsely billing me for their thievery.

9. I was called a "Terrorist" by a McNeil Island Captain, in response to my complaint about the staff doing illegal things, when the fact is that I am an honorably discharged hero who trained against terrorists at a level far above those disgusting pigs. It happened after the manager that I had sent the complaint to came down to my cell and ignored me, for the purpose of lying to the officers and telling them the lie that I wouldn't talk to her. The Captain of McNeil was probably the one who called Clallam Bay and told them to treat me like a terrorist. Then he drew me to his office and called me a terrorist himself! So, what did they do at Clallam Bay? Laughing at me, they placed me into a cell with an inmate who had put a Qur'an on my desk and told me that if I read or moved it, he would assault me. I went

and spoke to the manager of the unit I was in, and that prick got hostile and tried to start a fight between me and his officer. They moved me to a cell directly on the same side of the counsellor's office, which made it so that when she made me go to court inside her office, the inmates saw me at her desk during the trial. They thought I was ratting them out and threatened to beat me. That whole episode was done by a lot of evil officers who were trying to force me to be beaten when I didn't deserve it ... all in order to prevent me from explaining to the upper staff the lawbreaking they were doing. Every one of those pricks deserves to be sent to prison for what they did!

10. I was forced into a staff member's office to attend a hearing against my ex that was open by a window to the living area of the inmates - and the inmates who witnessed it thought I was ratting them out and threatened me ... both things that the disgusting staff member should have known,

11. I was told over the phone that my father David had committed suicide, and the prison staff tried to talk me into fighting them by saying it was something I deserved,

12. About a month later was sent to another prison, where they put me into solitary confinement for nearly a year and a half; what the press has said about Solitary Confinement is that it causes mental injury within the inmate forced into that sentence, a permanent one,

13. There Paris tried to talk me into attempting suicide, because that is likely what she had done to David,

14. One day a group of officers hit me with tear gas, then, walking me over to the medical unit, one of them gave directions to the other to push me into the floor: so he did and hit my head on the concrete so badly that it caused my head to bleed: the doctors tried to give me an X-Ray and the staff that did that tried to talk me into moving my head so that the X-Ray wouldn't work,

15. The psychologists and staff members of that prison wrote false reports about me, saying unlawfully that I had said things like "assaulting officers" when I said no such thing,

16. I was spoken to poorly by the psychologists, who gave me no assistance with finding a better avenue with thought. I had serious PTSD, and those despicable officers refused to help me cure at all. That is what they do to inmates within solitary confinement: they provoke and beat them, deny them their property, let them move elsewhere for only one hour out of the 23 hours forced to stay in the cell, they make fun of the inmates who speak out erroneous speech all day long, 24 hours per day, all day long, in such a prominence that it obstructs other inmate's ability to think or feel positive or think of something positive to say. Solitary confinement is such a horrible avenue of torture that the despicable guards who make it happen deserve to be placed inside cells like those forever, and never allowed to leave!

17. On my day of release, they directed me to speak to a psychologist who tried in depth to talk me into stating

the desire to assault a member of the grocery store who was threatening me; they were trying to invent a reason to keep me in prison past my release date, and I am sure that it was in retaliation for me calling for them to be held accountable for me complaining about them breaking the law, when the fact was that they were guilty and deserving punishment!

18. The day after release, I was sent to the VA hospital in San Diego for the purpose of having surgery on my stomach after the deep and long hunger-strike I had been on in prison. It nearly killed me, and I was put into the VA hospital for about a month to recover from it. I was also severely mentally ill from the unlawful solitary confinement they had me on.

That concludes what they did. I want the ACLU to use whatever means necessary to find out who the guilty parties are of those offenses, who tortured me unjustly, after I had spent 11 years putting my life on the line to protect them, and a) sue them, for a lot, b) find them guilty of their crimes in court, and c) put there asses in prison for the same 12 years that there unjust prison effect gave me mental damage!

6)

The illegal activities of Paris, Downlow, and my ex-wife (the names have been changed her to avoid lawsuit for this book).

In December 2016, I started to talk to Krishna about the PTSD and the negative things that Paris has done. We were in the car driving. At the exact same time, the song *Hotel California* by the Eagles came on, and it is about people getting swept under Satan. That was a sign from God that Paris is an agent of Satan.

I asked *The Brain That Changes Itself* book if Paris, Downlow, and my ex-wife were witnesses and requested the attempted homicide against me on Nov 29 or 30 2013. The first time I checked, the random spot with my finger was on the word "evidence" in notes. The second time it answered: ""That's the way the ball bounces." She said it meant "That's the way things are."" The third time I asked it, it answered "yes" and "pornography". That is because I was sexually abused.

Those three elements and searches are proof that they requested the attempted homicide against me. Also, I have ESP. I know this from my religious experience. Angels are talking to me. I know this because I have asked books over 100 questions in the last year, and every time the answers are accurate. That is the ESP of Angels. And I have a lot of religious experience.

To find the evidence of these three being in Phoenix on November 29/30 2013, the following should be looked at: credit card receipts, airline tickets, rental cars, hotel receipts, food receipts, gas station receipts, the Phoenix VA itself, online email receipts, computer wi-fi access info or access info, phone calls to each other or to elements in

Phoenix, ATM account records, bank receipts. Some of those elements will be proof that they were there. I very strongly doubt that they were able to keep those secret.

The illegal things Paris did

She attempted to kill my father in 1988, talked my father into suicide in 2007, tried to talk me into suicide in 2008, attempted to escape justice for my father's survival of her attempted murder by sending us to Concord California, trying to make me drop out of High School 5 different transfers in three years, telling Downlow to assault me in the tree when I was 12, Then in 2009 during Christmas trying to tell that story to Downlow's daughter to make her abusive to her son, refusing to take court documents to court hearing when I was in prison for visitation with little M, pressing fraudulent charges against me to the Yreka police and sending me to jail for 9 months when I was innocent, requesting 7 year sentence from prosecutor, violating 2012 no-contact order by: Requesting attempted murder in Nov. 2013, do-not-resuscitate at St. Joseph's in Phoenix, file false conservatorship papers during fraud at SSA stealing $4400.00 of my money, visiting and saying lies to the VA staff in Loma Linda in 2014, requesting Downlow go to conservatorship hearing so she can get money from the lawsuit against the VA, as it said in the Phoenix Newspaper.

Those crimes are, and some not listed, are: felony attempted murder against my father, felony promotion of suicide to me and my father (two counts), harassment, encouraging assault, abusing children, sexual abuse, filing false criminal charges, violating the 8th constitutional amendment by seeing additional punishment than is necessary, violating court access, fraud, attempted murder against me, requesting hospital do-not -resuscitate to avoid justice for attempted murder, theft, and attempt at theft. Those are a lot of crimes. She deserves prison for life for those.

The illegal things that my ex-wife did

Steal money from me when we were divorcing, try to create sanctions against me through the DCS/DSHS, tried to get me fired from Force Recon in 2001/2002 deployment by telling the Sergeant Major the lie that I had high-profile assaulted her – they did not kick me out, abusing my son little M, accusing me of cheating when I wasn't, in March 2005 telling McNulty and Pfaff lies about what happened and they believed her over my truths, she tells them the lie that she had succeeded at getting me kicked out of Force Recon and they put it on the lie letter to the judge, when I was in Clallam Bay she gets DCS to take 100% of my money illegally, we go to court in 2006 December and she lies to the judge about how long I was in their house and what happened and he believes her, then in Nov 29/30 2013 she was present and requested lethal off-duty cop attempted homicide against me in the coffee shop.

Those crimes are, and some not listed here, are: theft, lying to my command, applying for false sanctions, lying to my command about a crime that did not happen to get me fired, abuse of a child, harassment, lying to the police, pressing false charges, stealing money through DSHS or DCS, lying to the judge during a hearing – perjury and felony harassment, attempted homicide. Those are serious, and she deserves to be put in prison for life for those.

The illegal things that Downlow did

Trying to beat me when I was 12 in the tree, getting encouraged to do it by Paris, told about it to make her daughter abusive in 2009 Christmas by Paris, kicked me out of her house homeless after I returned from Force Recon deployment, telling me the lie that Krishna is a terrorist and that she had talked to the Attorney General about it, telling lies to the Phoenix news about me attacking police and carrying a weapon, asking for and attempting murder in 2013, refusal to be in contact with me at the Loma Linda VA, trying to make me a do-not-resuscitate at the Saint Joseph's hospital in Phoenix, protecting Paris's fraud through the SSA over the phone in 2014, taking me to court for the conservatorship hearing at Paris's request to get the millions of dollars from the lawsuit against the VA

Those crimes are, and some not listed here, are: assault, encouraging assault, abusing children, creating homelessness, lying about terrorism – harassment, lying to the police and news, attempted murder, attempt to eliminate charges for attempted murder, unlawfully requesting a do-not-resuscitate to make me die and avoid charges for attempted homicide, protecting fraud, attempt to take court funds by creating false court papers. Those are serious. And she deserves prison for the rest of her life for doing them.

Let me make this clear to you, ACLU, and I want it used in the investigation for the attempted homicide against me in 2013. I have a memory of Paris, Downlow, and my ex-wife requesting it from off-duty police officers. The reason I am certain that happened, is for one, my memory is very realistic and bright. I firmly remember it.

And the cause ... My ex-wife, in 2005, lied to the police and pressed charges based on lies about me. Then she stole much money from me illegally through the prison system. In addition, she requested that DCS take away my vehicle license for lies. She was in-touch with Paris when I was in prison, and I think she was part of the reason why Paris and Downlow would not tell me where my father was buried. If my memory of November 29 and 30, 2013 is correct, then I remember going to the coffee shop late at night and my ex-wife saying to two off-duty police officers repeatedly "do it! Do it!" In other words, to go ahead and murder me, at her request. And as she said it, I have a distinct memory of one of those officers taking a jimmy and hitting me so hard in the head 6 times that he broke my skull. My memories after that are proof of the conduct of cerebral hemorrhaging that I was getting.

Then there is Paris. She attempted to murder my father in 1988. She later talked him into committing suicide. She tried to talk me into suicide. Then, in 2012, she tried to press false charges against me and put me in prison for 7 years when I was guilty of nothing more than self-defense against her assault against me that hurt nobody. Her being present for the 2013 attempted homicide was because she was angry about my freedom and chose to violate the Judge Langford's no-contact-order from 2012. So, she was not only guilty in 2013 of attempted murder, she was also in violation of a no-contact-order multiple times… which is another crime. That is also a reason why it is very likely that she also asked the off-duty police to kill me.

Then there is what Downlow did. For one, when I was 12, she assaulted me with a nightstick. Then, after the attempted homicide I survived, in 2015 I got a newspaper article from the Phoenix news about how I am suing the VA there for millions of dollars. The article states that Downlow had told the police the lies, on record, that I had "assaulted an officer" – which has never happened – and that I was "carrying a weapon" – which was also a lie. She said those things to the police to turn them against me, probably at my ex-wife's request, for no good reason. Thus, her doing those negative things is evidence that she likely told the off-duty officers in 2013 that I was a "threat to them" and that they "needed to protect themselves". In addition, she probably told them that I was a felon, to really get their goats. That made them decide to kill me, at their request, in 2013.

And they did. I remember dying in the hospital, in the coma, and getting sent to God's Garden.

All three of them deserve prison sentences for attempted murder, even all their criminal activities, for life without parole.

---

7)

The positive aspects of Krishna.

For Christmas, Krishna bought me a fedora hat and suit jacket, telling me to wear them to look like an author. I did, and the people I have interacted with seem to really appreciate it. Then there was another guy who opened the door for me to walk out of with my walker. He said very pleasant things to me and said: "have a good day!"

Krishna is highly religious and respects my religious beliefs. She also respects me as a person. And she helps me out a lot. For example, the totality of money I make right now is Social Security money, a very small amount, and some $200 per month disability. She buys for me groceries, food to eat out, coffee, expresso, tea, clothes. She buys me way more than I can afford. It is because she is also a veteran of the USMC, and she appreciates my service.

She also lets me live here in her house for free, with no rent, which saves me enough for coffee while I write every day and to eat out.

I also have enough money to be able to buy enough books. I am actually about 5 books ahead right now. It takes time to read, because I am in the process of writing my 5th book right now.

Krishna goes above and beyond her call of duty. She is extremely helpful and supportive. She calls me a hero daily. And she has agreed to read this portion of the book so she can get a solid foundation of the evils I have had to face over and over and over again for so long. She is going to help me get justice. That is why she agrees that I should send this to my attorney and get his point of view.

---

8)

My current study of religion and the Torah on Nook

I purchased a Nook book of the Tanach, the Hebrew Bible. In addition, when we were at the Loma Linda VA earlier last month, I met a religious veteran there who liked my name and said that the name Krautant is Israeli. I looked online and went to a website of Hebrew names. So, he was right! I am a combination of Jewish, Christian, and Muslim. All three are real religions, I have found, with the same God, or Allah, or Jehovah, whichever name you choose, they are all to the same being, who speaks in different languages to different people for the same purpose!

9)

The Bible and Qur'an's version of after-death, per ESP.

(Krishna thinks I shouldn't write this because people will think I am crazy.) I asked the Bible on a random page what is going to happen to me since I am an Angel; it said that I was going to be made, like Jesus, to sit at God's right hand as a Son of God in Divine rulership as king over the people. I asked if that was true, and the Bible said, in *Daniel 7, 13* "I saw someone like a son of man coming with the clouds of Heaven … His rule is eternal – it will never end. His kingdom will never be destroyed."

So it is that, according to God and his Angels, after I die, I am to be put in a role of rulership to pay me off for my good deeds. The very many evils I have had to face, which would have killed many people, they were so thick with evil for so long, has been a lot, and it will be good when it is over. That is why I feel a need to start bringing justice down against those people who did evil things to me.

I hate the police. I hate the prison staff. And I hate all the attempted murderers. Those people put me under false prison sentences for 6 years when I was innocent. Then add to that the two years that I was fighting the war for God against evils for them. That is another two years of hell. Total, 8 years. Then there is the year I was in the hospital for attempted murder. That is 9 years. Then there are the three years that I was abused in High

School. That is 12 years. Then there is the whole time that I was abused by Paris, Downlow, and my ex-wife. That time is almost a total of 40 years.

That is fucking horrible, man. There is a reason why I cry so much from the PTSD I have. It is severe now. I need help. I need justice. Help.

Please charge me what you think is necessary to review this and give me legal advice, as you see fit. Please let me know what you think.

Now, this chapter is named the Final Chapter – but it is not the final chapter. When I was proofreading over it, it came to my attention that I haven't really written anything about when I died in the coma in 2013 and got taken to the Hereafter by God's Angels. Whole books have been written about that. So, I will add a chapter in this book about it.

And that will finalize this book! Enjoy!

CHAPTER 13

MOVEMENT TO THE HEREAFTER

What was it like for me to die in the coma in 2013?

I have a memory of it – even though I was in a coma and was after recovery unconscious for a total of 8 months in the hospitals. But I have a memory of dying and going to the Hereafter. With Angels. Even though the Angels told me that it was to be kept "Secret" and only used for special circumstances.

And it has given me Special Powers. I shall describe them herein.

My memory is interrupted, from the brain damage that I had in this life: compared to the elegant - but Secret - memories I have of being dead and within the Hereafter. I don't have a good memory of dying - because it is subliminal. But I DO have a good memory of flying in the sky instantaneously from the hospital in Phoenix (that I was in a coma and died in), to Huntington Gardens in California. That portion of my mind is accurate, because it occurred within the precision of a good memory of a person who was dead and within the elegant universes of the religious Hereafter.

I flew instantaneously through the atmosphere. I have a vision of the earth flowing rapidly and a long way away beneath me. Then I have an image of landing in a standing position suddenly by a bridge over a river next to the Japanese House within the Huntington Gardens. I looked to my side, along a concrete walkway with stairs on it at a table there. And there were three of Gods Angels standing there, with their hands up in a greeting of "Welcome!" I sat down on a bench. Two of the Angels sat down on the other side of the table. The third Angel stood next to the table, between us.

"I am the Archangel Michael", said the man sitting next to me. "I am the Archangel Gabrielle", said the female Angel sitting down. And the Indian-looking Archangel who was standing pronounced that he was: "The Angel of Death ... named Ariel." I knew from my subliminal mind that Ariel was responsible for me being dead then … (and I didn't know that she was going to bring me back to life: which she was!)

The Angels then told me some details about the Hereafter. Details like the fact that I was Dead and was instantly teleported there by a mysterious force in the universes that moves the Soul of a dead person to a special place called the Hereafter, (or the Afterlife by some religions). There, they are brought to the realization of the Fact that they have already been judged by God to go to either Heaven or Hell based on their beliefs, actions, thoughts, and performance - whether it is Holy or sinful - during their life here on Earth. So, why the Hereafter transition when the people have already been judged?

It is because, in that environment with that kind of knowledge and thoughts (the question of "how am I *dead* and still experiencing thing like I am *alive*?), a person is judged as to which level of Heaven or Hell they are going to go to for a long time. Heaven, you see, has 7 Heavens … or 7 levels. Each level has a different set of pleasure and enjoyment and bliss within it. And they are different for different levels. Thus, before the person goes to that level, God sees how they would operate if they were within that level. If they do good, then they are put there. If they do poorly, they are sent to another level. But know this: The decision to do things that will bring one to Heaven or Hell has already been done *and cannot be reversed!*

So, it makes sense to try to do the things that are the most Holy!

I was told, by the Angels, that things are going to be operating at different speeds for me now that I have experienced the Hereafter.

They told me about how the Physics of Information operate. They said that I would be able to use the "preservation of information" paradigm – which says that all information is preserved for all time (in one way or another) and is accessible with the right format to anyone, at any time – to search for information – at random locations – within a book and get the Answers to the Questions I have in my mind. That is a really interesting concept. I had no books but could tell by the tone of their voices and the particular words the Angels used that they knew what they were talking about. And the concept was sent to me, as the Angels were speaking, directly to my mind ... so that I didn't actually need to look at a random answer in a book to get the summary of the fact of what the Angels were talking about. Thus, it was also a demonstration of their Mind Power!

(Since I have become conscious and back alive in this life I have made it a habit to take the Angel's recommendations into mind and to think questions that I have to God and His Angels, and while I am thinking them to turn to a random page in a book I have or have not read, then open the random page by putting my unseen finger on a word ... then look at the word and think about it and thus see that the word is THE ANSWER TO THE QUESTION I ASKED! That is the way that God and His Angels operate with information! All it requires is that you: 1) think the question in your mind to God or His Angels; 2) allow Them to move your finger with your subliminal mind to the page and the answer on the page with your finger; 3) help your mind to perceive of the correct answer to the question when you actually look at the "random" (Godsent) word that your finger is on. That is how it works!)

Thus, you can see that God and His Angels have miraculous powers that our sciences and physics have no way of proving exist ... yet!

For example: I asked – mentally – the question of my book by Brian Greene titled: *Until the End of Time*. The question was one of God: "What do you want me to write in the story I am working on about my time in the Hereafter? What, do you say, is the Hereafter all about?" I turned the book to a random page and put my finger blind on a word. Then I opened my eye and read it. I have italicized the word in the next sentence that describes the sentence that my finger was on ... for you to peruse.

": quantum mechanics and eternity form a powerful union." That is the sentence that my finger was on at that question.

Think about it. Out of that whole book, THAT was the answer I got to a random location in a book to a thought out and unspoken question. That, my friend, is evidence that there IS a God and that He has mystical and magnificent powers!

And thus, the beliefs about His Angels are also factual! Thus, this story is all true! There is no doubt ... in case you had any! Now, it should be gone!

The three Angels – when I was in the Hereafter with them – told me that such things like Parallel Universes exist, that Heaven is within a Parallel Universe that is specially protected from the evils of Satan and Hell, that Jesus Christ is within Hell with special powers and there he will be working on eventually bringing the condemned people there to Salvation, and Jesus in Hell is going to take part in destroying Satan forever and thus freeing the people of Earth to be free and wholesome and happy. The Angels told me that Time Travel DOES exist to those with the special mentality to take part in it. They said that there are, indeed, multiple dimensions and parallel dimensions to ours – and that people in the Hereafter – those special ones – will have the ability to move inter-dimensionally through space and time to exist in independent locations and beings of existence. That was a tall order – but they explained it mathematically.

It is a miracle and a Gift from God that I am able to write this down the way I am. The Angels had told me in the Hereafter that the things that they were telling me were Secret, and to only be used when I was within the Hereafter – when I was dead for good. Then Arial told me that she was going to bring me back to life ... and when I was alive then I was to become an Author and write down books about my experiences. Holy books. Thus, I have written many books now ... and they have a lot to do with my experiences with Angels and demons and the devil and Satan and God Himself. Notice that the way I worded those beings was evil forces surrounded by Good ones. That is because the Good forces are going to, on Judgement Day, overwhelm the evil forces and totally defeat them. I totally believe in that. Just, as I was seen by Angels – I thus have Faith in them!

The Angels of God operated deep within my mind, using the forces of nature and environment, to draw most of my experiences with them to the subliminal mind. That makes it so that I do not have much direct knowledge of what we talked about – but I have the special remedies to the ideas that allow me to get the summaries of my subliminal mind on the subjects by doing things like asking questions in my mind to the TV while I am watching a program – then getting the answer to the question from the statements of the actors. They answer the questions! There is a timeframe equilibrium that allows for the time of my thought and the time that I even THINK to have the question to equal the preceptor to the time of the direct answer by the actor. Thus, I think that it is possible for Mind Reading and Time Travel to occur over long distances and over long periods of time. It is remarkable that the actors could, deep within themselves, know in their minds the questions that are being asked of them

... and then have their Soul answer the question with a parallel answer!

Believe it or not, there is a theory in science and physics that Information is preserved and always applicable to the interpreter – regardless of what amount of time has passed or what duration or length of space has come between the Answer and the Questioner. There is a *total preservation!* Thus, a person is able to apply that law of physics to their mind and body when they pick a random spot in a book to answer a question they have. It is a theory that applies to the fact that a person that – if they are open and relaxed in their mind – can think a question to a TV program or a movie they haven't seen and then instantaneously get an answer. The thing is, they have to be relaxed and calm when they do it. That way, they will get the question from their subliminal mind through the Angels of God influencing them – perhaps – or otherwise get it from the mental proclivities of the recipient of the Mind Power that they are invoking. Neat, huh?

You should try it to see how it works! Go with the first question that comes to mind ... and you will get the answer to that question!

Keep in mind that the answers are parallel to the question. They could mean the Answer ... but be in words that are meaningful towards the Answer ... but separate in pronunciation and vowel or verb or noun meaning. But the overall meaning of it – when thought through deep within the mind – means that the answer is profound.

And there could be a lot more to the Answer as seen by deeper thought than what is said. Think about it!

"This is only a sample of how the computer revolution will affect our health. We will discuss the revolution in medicine in much more detail in Chapters 3 and 4 where we will discuss gene therapy, cloning, and altering the human life span." P41, *Physics of the Future* by Michio Kaku. (The bold and italicized word "and" was the word that my unseen finger was randomly put on. That reflects that the summary of the data can be found on chapter 3 and 4 of this book: *Movement to the Hereafter*.)

So, I have experienced a Higher evolution of Holiness that has sustained an elegant power within my existence. I have learned, with my Angelic Secret discussions in the Hereafter, that I shall have an elegant sense of being and an elegant mission upon my death and time within the Hereafter. The Angels told me that, upon death, I was to go on board the Ark of the Covenant with 11 other selected individuals. We are then supposed to go to Hell and to use our mental and special powers to bring the people sanctioned there and being punished to thoughtful Salvation – at the assistance of Jesus Christ. And when the people have all been saved on Judgement Day, then we are going to take up magic against Satan and defeat and destroy him. That is what it says in the Bible within Revelations that will happen. So, it SHALL be done!

(I was going to write a story about the 12 within the Hereafter, but there is a passage in Revelations that says that nobody is to talk about or write a story about Judgement Day. The Bible and the Qur'an have already discussed it all. So, I am going to follow the Bible and write nothing more about it!)

That summarized what occurred when I was dead and inside of the Hereafter. The rest of the memories are subliminal. But I have become an Author, and the stories that I write are summaries of the thoughts that I have with an Angelic influenced subliminal mindset – that may potentially be the summaries of a Prophet of God. Granted, the Bible and the Qur'an both say that ALL the Prophets have been on the earth.

But there is a chance that they could be wrong about that. Perhaps I will not show my Prophet powers until Judgement Day. Perhaps.

Until then, I shall do as the Angels and God wants and write more books. I am currently working on writing a book about Angels.

Until that comes out, take care of yourself, your friends, your family, your mate, and people you interact with. I really enjoyed writing for you! And I hope you enjoyed it!

Take it easy!

(Thought to my book *The Future of Humanity* by Michio Kaku... I thought the question of this: "Dear God, please tell me if my images of Angels in the Hereafter were actual ... or if I made them up with mental disability?" I turned at random and put my finger blindfolded on a part of a sentence in the book. Then I looked. The part said: speed of light... That is the speed that Angels move at! That is a preclusion to the presence of Parallel Concepts that allow for God to put forth images in the exact, human words! Thus, I WAS seen by Angels of God ... and have been told so by Him today as I wrote this book ... and will have more experience with them later!

Wow! I think I AM a Prophet!)

Mitchell Krautant

Author,

writer of *Cheetah on the Wing* series

and *Movement to the Hereafter*

http://mkrautant.com

BIOGRAPHY OF MITCHELL KRAUTANT

Krautant, Mitchell (2020). California, USA. IngramSpark.com

Mitchell Krautant is a genius who tested with a 142 IQ when he was in the USMC. He served in SOC Force Recon there. He departed the Marines injured. Then he went to prison when he was innocent. They were highly illegal there and the prison staff gave him PTSD. He got sent to mind bending solitary confinement, which placed him under severe mental duress for 7 years after he was released.

When he was released, he went to college and was getting an A in calculus 2. But the mental trauma of solitary confinement overwhelmed him, so he dropped out of college and became homeless.

Mr. Krautant went homeless to the VA hospital and received no care there. He departed and was a victim of vehicular homicide. He died in the coma and was taken to the Hereafter by three of God's Angels. After he came back to life, he became an author.

He has written the *Cheetah on the Wing 1-4* books, *Movement to the Hereafter, Death and Life as a Victim of Vehicular Homicide*, and *The Elegant Lion Named George*.

There are even other books to follow!

www.mkrautant.com

CPSIA information can be obtained
at www.ICGtesting.com
Printed in the USA
LVHW020528101120
671253LV00010B/410